Autonomy and Foreign Language Learning

Advances in Digital Language Learning and Teaching

Series Editors
Michael Thomas
Mark Peterson
Mark Warschauer

Today's language educators need support to understand how their learners are changing and the ways technology can be used to aid their teaching and learning strategies. The movement towards different modes of language learning – from presence-based to autonomous as well as blended and fully online modes – requires different skill sets such as e-moderation and new ways of designing and developing language-learning tasks in the digital age. Theoretical studies that include practical case studies and high-quality empirical studies incorporating critical perspectives are necessary to move the field further. This new series is committed to providing such an outlet for high-quality work on digital language learning and teaching. Volumes in the series will focus on a number of areas including but not limited to:

- task-based learning and teaching approaches utilizing technology
- language learner creativity
- e-moderation and teaching languages online
- blended language learning
- designing courses for online and distance language learning
- mobile-assisted language learning
- autonomous language learning, both inside and outside of formal educational contexts
- the use of web 2.0/social media technologies
- immersive and virtual language-learning environments
- digital game-based language learning
- language educator professional development with digital technologies
- teaching language skills with technologies

Enquiries about the series can be made by contacting the series editors: Michael Thomas (MThomas4@uclan.acuk), Mark Peterson (tufsmp@yahoo.com) and Mark Warschauer (markw@uci.edu).

Titles in the Series
Interactive Whiteboards and Language Teacher Professional Development, edited by Euline Cutrim Schmid and Shona Whyte
Online Teaching and Learning, edited by Carla Meskill

Related Titles
Continuum Companion to Second Language Acquisition, edited by Ernesto Macaro
Available in Paperback as *Bloomsbury Companion to Second Language Acquisition*
Contemporary Computer-Assisted Language Learning, edited by Michael Thomas, Hayo Reinders and Mark Warschauer
Online Second Language Acquisition, Vincenza Tudini
Task-Based Language Learning and Teaching with Technology, edited by Michael Thomas and Hayo Reinders

Autonomy and Foreign Language Learning in a Virtual Learning Environment

Miranda Hamilton

BLOOMSBURY
LONDON · NEW DELHI · NEW YORK · SYDNEY

Bloomsbury Academic
An imprint of Bloomsbury Publishing Plc

50 Bedford Square   175 Fifth Avenue
London   New York
WC1B 3DP   NY 10010
UK   USA

www.bloomsbury.com

First published 2013

© Miranda Hamilton, 2013

All rights reserved. No part of this publication may be reproduced or transmitted in any form or by any means, electronic or mechanical, including photocopying, recording, or any information storage or retrieval system, without prior permission in writing from the publishers.

Miranda Hamilton has asserted her right under the Copyright, Designs and Patents Act, 1988, to be identified as Author of this work.

No responsibility for loss caused to any individual or organization acting on or refraining from action as a result of the material in this publication can be accepted by Bloomsbury Academic or the author.

British Library Cataloguing-in-Publication Data
A catalogue record for this book is available from the British Library.

ISBN: HB: 978-1-4411-5064-6
PDF: 978-1-4411-5368-5

Library of Congress Cataloging-in-Publication Data
Hamilton, Miranda.
Autonomy and foreign language learning in a virtual learning environment / Miranda Hamilton.
pages cm. – (Advances in digital language learning and teaching)
Includes bibliographical references and index.
ISBN 978-1-4411-5064-6 (hardback) – ISBN 978-1-4411-5368-5 (epdf) – ISBN 978-1-4411-8980-6 (epub) 1. Language and languages–Study and teaching–Technological innovations. 2. Language and languages–Computer-assisted instruction. 3. Educational technology. I. Title.
P53.855.H36 2013
418.0078–dc23
2013000815

Typeset by Newgen Imaging Systems Pvt Ltd, Chennai, India
Printed and bound in Great Britain

Contents

List of Figures		vi
List of Tables		vii
1	Paradox and Promise: Autonomy, Foreign Language Learning and Technology	1
2	Understanding Autonomy: An Overview	17
3	Technology: Virtual Promise or Virtual Reality – the Pedagogical Challenge	49
4	Shadow Dancing: Autonomy in Action	71
5	Learner Reflections about Learning English as a Foreign Language and the Role of Technology	111
6	Perceptions and Reality 1: Students' Response to Using a VLE in Computer Room Lessons	133
7	Perceptions and Reality 2: Beyond the Classroom – Students' Free Time Use of the VLE	171
8	An Ecological Perspective of Autonomy, Foreign Language Learning and Technology	197
9	Looking Back, Thinking Forwards	219
Bibliography		232
Index		244

List of Figures

4.1	Conceptual framework for autonomous learning behaviour in a learning environment	79
5.1	Task-based interaction between the learner and the computer	121
5.2	Communicative interaction mediated through the computer not face-to-face	124
8.1	Conceptual framework for autonomous learning behaviour in a learning environment	199

List of Tables

1.1	The pedagogical rationale for understanding the nature of the relationship between autonomy and technology	10
2.1	Difficulties with the psychological and cognitive dimensions of autonomy in a VLE	31
2.2	Autonomy framework 1	39
2.3	Autonomy framework 2	40
2.4	Autonomy framework 3	42
2.5	VLE autonomy framework with *EI* – blended learning and free time	45
4.1	VLE autonomy framework with *EI* – blended learning and free time	73
4.2	Criteria in selecting students as members of the core student group	85
4.3	*EI* teaching and learning tools and modes of delivery	89
4.4	Stage one: Overview of *EI* blended lessons	92
4.5	Stage two: Overview of *EI* blended lessons	93
4.6	Integrative CALL approach to an example *EI* lesson	97
4.7	Topics *Read, Think and Reply* weekly, free-time, expert-generated threads	100
5.1	Whole-class access and use of technology – opening questionnaire	120
5.2	Zarita – access and use of technology – opening questionnaire	122
5.3	Monse – access and use of technology – opening questionnaire	123
5.4	Maribel – access and use of technology – opening questionnaire	123
5.5	Summary of student perspectives on their learning environment before introducing *EI*	128
6.1	VLE blended learning autonomy framework with *EI*	134
6.2	Closing questionnaire – language used in the *classroom* – core students	135
6.3	Closing questionnaire – language used in the *classroom* – whole class (21 students)	136
6.4	Closing questionnaire – language used on *EI* – the VLE – core students	136
6.5	Closing questionnaire – language used on *EI* – the VLE – whole class (21 students)	136
6.6	Closing questionnaire – under what circumstances would you use Spanish on *EI*? (21 students)	137

6.7	Assignments and associated posts submitted (whole class)	144
6.8	Recurring themes – texting and context	146
6.9	Recurring themes – texting, young people and fashion	146
6.10	Recurring themes – texting and saving time	147
6.11	Blended classroom 'Learner' autonomy in *EI*	150
6.12	Mid-course questionnaire 1 preferences: *EI* in the classroom or computer room – whole class (21 students)	151
6.13	Mid-course questionnaire 1 preferences: *EI* in the classroom or computer room (core students)	151
6.14	Interview data preferences: *EI* in the classroom or computer room (core students)	151
6.15	Learner autonomy – students controlling the technology	152
6.16	*EI* access – screen hits in class versus free-time hits to the same screens	157
6.17	Student interaction with VLE following *EI* classroom lessons and *EI* computer room lessons	158
6.18	Core students' interactivity between stages of 12 *EI* blended lessons	160
6.19	Learner autonomy – decision-making and learning outcomes in *EI*	161
7.1	VLE free-time autonomy framework for student interaction with *EI*	173
7.2	*EI* forums – free-time threads, posts and views	177
7.3	*Read, Think and Reply* – free choice or obligation?	178
7.4	Free-time expert and student threads and responses to *EI* forums	179
7.5	Mid-course questionnaire – reasons for not generating threads	180
7.6	Mid-course questionnaire 1: Which students' postings would you be most likely to read?	184
7.7	Thread – *'The Best Age to Be . . .'*	186
7.8	Thread – *'If You Had to Choose . . .'*	189
7.9	Number of postings and threads generated in forums (core students)	195
9.1	Implications of the transformative qualities of a VLE on the learning experience	230
9.2	Recommendations for further research	231

1

Paradox and Promise: Autonomy, Foreign Language Learning and Technology

Assumptions about autonomy and technology

> ...educational technology demonstrates its effectiveness as a purveyor of learner autonomy. (Murray 1999:296)

> One obvious benefit of technology for language learning is the creation of opportunities for students to use language in authentic contexts. Such activities encourage students to strive for autonomy in the target language. (Kessler 2009:79)

These are indeed bold suggestions, expressed with some certainty. But how can we be so sure? Are we beguiled by the promises for our brave new digital classroom, in danger of being blinded by style over substance?

Though published ten years apart, these two observations convey a common sentiment, which is that the introduction of technology into a context for learning can provide opportunities for learners to exploit their capacity for independent learner and language behaviour beyond the constraints of their traditional learning environment. Autonomy lies at the heart of this book although it is an elusive construct to pin down and often confused with independence. The construct as I have interpreted it corresponds with the distinction made by Deci and Flaste (1996:89):

> Independence means to do for yourself, to not rely on others for personal nourishment and support. Autonomy, in contrast, means to act freely, with a sense of volition and choice. It is thus possible for a person to be independent and autonomous (i.e., to freely not rely on others), or to be independent and controlled (i.e., to feel forced not to rely on others).

I am interested in examining the sense with which the learner feels capable of acting of his own volition and choice but that this might be enhanced within a technological learning context by the nourishment and support received from his environment.

This book contextualizes the examination of the nature of the relationship between autonomy and technology through the teaching and learning of a foreign language. Perhaps more than any other academic discipline, the aim for foreign language teachers is to support their learners to take ownership of the target language so they can set their sights beyond the remit of the classroom and use the language freely and spontaneously. The foreign language in the context I describe in this book is English, but this is not to say that the insights about autonomy and technology that emerge in this book bear no relation to learning other foreign languages. But why English? I taught English as a foreign language for many years so it is a learning environment I am familiar with. But significantly English has become the lingua franca of the internet and we are living through the global explosion of online communication which means that there is a need identified around the world to be able to use English online. Technology creates hitherto inaccessible opportunities for real-world, meaningful interaction and engagement in the socially constructed setting of the classroom. The teaching of English as a foreign language is therefore well placed to harness the energy of technology, shedding insights into notions of autonomy and taking us beyond technological wizardry and towards well-grounded pedagogical practice that might then be usefully extrapolated and applied not only to other languages and but also to other academic disciplines.

Despite indications to suggest that we are living through a digital revolution, and the conceptual complexities of the notion of autonomy, we continue to read that the 'obvious benefit' (Kessler 2009:79) of technology lies in its capacity to '[purvey] learner autonomy' (Murray 1999:296) do we understand the nature of this relationship and the basis upon which is it founded? Embedded within these references is the problematic implication that the conventions of traditional language learning make it difficult for students to behave autonomously, with the suggestion that they are otherwise 'thwarted by institutional choices' (Ciekanski 2007:112), which overlooks the possibility that it is possible to be autonomous in the classroom. This sentiment is compounded by the suggestion that technology creates hitherto unheralded opportunities for communicative independence in the target language.

Consider the following broad interpretation of an autonomous individual:

> A person charts his own course through life by self consciously choosing projects and assuming commitments from a wide range of eligible alternatives, and making something out of his life according to his own understanding of what is valuable and worth doing. (Wall 2003:307/8)

It could be argued that technological functionality has the potential to enhance the learner's freedom to choose by presenting an extensive 'range of eligible alternatives' (ibid.) with which to engage, according to a personally held criterion of 'what is valuable and worth doing'(ibid.).

The suggested relationship between autonomy and technology has widespread appeal, but Hawisher and Selfe (2000:56) caution against the 'uncritical enthusiasm' of technology and Lamy and Hampel (2007c:82) argue that 'for many of the positive aspects [...] there is a corresponding negative impact'. The union is more complex than it might at first seem. The aim of this book is to examine the nature of the relationship, because in so doing, this might offer some insights into the reasons why, despite great optimism and promise, the ESRC (Economic and Social Research Council) research group, PACCIT (People at the Centre of Communication and Information Technologies) (2005:3) have expressed concerns that 'huge technological developments [...] have not always delivered their intended benefits to end-users', with this sentiment reflected in PACCIT's research objectives:

> To develop a greater understanding of the psychological, social and organisational characteristics of individuals and groups as they relate to, and interact with, information technologies and to feed this knowledge back to the evaluation and design of more effective IT systems and products.[1]

The problem: Understanding the nature of the relationship between autonomy, language learning and technology

Autonomy has been identified as a pedagogical ideal, such that it has achieved 'buzzword status' (Pemberton 1996:2), and with the increasingly ubiquitous presence of computers in education, it has been affiliated to technology. Yet

---

[1] Retrieved 26 May 2010 from: www.csrcsocietytoday.ac.uk/ESRCInfoCentre/research/research_programmes/PACCIT.aspx.

burgeoning popularity has given rise to some ambiguity, which Pemberton (ibid.) suggests becomes apparent when one considers how many terms referring to the notion of autonomy are used to describe the same phenomenon, and that a single term is often used to describe different phenomena. In light of the complexities associated with what it means to be autonomous and how it might therefore be applied to learning with technology, it is helpful to consider the two conditions proposed by Holec (1981:7) which are that in order for the learner to behave autonomously.

> ### Box 1.1 Two conditions necessary for autonomy (Holec 1981:7)
>
> First, the learner must have the ability to take charge of his learning, that is he must know how to make the decisions which this involves.
>
> Secondly, there must be a learning structure in which control over the learning can be exercised by the learner, that is in which the learner has the possibility of exercising his ability to take charge.

Holec's two conditions indicated in Box 1.1 point to the relationship between the internal and external dimensions of autonomy, reflecting the view held by Little that 'as social beings our independence is always balanced by dependence, our essential condition is one of interdependence' (Little 1990:7).

Esch (2009:31) reflects that the integration of autonomy into educational practice appears to have been successful but she argues that in the processes of 'mainstreaming' (ibid.) there has been some distortion in the interpretation of what it means to be autonomous, and considers two misconceptions identified by Little (1991:3, cited in Esch 2009:31) that prevail: autonomy equates to self-instruction and that by implication teacher input is detrimental to the development of autonomous behaviour.

Critically these misconceptions fail to observe the element of 'interdependence' (Little 1990:7) between the individual and the learning structure that bring Holec's two conditions for autonomy (Box 1.1) together. These misapprehensions can be seen in the multiplicity of computer programmes designed so that students can learn independently of the classroom and the teacher. As an approach, this diminishes what it means to be autonomous by overlooking language and learning as socially situated constructs, where students are the 'creative products of their social context' (Esch 2009:43). Technology may have failed to deliver intended benefits when, by design, digital grammar games and exercises offer little in the way of meaningful feedback, and autonomous learning mediated by technology has been confused with learning in isolation and individualization. But the relationship between autonomy and technology is more complex than this. More recently, the provision of virtual space has the potential to bring learners and teachers together, with the promise and pedagogical value of online L2 interaction, yet Mason (2001:69) found that, despite the apparent potential, 'simply providing an environment in which students and teachers could interact did not guarantee successful engagement,' because of the need for the stimulus of human interaction. A virtual environment is simply an empty space because as Hutchby (2001:20) says, 'there are no inherent or necessary features of technological artefacts which lead to determinate social consequences.'

Concerns expressed by PACCIT (2005:3) indicate that technological developments have not lived up to expectation, and the group's research objectives highlight the need to understand more about the design of technology to maximize the benefits to the learner. In the context of this book the suggestion could be interpreted to mean that improved design might encourage autonomous learner behaviour. Although Kern and Warschauer (2000:2) reflect on the significance of the context within which the technology is used and Ganem Gutierrez (2006:244) considers that the success of an activity cannot be attributed to the medium of implementation, much of the debate has been focused on the connection between the learner, the technology and pedagogical outcomes, whether this is in terms of the computer-as-tutor, task-based learning or promoting authentic L2 interaction.

The search for understanding

If we are to understand something more of the nature of the relationship between autonomy and technology, while consideration should be afforded to its internal and external dimensions, the notion of interdependence should include the wider implications of introducing technology into the learning environment. I am therefore interested in the ecological approach where context is 'at the heart of the matter' (van Lier 2004:5). But what of the context that lies at the heart of this book?

Context, autonomy and language learning in Mexico

The work represented in this book was conducted in the context of a university in Mexico, an educational setting that lends itself very well to our search for understanding, through an examination of assumptions, theories and current thinking about the nature of the relationship between technology and the development of autonomy. The teaching of languages in Mexico has been going through a period of pedagogical transition over a period of years. Not only have different traditions of autonomous learning evolved but they exist in tension with one another.

The voices of the students who appear in this book were advanced learners of English enrolled on a full-time English language learning programme at a university in Mexico, an educational setting that lent itself very well to our search for insights into the nature of the relationship between technology and autonomy in the context of foreign language learning. In recent years, the teaching of languages in Mexico has been going through a period of pedagogical transition with autonomous learning identified as a priority. These students straddled the 'fault line' between one era and another, therefore offering a unique opportunity to research notions of autonomy, new classroom methodologies and technologically mediated learning opportunities.

Background to the Mexican context

In the state sector in Mexico, the pedagogical approach to teaching English as a foreign language has evolved from the classic tradition of grammar-translation (Manteca Aguirre et al. 2006:10). Historically, the ability to manipulate the written word has been more highly valued than communication through the spoken word. By way of contrast, privately run British, American and Australian language schools in Mexico adopt a different pedagogical approach with communicative language teaching (ibid.). New language education policy in 1993 recommended a realignment of priorities so that rather than focusing exclusively on formal aspects of language and translation, students should work towards becoming competent users of the language. Such a paradigm shift in the conceptualization of language and basic language education (ibid.) has proved more difficult to achieve in practice. An exploratory study conducted across more than 100 secondary schools in 2001–2 revealed that students were still leaving secondary school with poor language skills and unable to communicate in the target language.

Fostering autonomous learning in Mexico: The British Council approach

Following consultation with the British Council, Mexico has seen significant public investment in the development of centres for self-directed foreign language learning at universities (Hernández Cuevas 2004). The British Council website[2] advocates that teachers should 'attempt to foster autonomy through practices in EFL classroom'. The role of the teacher is identified as central to promoting autonomous learning, with the classroom as the environment where students can explore and develop the necessary skills and strategies through classroom activities, working towards becoming more self-reliant and motivated lifelong learners. Many educational institutions in Mexico have adopted a British Council approach to self-directed learning as a component of classroom learning. The self-access centre complements and supports classroom teaching, as a means of promoting independent learning. Learners are guided towards a less dependent culture for learning, as educational institutions provide students with structured self-access learning pathways that are formally integrated into the syllabus, using the students' course-book as a guide, and adapting commercially available materials. However, self-access centres have largely been run by busy teaching staff with limited training in self-directed learning and have been found to be underutilized by students (Groult Bois: no date[3]).

This mode of self-directed learning is ultimately managed by the institution, so that the learners' potential for autonomy is determined and controlled by their context for learning and their teacher. Arguably, this runs contrary to the notion of autonomy posited by Benson and Voller (1997:4) as 'freedom from external control' and is remote from the more expanded notion of learner autonomy suggested by the wider literature.

Fostering autonomous learning in Mexico: The CRAPEL approach

An alternative approach towards self-directed language learning in Mexico is offered to students at the *Centro de Enseñanza de Lenguas Extranjeras* (CELE) at the *Universidad Nacional Autónoma de México* (UNAM). In 1995, CELE opened its centre for self-access language learning set up following the guidelines for

---

[2] Retrieved 8 June 2010 from: www.englishonline.org.cn/en/community/featured-blog/jane/autonomy.
[3] Retrieved 30 October 2010 from: www.santiago.cu/hosting/linguistica/Descargar.php?archivo...groult.pdf.

self-directed learning proposed by CRAPEL and founded on the premise of creating opportunities and extending language education to non-specialists. Central to this approach is the notion of self-directed learning that need not emanate from the classroom. The centre strives to support learners by stimulating the development of cognitive and metacognitive learning strategies and encouraging their capacity for reflection and self-evaluation through carefully designed learning materials and students can attend counselling sessions.

Development needs emerge on two levels: first, in supporting the processes associated with the development of the learners' cognitive and metacognitive skills so that they make the transition towards becoming independent learners. Secondly, the need emerges for teacher education programmes to prepare educators to understand the complexities of self-directed learning, so that they might be better placed to support their learners in their efforts to achieve autonomous learning as opposed to merely independent learning.

Tensions between two schools of thought: The British Council and CRAPEL

In Mexico these two schools of thought exist in parallel, yet in conflict, each sharing a common belief in the value of supporting the individual's potential for autonomy. From the British Council perspective, the development of learner autonomy is a component of classroom learning. By way of contrast, the CRAPEL approach has evolved so that non-language specialists can engage with language education through self-access, enrolling, participating and learning at the time and pace that suits them. Without the presence of the teacher or the existence of the classroom, students are faced with the cognitive and metacognitive challenges in managing their own learning. For the students in this book, the approach adopted by their institution corresponded to that of the British Council, rather than the CRAPEL model, making it an ideal setting to introduce a virtual learning environment (VLE) for use in the students' computer room lessons with free-time access to VLE-mediated language development content and forums.

The aims of this book

What does this book set out to achieve? There are three main aims, the first of which is to review current thinking and examine the relationship between autonomy and technology from a theoretical perspective. A second aim is pedagogical because enhanced understanding about the effective integration of technology has the potential to inform teachers, developers and writers and promote good learning. The third aim is research-based, looking beyond learning outcomes and instead taking a contextualized, ecological perspective in the examination of interactions between participants in a VLE-mediated language learning programme to see whether this might reveal fresh insights into the nature of the relationship between autonomy and technology.

Theoretical aims

The debate has revolved around whether new technologies lead to better learning, with current theories about language learning adapted, applied and evaluated for new technological realities, with consideration afforded to the following: teaching aims; technological functionality; optimal task design; L2 interaction and discourse analysis. We have been in danger of confusing the tool with methods and outcomes (Ganem Gutierrez 2006:233). Although research has indicated how autonomous behaviour might emerge in response to a technological stimulus, 'one cannot attribute the success [. . .] of a task solely to the medium of implementation' (ibid.). In terms of the link between autonomy and technology, the theoretical literature has yet to conceptualize the 'totality of relationships of an organism with all other organisms with which it [technology] comes into contact' (van Lier 2004:3) and the transformative qualities that technology brings to the learning environment. In light of the concerns expressed by PACCIT (2005:3) that new technologies have 'not always delivered their intended benefits', it is necessary to look beyond the question of whether technology leads to good learning where technological elements have been examined in isolation from the context within which they exist. The theoretical aim of this book is to examine how the introduction of technology impacts upon the dimensions and interconnectedness between elements in a learning environment relative to autonomy. Closer analysis of examples of autonomy in response to technology should be considered in light of the context within which learning takes place. In so doing we enlighten our understanding of the nature of the relationship between autonomy and technology in a language learning environment, thereby allowing us to build a theoretical representation of the link between the two constructs.

Given the high level of investment associated with the introduction of technology, it is not unreasonable that the debate has focused predominantly on whether technology leads to better language learning, but to what end does an improved understanding of the relationship between autonomy and technology serve? This leads us to consider the pedagogical aims of this book.

Pedagogical aims

The value of autonomous language learning, whereby students are encouraged to learn and communicate independently in the target language is a valid pedagogical aspiration. Educators, materials writers, software developers and researchers have long since identified technology as a platform which students might use to realize their potential for autonomy. In our haste to harness the apparent potential of technology in response to this intuitive relationship, our attention has been drawn to its value in terms of pedagogical outcomes. In so doing we have failed to comprehend the significance and impact of introducing a socially transformative tool into the language learning environment. This has cast a shadow in comprehending the effects of learning in a digitalized environment. If, as educators, our aim is to create 'the conditions in which it [autonomy] can flourish' (Benson 2009:26), it is necessary that we have a clearer understanding about the nature of the relationship between technology and autonomy. Improved understanding will enable teachers, teacher educators, materials developers and software designers to maximize the benefits of the technology for the learner, as shown in Table 1.1, so that technology might be more effectively exploited to stimulate autonomous learner behaviour.

Table 1.1 The pedagogical rationale for understanding the nature of the relationship between autonomy and technology

Facilitators	Pedagogical aims
Teachers	1. Recognize, understand and evaluate the significance of events as they take place in a technological learning environment. 2. Respond and build on events as they take place in a technological learning environment. 3. Build on opportunities for autonomy as they emerge from learners' response to learning in a technological learning environment.
Teacher educators	To train teachers to exploit and understand the impact brought to the dynamic of the learning environment by the introduction of technology.
Materials designers and software developers	Create a context and activities that embrace and incorporate the transformative effects of introducing technology into the learning environment.

Research aims

The suggestion is that technology has not always delivered its intended benefits (PACCIT 2005:3). The research aims in writing this book have been to evaluate how the introduction of technology into a learning environment impacts upon elements with which it comes into contact relative to instances of learner autonomy and use of the target language. Other studies have identified the significance of context in terms of learners' response to technology, adopting sociocultural theory as a theoretical framework from which to analyse the 'social and cultural situatedness of learner activity' (Kern 2006:187). However, sociocultural theory adopts a more profoundly psychological stance, with an emphasis on the psyche of the individual. As an approach this does not satisfactorily address the interconnectedness between wider contextual factors in the learning environment, and the transformative qualities brought about by the introduction of technology.

With this in mind, the ecological approach underpins the theoretical framework of the book. The ecological approach embraces the 'totality of relationships of an organism with all other organisms with which it comes into contact' (van Lier 2004:3) to see what this might reveal about the nature of the relationship between autonomy and technology in the context of learning English as a foreign language.

In this book I am concerned with the nature of the relationship between autonomy and technology so the purpose is to look beyond the question of learning outcomes, matters about whether computer-assisted language learning (CALL) improves learning and the effects of context on the psyche of the learner. I am interested in taking a more holistic view of learning with technology, reflected in the research aims of the project described in Box 1.2.

Box 1.2 The research aims of the project

1. The co-existence and interconnectedness between objects within a learning environment and how this relates to indications of autonomous behaviour.
2. How, and if, learners perceive and act upon and value technologically mediated opportunities for autonomy and the independent use of the target language.

In terms of building understanding about the nature of the relationship between autonomy and technology, in this book, context is paramount by examining:

> ... the learner in action in a learnable environment, appropriating meaning [...] in action, and jointly with others. [. . .] Learners must be engaged, so that the learning emanates from them, rather than being delivered to them. (van Lier 2004:222)

The research problem

The theoretical literature reports that the notion of autonomy is widely described as 'freedom from external control' (Benson and Voller 1997:4). Considered in isolation, this misrepresents the complexity of what it means to be autonomous, overlooking the philosophical notion that absolute freedom is unattainable and is relative to the sociocultural context within which we live. If one considers the view that 'successful autonomous use of the target language should be the ultimate goal in language instruction' (Kessler 2009:81), the significance of the dynamic between the learner and the context for learning emerges in the individual's quest towards 'develop[ing] the ability to use the language freely and spontaneously' (Lantolf 2003:367).

Theorists report on the duality of meaning where autonomous learning is an internal construct, relative to the individual's capacity for self-determination, notwithstanding his ability to engage with, and make sense of, new information in light of existing knowledge. But this perspective is held in tension with the view of autonomy as simultaneously an external construct whereby the individual responds to his environment, guided in a 'principled way' (Dickinson 1987a:24) towards autonomy by the activity, the lesson and the teacher.

A delicate 'interdependence' (Little 1990:7) emerges between the individual's innate capacity for autonomy and the responsibility of educators to support learners' autonomy to create an environment where learners can express their capacity for autonomy. The role of the teacher and a structure for learning cannot be overlooked because ultimately the student does not know the language he is learning (Esch 1996:36). If, as Holec (1981) proposes, that there should be a structure within which the learner can exercise control, it seems that autonomy is possible in class.

I am interested in the notion of interdependence and the student's ability to express his potential capacity for autonomy but that this is in response to activities and interactions within the structure of a technological learning environment.

The research literature points to the ambiguity that has emerged in terms of how the concept is to be interpreted in the context of a technological learning environment. A polar spectrum of learning with technology has emerged and confusion ensued relative to what it means to be an autonomous learner with technology. At one end of the spectrum technology is associated with self-access, where the learner is liberated from the external constraints of the classroom. The technology provides a clearly defined structure within which the learner can exercise control and chart 'his own course through life' (Wall 2003:308), but he is guided by screen-mediated content and works in isolation. Yet this represents a diminished sense of what it means to be autonomous. This view of technology and autonomy overlooks language and learning as socially situated phenomena and the ways in which the structure of a technological learning environment has the potential to create opportunities for the learner to exercise his potential capacity for autonomy.

At the other end of the spectrum, there is the suggestion that 'technological artefacts, in both their form and meaning are socially shaped' (Hutchby 2001:14). Dillenbourg et al. (2002:5) point out that 'a set of *cf* Web pages does not constitute a virtual learning environment unless there is social interaction about or around the information.' More recently, Web 2.0[4] technologies have created the potential to populate virtual space, providing a 'designed information space' (ibid.) and a technologically socially situated context for learning within which individuals can construct meaning. However, as Mason (2001:69) found, the provision of a technological learning environment where students and teachers could interact was no guarantee of success. At each end of the technological spectrum, from the 'principled' (Dickinson 1987a:24) approach to the 'socially shaped' constructivist view of technologically mediated learning, we see indications of the 'reciprocal interdependency between internal processes and external environment' (Shachaf and Hara 2002:2).

Questions begin to emerge relative to the relationship between how learners perceive and value opportunities for autonomous learning in a technologically mediated context, and whether they choose to respond to those opportunities. Analysis of learners' perceptions considered in parallel with their use of the technology should reveal something about what it is that transforms 'potential effects into actual effects' (Dillenbourg et al. 2002:9) in the context

---

[4] Web 1 – users are limited to the passive viewing of information provided to them. Web 2.0 allows users to interact and contribute to the website, for example wikis, blogs, chat, message boards, social networking.

of a technological learning environment. We might then begin to understand something of the nature of the relationship between autonomy and students' the use of a technological learning environment in an EFL context.

Layout of the book

In the chapters that follow I begin by presenting a discussion of the literature. This has been divided into two chapters. Chapter 2 is a discussion of the literature relating to autonomy, which begins by considering the broadly philosophical and political dimensions of the concept. I discuss the link between autonomy and education and language learning, different versions of autonomy and the ambiguity between ideologies, enabling me to locate and suggest a theoretical definition of autonomy. The chapter concludes with a presentation of three frameworks drawn from the literature for autonomy in language education that contributed to the construction of my own framework for autonomy in a VLE so that I might then identify instances of autonomous behaviour in a response to the VLE. Chapter 3 is a review of the literature relating to technology and considers the promise and paradox of introducing technology into the language learning classroom, as well as the theoretical distinctions between different approaches to using technology, and how they might be deemed to support the development of autonomy.

Following the literature review, Chapter 4 considers the aims of the book and presents a discussion describing the construction of the theoretical and conceptual frameworks, tools that enabled the examination and evaluation of learner behaviour relative to notions of autonomy. This chapter provides a profile of the students and the educational setting, and describes the development of the technological platform that mediated the language development programme known as *English International* (*EI*).

Chapter 5 is the first of three chapters of analysis which provides a baseline evaluation of the students' perceptions and experiences of language learning with technology before the introduction of the VLE. I present the analysis of the students' response to the technology in their computer room lessons in Chapter 6 addressing the data-based research questions, taking the same approach in Chapter 7 in response to the students' free-time engagement with the VLE. I return to the main themes that emerged from the literature and the analysis and I draw on the theoretical framework in Chapter 8, attempting to work towards a theoretical representation of autonomous and virtual language learning. The concluding chapter provides a summary of the students' perceptions of the value of their VLE-mediated language development programme compared with their online activity relative to notions of autonomy. In light of this, I make recommendations about the nature of the relationship between autonomy and technology in the context of learning a foreign language and consider the contribution and implications of this project to the current debate, making recommendations for further research.

2

Understanding Autonomy: An Overview

The central premise of this book pivots on working towards a more profound understanding of the nature of the relationship between autonomous learner behaviour and technology through the examination of learners' personal response to a VLE and to consider how far indications of autonomous behaviour might be influenced by the technology. The notion of 'personal response' is defined as the students' onsite activity and their observational reflections about the experience. In this chapter, I critically engage with different interpretations of autonomy in relation to language learning as presented in the literature, in order to problematize the construct and to arrive at a framework to examine the notion of autonomy in the context of foreign language learning in a virtual learning environment.

Examining the tenets that underpin the philosophical assumptions within the construct of autonomy and the categorization the different dimensions of autonomy adopted by the theorists informs my own response to the theoretical literature. I review three frameworks for autonomy described by different writers in their attempts to operationalize the concept in a language-learning context. This chapter concludes with a framework for autonomy designed as a tool with which to interrogate the data for signs of autonomous engagement in terms of students' personal response to the VLE relative to what they *did* and what they *thought* about the technology, to see what this might reveal about the nature of the relationship between autonomy and technology.

Holec's (1981:3) broad definition of learner autonomy as the 'ability to take charge of one's learning' is cited extensively across the literature, serving as a useful starting-point for closer scrutiny of the concept by the theorists. Autonomy is problematic not only to define, but also to operationalize and evaluate. This is reflected across the theoretical literature where conceptually diverse interpretations of the notion are represented, which may explain Holec's (1981:3) description of the 'semi-anarchical' application of autonomy in education and the 'conflicting ideologies' (Oxford 2003:75) between the theorists.

Nevertheless, wherever on the ideological spectrum the theorists locate themselves, the pursuit of autonomy in learning is acknowledged across the literature as pedagogically beneficial, because it is suggested that 'we learn better when we are in charge of our own learning because of cognitive, social and affective aspects involved in the learning process' (Ciekanski 2007:112); furthermore, Ellis and Sinclair (1989:2) advocate:

1. Students who take control of their own learning are ready to learn and learning is more effective.
2. Students who are responsible for their own learning can carry on learning outside the classroom.
3. Learning strategies can be transferred to other subjects.

In terms of learning a foreign language, the value of being autonomous is far reaching, because it involves the individual's ability not only to learn, but also to communicate independently, which Littlewood (1996:429) describes as 'major factors enabling a person to make choices in life, they also contribute to each learner's autonomy as an individual'. The notion of the value of meaningful, autonomous communication in the target language emerges as a significant factor of autonomy in language learning. Kern (2000:17) considers that interaction should go beyond the rehearsal of language skills and towards an engagement with 'real literacy events' where students learn to 'deal with uncertainties and ambiguities rather than relying on simplistic and rigid form-meaning correspondences', challenging them to organize their thoughts and ideas into the target language.

The difficulty lies in defining the key construct of autonomous behaviour because autonomy is essentially an abstract concept, described as 'divorced from any particular situation' (Boud 1988:20). Despite divergence between the theorists in terms of defining and operationalizing the concept of autonomy in the learning environment, as a construct it is one that is difficult to oppose (Pennycook 1997:39) and Benson and Voller (1997:1) consider that concepts with which we can hardly disagree are often those in need of the greatest clarification. To this end, the purpose of this chapter is to work towards a definition in response to the literature. If we are to make sense of the construct it is of value to begin by considering the philosophical dimensions of the concept before turning to the different versions of autonomy as represented in the theoretical literature.

Philosophical dimensions of the concept of autonomy

The notion of autonomy as it has been interpreted in twentieth-century Western thought is grounded historically in the political field where it suggests a sense of 'freedom from external control' (Benson and Voller 1997:4) of government, institution or group. Conceptually, autonomy carries a duality of meaning. On one level autonomy might be understood cognitively as the individual's ability to chart 'his own course through life [. . .] according to his own understanding of what is valuable and worth doing' (Wall 2003:308). This strand of autonomy could be described as 'internal' or a 'form of self-mastery over oneself' (Pennycook 1997:36). On a second level, from the perspective of the individual, autonomy has an external dimension reflecting 'freedom from mastery exercised over oneself by others [. . .] external, social and political freedom' (ibid.) where the individual is not 'thwarted by institutional choices'(Ciekanski 2007:112).

In the eighteenth-century Western society the concept of autonomy evolved and 'increasingly emphasized the responsibility of the individual as the social agent' (Benson and Voller 1997:4). Autonomy can be conceptualized as having internal and external elements existing simultaneously, yet in tension with one another. In order for the individual to realize his capacity for autonomy, Wall (2003:308) suggests that he:

1. Can plan and strategize his intentions.
2. Can decide what is important and worth doing.
3. Has a desire to take control of his life.
4. Has access to an environment that provides a wide range of options.

According to these criteria, the balance of responsibility seems to lie predominantly with the individual in the realization of his capacity for autonomy; however, this does not mean to say that responsibility on the part of the institution is relinquished. If the institution were to overlook its responsibilities, this would not provide an environment with a 'wide range of options' that would lead to autonomy. As Wall (2003:313) explains in his analogy, 'the slave remains a slave even if his master allows him, for the most part, to do as he pleases. A slave is still a slave even when he has a liberal master'. Similarly, Trebbi (2008:35) argues that absolute freedom within the concept of autonomy is misleading considering the philosophical notion that humans are not entirely free agents, and that freedom is relative to the sociocultural context within which we live. For Trebbi, (ibid.) autonomy is less a matter of freedom than of 'whether we are victims of constraints or not'.

Benson (2009:26) points out that learners have an innate capacity for autonomy and that it is the role of educators 'to support their autonomy as far as we are able by creating the conditions in which it can flourish' so that they might 'lead the kinds of lives that they wish to lead, rather than to fit them out with the skills and attributes that society demands of them' (ibid.). This resonates in the context of the students who appear in this book in terms of creating the conditions within a VLE where they either felt empowered by their participation, or duty-bound by expectation. Although autonomy brings with it a sense of a democratic and empowering ideal, there is less control than might be suggested by the model of the 'rationally autonomous being' (Pennycook 1997:39) because the individual is the product of the discourse within which he exists, and technologically 'one cannot separate the tool from how it's used or embedded in social interactions' (Blake 2008:132). The autonomous learner does not exist in isolation from his environment but rather there is an interdependent relationship between the individual and the context within which he exists; as Little (1990:7) suggests, 'As social beings our independence is always balanced by dependence, our essential condition is one of interdependence.' Pemberton (1996:3) reflects that many theorists consider that 'Autonomy is seen generally as a capacity that is rarely, if ever, realised in its "ideal" state,' complicated further by the sense that to be autonomous is not an absolute state, and an individual can be 'autonomous in one situation but not in another'.

Autonomy might not relinquish the institution from responsibility, but nor does it release the individual from responsibility for himself and interactions with others within his social context. The notion of interdependence within the concept of autonomy is described by Kohonen (1992:19) as 'being responsible for one's own conduct in the social context: being able to cooperate with others and solve conflicts in constructive ways'. The historical, political and philosophical legacy of autonomy is underpinned by the marriage between independence and responsibility that is challenged by, yet dependent upon, the confines of authority and structure. Autonomy is both an external, interdependent construct as well as internal and independent. It is helpful to group the theorists according to their ideological interpretation of autonomy.

Theories of knowledge and approaches to learning

The concept of autonomy has been widely scrutinized and variously interpreted across the literature but Wiśniewska (2009:13) suggests that differences in approaches between the theorists' interpretations depends on the aspects of autonomy they prioritize. Benson (1997:19) locates his 'versions' of autonomy within the domains of theories of knowledge and learning, drawing on theories of positivism and constructivism, suggesting that this serves as a useful position from which to gain useful insights and explore the relationship between autonomy and language learning. He expressly cautions against the oversimplification of these theories; however, he considers they might shed light on Holec's (1981:3) description of the 'semi-anarchical' application of autonomy in education, and the challenges facing learners in achieving their 'potential capacity' (ibid.) for independence. Positivism and constructivism are more usually applied to theoretical assumptions about knowledge in the humanities and social sciences and not recognized as pedagogical terms, neither are they specific to language learning. To avoid confusion I have adopted the terms 'guided learning' adapting Crook's (1994:79) reference to guided instruction as 'the most orthodox of situations: that involving organized asymmetry of expertise (expert and novice; teacher and pupil)' (ibid.). I also use the term 'autonomous' learning rather than 'constructivism' (Benson 1997:23) to reflect the notion of independent, psychological engagement with the processes of learning organization of thinking and working towards understanding (Little 1990:11).

A guided approach to learning

Conceptually positivism works from the assumption that knowledge is a reflection of objective reality. In the classroom the teacher presents knowledge from the perspective of his own reality, reflected in the traditional teacher/learner relationship (Benson 1997:20). So-called student-centred pedagogies can be misleading. For example, Benson (ibid.) suggests that the theory of discovery learning in which the learner ascertains knowledge for himself is essentially underpinned by positivist principles because the 'knowledge to be acquired is pre-determined but with-held from the learners' (ibid.). Allford and Pachler (2007:149) challenge the association made by Benson between the positivist view of knowledge and autonomy on the basis that his analogy is too vague, uncertain as to which 'positivist' ideologies Benson refers, expressing concern that the association is simply drawn from the 'reprehensible notion' (ibid.) of traditional notions of transmissive education and objective reality, a view they consider to be less than compelling. In this book the term 'guided' learning (Crook 1994:79) is used as a label to acknowledge the presence of the teacher or expert who has a hand in guiding or structuring student activity.

An autonomous approach to learning

In contrast, constructivism emanates from the assumption that through psychological engagement and interaction with the world, the individual acquires and makes sense of new information, reflecting upon it in the light of existing knowledge where 'language does not reflect reality; [...] it constitutes the means by which subjective realities are constructed' (Benson 1997:21). Constructivism considers the inherently social nature of the individual, where learning mediated by interaction in the target language is dependent upon having adequate 'time and psychological space' (Little 1990:9) to construct understanding; nevertheless, the individual might feel compromised by his learning environment where 'Learners and teachers alike are caught in a tug-of-war between one relatively explicit set of beliefs and values [...] and another inexplicit set' (Riley 2009:46). Allford and Pachler (2007:150) criticize Benson's explanation of constructivism because social interaction is seen as a subjective experience that does not reflect reality, overlooking the function of language in mediating our engagement with the world. I have therefore used the term 'autonomous learning' as a label to indicate how the students exploit the time, space and opportunities mediated by a VLE to construct their own understanding and formulate their own response.

Towards autonomy: An eclectic blend of guided and autonomous learning

If guided learning considers the acquisition of knowledge as experience enabled by others, and autonomous learning as the individual interpretation of information mediated by social interaction, it might seem these paradigms cannot co-exist. Yet Macaro (1997:168) observes that 'the presence or the absence of the teacher is not the yardstick by which one can judge autonomous learning skills.' Furthermore, Esch (1996:36) suggests that while the premise of the learner taking charge of his own learning is to be encouraged, ultimately he does not know the language he is learning, so needs the support of a teacher. An eclectic blend of the two theoretical perspectives might be an effective approach, enabling the learner to exploit his innate potential for autonomy.

In Murray's study it is suggested (1999:300) that while students liked being able to work at their own pace, they also felt comfortable with the 'coercive nature' of the classroom, because it absolved them from the burden of responsibility for their own learning. This substantiates Holec's (1981:3) view that although being autonomous means taking charge of, and making decisions about learning, autonomy is fundamentally the individual's 'potential capacity to act in a given situation', which supports Murray's view that autonomy is 'a highly individual construct' (1999:301) meaning that students might be 'autonomous in one area while dependent in another' (ibid.).

Holec goes on to suggest that 'there must be a learning structure in which control over the learning can be exercised by the learner' (Holec 1981:7). The challenge for the institution lies in providing a structure within which the student can spread his wings, but this leaves educators with the problem of treading 'a fine line between propagandizing on the one hand and abandonment of responsibility on the other' (Benson 1997:34), raising the question of 'where on the continuum between fully directed tasks and complete learner autonomy does good learning lie' (Fisher et al. 2004:57).

Versions of autonomy

Benson (1997:19) urges caution in expressly attributing 'versions' of autonomy to different writers, because this would suggest that they exclusively represent one approach, Wiśniewska (2009:13) reminds us that they should not be identified as separate entities because of the overlap between dimensions. Versions of autonomy, as explicated in the literature, problematize the concept beyond the broader understanding of autonomy as the capacity to take control of one's learning. Theorists variously define their versions of autonomy and Benson (2007:24) cites the following as examples: convergence, divergence/convergence and convergence/divergence view (Ribé 2003); internal-cognitive, social-interactive and exploratory-participatory (O'Rourke and Schwienhorst 2003); native-speakerist, cultural-relativist and social approaches (Holliday 2003). Wiśniewska (2009:13) refers to the dimensions of autonomy that are widely cited in the theoretical literature and I have adopted this as a general organizing principle in my orientation of the literature. I consider and critique four categories: technical, psychological, political and cultural versions of autonomy.

Technical autonomy

The most commonly cited definition of autonomy is 'the ability to take charge of one's own learning' (Holec 1981:3), which includes the capacity to make decisions about the direction, management and organization of learning at different stages.

The emphasis of the Holec paper (1981:1) and the Council of Europe Modern Languages Project was the promotion of autonomous language learning for adults with a move towards self-directed learning. In turn, this stimulated an association between autonomy and the management of the processes of learning, referred to by Benson (1997:23) as 'technical' autonomy. Benson (1997:23) defined technical autonomy as equipping the learners with the necessary skills to manage their learning beyond the classroom, suggesting that this corresponded to the notion of 'positivist' (Benson 1997:23) or guided approaches to learning. Yet the construct of technical autonomy can be expanded to include learning strategies within *and* beyond the classroom, with implications for the following perspectives, indicated in Box 2.1.

Box 2.1 Technical autonomy: Factors to consider in taking charge of one's learning

Situation	Supporting students to work effectively in alternative contexts for learning.
	Examples: self-access centre; computer room; home; classrooms with a laptop and overhead projector; VLE-blended lessons; VLE free-time affordances.
Training and development	Raising awareness of cognitive learning strategies and techniques supporting learners towards fulfilling their potential capacity to take charge of their learning in new learning environments.

Technical autonomy: The situational aspect

Early work following the Council of Europe's Modern Language Project in the 1970s led to wider interest in the value and practicalities of fostering learner independence. Benson and Voller (1997:9) suggest that there has been a tendency for the literature to assume that self-access and self-instruction to be a natural means by which autonomy might be realized. This is not the only view characterized in the literature by the 'technical autonomists'. Dickinson (1987a) proposes that contexts for learning need to be organized in such a way as to accommodate individual needs within and beyond the classroom, arguing for greater flexibility in institutions and in language classrooms, with implications for the role of the teacher in both teaching and supporting the development of skills so that the learners might 'strive towards autonomy in learning' (1987a:2).

Intuitively, the suggestion is that self-instruction means working independently of the teacher, or the classroom, corresponding to a view of autonomy as freedom from external control, in which the learner has temporal and spatial control. Yet Dickinson defines self-instruction as 'situations in which a learner, with others or alone, is working without the direct control of a teacher' (1987a:5), whether for short periods in class, whole lessons or undertaking a learning programme without a teacher. The difficulty is that assumptions about learning have evolved from a culture of teacher/learner dependency. Despite years of research identifying strategies, approaches and tools that might be adopted in class to cultivate autonomy, Leni Dam (2009:125) reflects that it is surprisingly difficult for teachers to change from a traditional approach to one that actively creates opportunities for learners to get involved in their own learning. An autonomous approach to language-learning challenges notions of classroom hierarchy, requiring a redefinition of teacher–learner relationships (Villanueva et al. 2010:5).

Self-directed learning emerges as more than a matter of creating the external conditions in which students can work independently of the teacher. Simply by creating a resource-rich educational context, but one in which de facto the situation determines that learners have no choice but to self-direct, is no guarantee of success, either in class *or* beyond. The realization of the learner's capacity for autonomy therefore emerges as an attribute of the learner, rather than the learning situation; as Dickinson (1994:4) says, 'autonomy is primarily a matter of attitude to learning rather than the physical setting of the learning'.

In one sense autonomy can be identified 'technically' as a matter relating to creating the conditions within which the learner can realize his capacity for autonomy, which has design implications for the development of an effective technological learning environment. But considered in isolation the difficulty is that autonomous behaviour emerges as a personal response to external stimuli, overlooking the cognitive complexity of the construct. Dickinson counters this argument with the suggestion that autonomy is a matter of attitude to learning (ibid.). The weakness with this argument is that attitudes are influenced by expectations about roles and relationships in an educational setting and are affected by past experience. The students and teacher who appear in this book were accustomed to a culture of teacher-led learning. Simply creating a resource-rich VLE context designed to stimulate signs of autonomous engagement would be no guarantee of success. The role of learner training arises in the literature as a means of raising awareness and developing cognitive strategies in order to explore students' potential for autonomy.

Technical autonomy: Learner training and development

Benson (2007:23) argues that while Holec (1981:3) describes the exercise of autonomy and *what* the autonomous learner is able to do in terms of the mechanics of learner management, he does not offer any practical suggestions as to *how* this might be achieved. Dickinson proposes that very few individuals are 'spontaneously self-directed' (1987a:1), so learner training emerges as an aspect of 'technical' autonomy (Benson 1997:23) guiding the learner towards maximizing the advantages of autonomous learning (Dickinson 1989:45). In suggesting that spontaneous autonomy is a rarity, Dickinson (1989:45) indicates the cognitive challenges associated with raising learner awareness so that learners are capable of embracing increased levels of responsibility for learning. Dickinson (1994:5) identifies learner autonomy as a goal that he describes as a 'co-operative enterprise between teacher and learners' with Weaver and Cohen (1998:67, cited in Wiśniewska 2009:24) seeing learner training as a means of guiding learners towards the application of cognitive strategies in order to manage different tasks and contexts for learning and to promote learner autonomy. Allford and Pachler (2007:158) adopt a 'gradualist position' where autonomy is identified as an 'eventual goal rather than a starting point or right' and argue that although in *practice* Holec took the gradualist position, where autonomy is 'not inborn but must be acquired' (Holec 1981:3), *in principle* he insisted that autonomy should be the starting point, otherwise the teacher undermines the learner's capacity for autonomy by adopting an overly dominant position. Although advocates of learner training (Dickinson 1994:5) have emphasized the sense with which the process should be integrated into the learning programme as a co-operative enterprise, Esch (1997:164) expresses concern that over the years the debate about the aims of learner autonomy has fallen prey to short-term goals, management issues and organizational matters, reducing autonomous learning to a set of learnable skills. But these approaches need not exist in isolation from one another. Foreign language courses can be organized systematically so that as an outcome, learners can become increasingly aware and explore their capacity for autonomy. Nevertheless, with its promise of far-reaching transformative properties, the role of technology emerges as a strategic tool in supporting this process; as Esch and Zähner (2000:9–10) reflect, 'ICTs can be used to activate cognitive and metacognitive language-learning strategies which force learners to think and concentrate more on their engagement into the process of knowledge creation and the way they conceptualise the information.'

The move towards learner training reflects the pedagogical view where the teacher supports the learner in developing his/her capacity for increasing levels of independence in learning. Dickinson et al. (1989:3) suggest that complete autonomy is a rare state but that 'learner training espouses the belief that everybody has the right to develop the capacity for taking charge of his or her own affairs'. The premise of learner training is to furnish learners with strategies and the confidence to embrace increased responsibility, preparing them for independence, focusing their attention on the processes of learning, with an emphasis on *how* rather than *what* to learn. Ellis and Sinclair (1989) propose that learner training is based on the following assumptions:

1. Individuals learn in different ways, and can use a variety of strategies at different times, depending on how they feel, what they are doing.
2. The better informed the learner is about language and learning, the better they will be at managing their own learning.

Allwright (1988:35) advocates a minimalist approach to learner training in the classroom, based on the nurturing of naturally occurring instances of autonomy generated as a feature of classroom interaction such that:

1. Each lesson is a personal response to a shared experience. Each student takes something different from the lesson. From this perspective, 'Perhaps the learners are already "autonomously individualising" their classroom experience' (Allwright 1988:36).
2. Co-productive nature of classroom lessons: classroom discourse makes a difference to the turn of events in the lesson, where linguistic choices influence the lesson.
3. Learners individualize the lesson by responding to one another, as well as the teacher, taking something unique from the experience.

The value of reflection emerges as a means by which learners might be encouraged to realize their capacity for autonomy; as Cotterall (2000:112) says, 'The potential for autonomy increases as an individual's awareness grows. Therefore activities which prompt learners to reflect on their learning aim at enhancing learners' insight into their learning process.' Learner training is a component identified by the 'technical' theorists as a way of supporting the individual towards taking control of his own learning, whether explicitly in the development of learning strategies or the exploitation of the seeds of autonomy occurring naturally in the classroom (Allwright 1988:35). Terminology can be misleading and used interchangeably between the theorists. In writing about self-access, Sheerin (1997:59–60) makes the distinction between learner training and development. She suggests that training implies the transmission of skills, something that is done to someone by another, such as how to use a computer programme. On the other hand, learner development involves raising the learner's awareness in becoming more proactive and accepting responsibility for his learning, which is cognitively more gradual and complex to define.

There is a place for institutions to provide a robust context and conditions for learning with development opportunities embedded in the learning programme so that individuals can be encouraged towards autonomy. However, in attempting to visualize, package and operationalize the ways in which learners can take charge of their learning, I reiterate the point raised by Esch (1997:164) that the debate reduces the idea of autonomous learning to a set of learnable skills. I would add that there is a danger in overlooking the notion of learner agency and self-determination.

Balancing the external conditions and internal cognitive dimensions of the concept is difficult to achieve, but in this book I am not interested in training and modifying student behaviour. I am interested in the examination of the learners' personal response to the introduction of a VLE in terms of what they thought and what they did in response to the technology and how far signs of their engagement could be described as an autonomous personal response to the VLE. In so doing this might reveal something of the nature of the relationship between autonomy and technology in the context of foreign language learning. The technical approach is a more descriptive, practical view of autonomy that relates to the development of the individual's ability to perform tasks in different contexts, thereby realizing his potential for autonomous learning, rather than as 'a particular psychological relation to the process and content of his learning' (Little 1991:4).

Psychological autonomy

Benson (1997:23) makes the association between constructivist approaches to learning and the psychological version of autonomy which is concerned with learner behaviour and attitudes. This perspective corresponds with Little's (1996:203) description of learner autonomy as 'a special instance of a socio-psychological phenomenon.'

There are repeated references throughout the literature to autonomy as the individual's capacity to take charge of his learning. However, Little (1999:11) proposes that the fundamental premise of learner autonomy is that the learner accepts responsibility for his own learning. Furthermore, Scharle and Szabó (2000:4) suggest that responsibility implies that the individual has to deal with the consequences of his actions, alerting us to the cognitive and psychological aspects of autonomy, going beyond the matter of autonomy as the management of the processes of learning. Wiśniewska (2009:17) points to the view that learner autonomy has a psychological dimension because 'the cognitive and emotional side of the individual are engaged in the process of learning' but that simultaneously it also has a social aspect since 'learners do not operate in a social vacuum and their learning is more successful when supported by others' (ibid.). I argue that the cognitive and social dimensions are two sides of the same coin relative to the psychological approach to autonomous learning; as Little (2000:17) suggests, 'social context and interaction play a vital role in stimulating and shaping the cognitive processes'. From an ecological perspective, van Lier (2000:258) connects 'cognitive processes with social processes', where language and learning are identified as the relationship among and between learners and their environment. Esch (2009:33–42) considers the choice between two 'roads' (ibid.) that exist in tension with one another, facing teachers' and researchers' practice: 'individual personal autonomy' and 'autonomy as a capacity to exercise critical thinking about learning as a participant in a social milieu.' Each 'road' (ibid.) might however be considered to be an illustration of the psychological dimension of autonomy.

Contrasting: 'Individual Personal Autonomy' and 'Autonomy as a Capacity for Socially-Mediated Critical Thinking about Learning' (Esch 2009:33–42)

Esch (ibid.) considers the moral dimension of personal autonomy and the Rogerian tradition in which the individual's capacity to take responsibility for his actions and their consequences is necessary in the quest for self-fulfilment. In their evaluation of what it means to be an autonomous learner, Breen and Mann (1997:135) reflect that metacognitive ability allows the learner to make conscious choices about what, when and how to learn. They go on to suggest that this capacity allows the individual to evaluate, respond and adapt to available resources; in other words, to express his potential for personal learner autonomy. There is a danger that in prioritizing individual personal autonomy, we overlook the notion of learning as a socially mediated, participative construct, so endorsing an individualistic culture of *self*-centredness rather than *learner*-centredness in the quest for self-determination (Esch 2009:35). Little (2000:16) acknowledges the intuitive association between autonomy as independence and learning in isolation, but in addition argues that higher cognitive functions are shaped by the processes of social interaction, because we are social beings and learning is essentially a collaborative activity. Little (2009:48) reflects upon the idea that 'connectedness' might conflict with autonomy but suggests that this confuses autonomy with independence, citing Deci and Flaste (1996:89) in differentiating between the two constructs. The notion of connectedness supports Little's (1990:7) view of interdependence and the balance between independence and dependence. If the construction of knowledge and understanding emerges from the individual's interactive involvement, which is then expressed communicatively as speech or writing, language is therefore the tool for both metacognitive and metalinguistic processes (Little 2007:21).

It might be argued that Esch's (2009:33) notion of 'autonomy as a capacity to exercise critical thinking about learning as a participant in a social milieu,' corresponds to the Vygotskyan view of language as a tool that mediates the individual's capacity to articulate higher-order mental activity, such as thinking and meaning, representing the 'relation between human beings and their environment, both physical and social' (Vygotsky 1978:19). Applied more specifically to language learning, the experience becomes 'more than acquiring new signifiers [...] it's about acquiring new conceptual knowledge and/or modifying already existing knowledge as a way of re-mediating one's interaction with the world' (Lantolf and Thorne 2006a:5) whereby the exchange of ideas is conveyed between interlocutors by language so that 'publicly derived speech completes privately initiated thought' (Lantolf 2000:7). Vygotsky (1978:53) considered the idea that 'the tongue is the tool of thought' as somewhat fanciful; nevertheless, as an idea it conveys the interconnectedness between cognition and language, and the psychological dimension of autonomy and language development. The difficulty for the language learner is in precisely articulating his thinking in the target language and the degree of spontaneity with which he is able and willing to do so. By virtue of being an L2 learner, his 'behaviour is enhanced or constrained by the tools [he has] available' (Swain and Deters 2007:821).

In this book I am interested in the examination of students' personal response to a VLE-mediated language development programme in terms of their perceptions of its value and their online activity relative to autonomy to see what this might reveal about the nature of the relationship between autonomy and technology. The premise of psychological autonomy is therefore intellectually appealing, considering the view held by Little (2007:18) that human nature is simultaneously 'internal-cognitive and social-interactive' and that individuals have the capacity to respond *to* ideas *in* the target language, as indicated in Table 2.1. However, as an approach it is difficult to operationalize in terms of evaluating the learners' personal response to the technology.

Table 2.1 Difficulties with the psychological and cognitive dimensions of autonomy in a VLE

Psychological autonomy in a VLE	Difficulties associated with psychological autonomy in this study
Learners individually cognitively (Little 2007:18) reflect, evaluate and adapt to the range of available resources in a VLE environment.	Tracking VLE movements as observational data is possible but identifying and capturing 'internal-cognitive' (ibid.) strategies of signs of engagement in navigating the VLE is challenging.
Learners perceive their 'social-interactive' (ibid.) capacity to articulate and exchange personally held ideas with others in the target language in a VLE-mediated context.	Capturing the interconnectedness between cognition and language is difficult to achieve. Difficult to corroborate learners' perceptions of their ability to articulate and exchange their own opinions. Difficult to evaluate the impact of the VLE from the learners' personal response.
Learners are individually cognitively (ibid.) reflective and attribute value to their participation in VLE-mediated language development programme.	Challenging to identify the means of reliably capturing the cognitive reflective process.

Littlewood's (1999:74–5) interpretation of autonomy corresponds to Little's (1990:7) notion of interdependence and he cites Ryan's (1991:210) view of autonomy as the 'mutually supportive relationship' between 'self-regulation' with 'relatedness'.

The idea of relatedness might be thought to correspond to the notion of ecology posited by van Lier (2004:3) and the 'totality of relationships of an organism with all other organisms with which it comes into contact'. In this book, conceptually, the ecological dimension emerges as a means of evaluating the learners' personal response to the VLE because it acknowledges the inextricable cognitive links between self and others with the unpredictability of a web of social interaction. However appealing the notion of interconnectedness, in isolation the difficulties associated with psychological autonomy still remain. The need emerges to step back, take the overview and examine what the learners are responsive to. Mindful of the connection between self-regulation and relatedness, Littlewood (1999:75–6) refines his interpretation of autonomy further, adopting the terms 'proactive' and 'reactive autonomy', which he draws from Flannery's (1994) distinction between group-oriented 'cooperative' and 'collaborative' learning strategies. Boxes 2.2 and 2.3 summarize the distinction Littlewood makes between the two concepts.

Box 2.2 Summary of proactive autonomy (adapted from Littlewood 1999:75–6)

Proactive autonomy: Action	Impact and outcome
'regulates the direction of the activity undertaken by the individual as well as the activity itself'. (Littlewood 1999:75) Direction initiated by learner so that he: 1. Takes charge of own learning. 2. Determines own objectives. 3. Selects methods and techniques for learning. 4. Evaluates learning.	Process of learning is as important as the product as: 1. Learner establishes the direction of learning. 2. Self-affirmation of individuality.

Box 2.3 Summary of reactive autonomy (adapted from Littlewood 1999:75–6)

Reactive autonomy: Action	Impact and outcome
'regulates the activity once the direction has been set' (ibid.) Direction initiated by *others* so that learner: 1. Can organize learning resources and reach goals. 2. Can work with others to complete task. '*Expert*' selects learning methods and content for learners to work with.	Complements rather than challenges traditional learning. Either: 1. Preliminary step towards proactive autonomy. Or: 2. A goal in its own right.

Littlewood indicates that there is a tendency for proactive autonomy to be deemed to hold greater value because with reactive autonomy learners do not initiate the activity, but he points out that 'once a direction has been initiated learners can organize their resources autonomously in order to reach their goal' (1999:75). Reactive autonomy suggests a view that allows the concept of autonomy to be operationalized and evaluated without the need for radical

> **Box 2.4 Proactive and reactive autonomy in the context of a VLE**
>
> 1. **Proactive autonomy**: The VLE creates a context in which learners can proactively navigate and respond to VLE-mediated affordances; student-led forums provide electronic spaces for student-generated communicative activity.
> 2. **Reactive autonomy**: By design and with the facilitative support of the teacher, learners respond to the direction set by VLE-mediated blended lessons and weekly expert-generated forum threads. Conditions might be created which might stimulate learners to marshal resources and work together, going beyond the remit stipulated by the trigger of the 'expert' voice.

restructuring of the classroom. Littlewood's notion of proactive and reactive autonomy resonates in the context of a VLE as indicated in Box 2.4.

It allows for fresh insights into the interpretation and analysis of students' personal responses by acknowledging the significance of an external structure in mediating the activity or resource to which the students can personally respond. Our view need not be restricted to an examination of learners' responses to a context purposely designed to liberate them from the rigours of external control.

It is possible to manifest signs of autonomous engagement triggered by a stimulus, for example responding to instruction provided by the teacher or computer screen. What emerges is the difficulty in determining how far signs of student engagement are directly a response to the stimulus, or a response to the network of subsequent interactions – indirectly a response to the stimulus, raising questions about the nature of the relationship between autonomy and technology. This leads us towards the possibility of considering autonomy from an ecological perspective, with its emphasis on context, broadening our view beyond the learner's 'solitary performance' (van Lier 2000:259) in response to the task, the pedagogical approach and the medium (ibid.).

In acknowledging a relationship between guidance and autonomous behaviour, the challenges associated with working towards social equilibrium between the voice of the expert and the student emerge because, as Pennycook (1997:39) suggests, 'as both political and psychological beings we have far less control over what we do or say than is suggested in the model of the rationally autonomous being'.

Political autonomy

Mindful of the association between autonomy as self-determination and freedom from external control, autonomy can be considered a political construct because the learner has the 'right to have control over his/her learning' (Wiśniewska 2009:17), encouraged in the development of his ability to manage his learning so that he might become the author of his own world (Benson 2009:26). In an educational setting this perspective unsettles conventions of institutional power structures (Little 1996, cited in Pemberton 1996:6), leading to the suggestion that constraints imposed upon learners by external forces, such as the institution, have the potential to suppress their capacity for autonomy (Candy 1989, cited in Benson 1997:23). A less didactic approach to classroom learning can seem 'less rather than more purposeful and efficient' (Little 1991:21, cited in Benson 2001:37) proving problematic because expectations and assumptions about learning are learned from an early age. In practice 'many learners [...] have been socialized into a dependent relationship with the teacher' (Breen and Mann 1997:143) so traditional education does not create the conditions within which learners can exercise their potential for independence. Benson (2000:114) argues that this might be because 'the interests of society have priority over the interests of the individual'. In the context of the classroom the direction of learning is traditionally weighted in favour of the voice of authority, with opportunities for autonomous behaviour awarded by degree at the behest of the teacher. However, Little (1990:11) counters this view, with the suggestion that autonomy is less a matter of external organization and more a matter of the learner's psychological relationship with the processes of learning.

On a macro scale, in the interests of the global economy, there are growing expectations that workers will engage in training and take more responsibility for their development, thereby improving productivity (Benson 2009:24). In our increasingly digitalized world where English is the lingua franca of the internet, policy decisions to teach English in preference to other languages prove far from politically neutral (ibid.). On a micro-scale, the classroom emerges as a politicized environment, mediated by the trend towards empowering and recognizing the rights of the individual, and promoting independent learning, where learners are 'called upon to act as agents of our own socialisation and subordination' (Benson 1997:29). In her quest for a model of L2 learner autonomy, Oxford (2003:90) considers the need to challenge the status quo of the classroom and assumptions about traditional power structures. The macro and micro political stances regarding autonomy correspond to Pennycook's view that 'the notion of the freely acting political agent within a democratic state has been one of the great obfuscatory myths of liberal democracy' (Pennycook 1997:37). In his study of young language learners in a school in Northern England, Lamb (2009:86) suggests that in working towards learner autonomy, teachers need to be prepared to relinquish rather than tighten control, but in so doing this requires the development of structures within which learners feel able to express their views, negotiate and compromise. In his 'expanded notion of political autonomy' Benson (1997:31) proposes that consideration should be afforded to matters such as social context; learning tasks and content; and roles and relationships within and beyond the remit of the classroom.

A VLE can be described as an externally developed tool with the potential to facilitate collaboration between learners. The difficulty lies in the development and construction of VLE-mediated content and the creation of the conditions that balance the voice of the external agent with that of the learner so that the individual feels capable of expressing his right to take control of his learning. Nevertheless, Esch and Zähner (ibid.) suggest that the learner is central in the appropriation of technology into a language-learning environment, revealing the potential of new technologies by conceptualizing and evaluating the perceived relevance of ICT tools to support language development.

Autonomy could be conceptualized in this study as an undercurrent affecting internal-cognitive processes and collaborative social interaction (Benson, ibid.). I acknowledge the challenges associated with political autonomy and the literature indicates the notion of learner autonomy as an ideological Western construct, alien to learners from other cultures which resonates in the context of language teaching around the world. However, the focus of this book is directed towards an examination of the balance of power between external forces and individual autonomy. The emphasis lies in the interrogation of the nature of the relationship between autonomy and technology through an analysis of students' personal response to the technology in terms of: VLE-mediated student behaviour and student reflections about the VLE. I am interested in the notion of interdependence between the learner and the context suggested by proactive and reactive autonomy (ibid.).

Cultural autonomy

Pennycook (1997:43) expresses concern that the global promotion of learner autonomy might be perceived as 'another version of the supposed emancipation to the unenlightened, traditional, backward and authoritarian classrooms of the world'. Oxford (2008:50) argues that if we are to understand autonomy, an awareness of cultural values is particularly important, citing Cotterall (1995) who suggests that learners' beliefs are affected by sociocultural context influencing autonomy. Littlewood (1999:72) reflects on the view that conceptually autonomy is culturally laden, arguing that although trends within and between groups of learners can be observed, learners are essentially individuals. Oxford (2008:50) expresses doubt that generalizations can be applied 'en bloc' (ibid.) to every member of any given culture, within which cultures and subcultures co-exist. Littlewood (1999:72) argues that, regardless of culture, the aim in language teaching should be to encourage learners to work towards autonomous communication and learning, without the support of their teacher where opportunities for autonomous interaction and independent thinking are incorporated into the classroom. Furthermore, Little (1999:12) raises the following points:

1. Autonomy is an elusive concept to operationalize, whatever the educational context.
2. The encouragement of critical thinking in learning is not exclusive to the West.
3. Our capacity for awareness of our conscious selves is a universal human capacity, not only a matter of culture relative to ethnicity.

Little (2003: n.p.) proposes that despite evidence to suggest that the capacity for autonomy is essentially a psychological phenomenon that goes beyond cultural differences, research indicates that learning and behaviour are 'always and inevitably culturally conditioned' (ibid.), with Palfreyman (2003:13) suggesting that 'all learning is cultural since it involves interacting with one's context [. . .] as well as other people and their words and ideas in order to develop meanings.' Furthermore, it would be wrong to suggest that culture is exclusively a matter of nationality and ethnicity, and Palfreyman (2003:1) sees that cultural autonomy relates to:

1. The values and beliefs of a community, such as a classroom or a school.
2. The learner who exists within a sociocultural context.

Dickinson's view that autonomy is essentially an 'attitude for learning' (1995) is affected by the cultural conditions that might be reflected in students' personal response to the VLE experience. However, in this book the focus is not expressly concerned with the examination of the cultural dimensions of the relationship between autonomy and technology, nor is this a book that explores the technologically mediated emancipation of students from the cultural constraints of their learning environment. The focus of this book is the analysis of the learners' personal response in terms of their onsite activity and their reflections on their VLE experience to see what this might reveal about the nature of the relationship between autonomy and technology. It is timely therefore to propose my own theoretical definition of autonomy in a VLE.

A theoretical definition of autonomy in a VLE

The underlying conceptual premise of autonomy is that the individual has the opportunity to chart 'his own course through life [. . .] according to his own understanding of what is valuable and worth doing' (Wall 2003:308) and that he is not 'thwarted by institutional choices' (Ciekanski 2007:112). But we do not exist in isolation from others, making this an idealistic view. Freedom is relative to the constraints of the sociocultural context in which we live. Autonomy is characterized by the interdependence between its internal, cognitive dimensions and its external dimensions mediated by the multiple stimuli to which we respond. The difficulty lies in balancing the internal and external dimensions of autonomy, so that the construct becomes less a matter of freedom but 'whether we are victims of constraints or not' (Trebbi 2008:35). In translating this notion into the context of a technological learning environment, students cognitively engage with, and respond to, the dynamic processes of learning in response to external stimuli mediated by the teacher, classmates and activities, stimulating social interaction.

Autonomy might be identified as the interdependence between internal-cognitive and external social-cognitive (Little 2007:18) and contextual dimensions. However, my concern is that this represents a linear and therefore reductive perspective of the dynamics of autonomous learning. I draw on the metaphor of ecology, identified by van Lier (1997, 2000, 2004, 2007) to reconceptualize language learning and teaching beyond notions of input and output where context and interaction are central to the analysis. Lantolf (2000:25) argues that the ecological perspective means that everything is connected to everything else where individual elements cannot be considered in isolation but should be considered in relation to other factors. I propose an ecological version of learner autonomy. This dimension acknowledges the more fluid interrelationship between elements that contribute to the unravelling of events in the learning environment and the individual's realization of his potential for autonomy.

I define ecological learner autonomy as: an internal-cognitive response to a socially interactive web of unpredictability; it is a version of autonomy characterized by the significance of the 'totality of relationships of an organism with all other organisms with which it comes into contact' (van Lier 2004:3). From this perspective we enrich the notion of interdependency between the internal and external dimensions of autonomy by accounting for the transformation of an activity as it is variously, individually and unpredictably interpreted between participants. Autonomy emerges as a fluid, responsive state, a web of cognitive and socially interactive engagement. According to the ecological view of learner autonomy, the dynamics of learning are set in motion, anchored by the task and mediated by the teacher and the technology, but cognitively learners make judgements and choices, reflecting and responding in a non-linear way to the voices of those who go before and around them.

Technological functionality makes it possible to probe more deeply, examining intricate patterns of interaction from the guided/didactic environment to the autonomous/constructivist context. Technology allows us to observe and scrutinize signs of engagement in response to expert-generated tasks (reactive autonomy, ibid.) and learner-generated activity (proactive autonomy, ibid.), privileging us with previously inaccessible insights into learner behaviour. Considered alongside learners' reflections about the VLE-mediated experience, we can examine and arrive at more profound insights into the nature of the relationship between autonomy and technology.

Given the complexity and multiplicity of interpretations of the concept of autonomy, the difficulty lies in operationalizing autonomy, so making the transition from the pedagogical ideal to which 'we can aspire' (Boud 1988:20) to meaningful application in a learning environment. In attempting to operationalize autonomy in the context of language learning mediated by a VLE, it is helpful to provide an overview of three frameworks for autonomy proposed by Benson, Littlewood and Macaro.

An evaluation of three conceptual frameworks for autonomy in language education

I have looked for the commonalities, differences, strengths and limitations between three different frameworks for autonomy. I have borne these factors in mind in considering how instances of autonomy might be identified and evaluated within the context of the VLE, and in the construction of the VLE autonomy framework.

Framework 1 – Benson

This framework is widely cited and critiqued across the literature, (see Table 2.2) creating a useful base from which to operationalize the notion of autonomy. Oxford (2003) critiques the merits and interrelationship between these different versions of autonomy. However, she expresses concern that there has been an overemphasis of the political dimension arguing that this should not be at the expense of other relevant perspectives (2003:90). Oxford expressly cautions against an over-reliance on a single viewpoint 'No single perspective should be considered antithetical to any other' (ibid.).

While psychological autonomy incorporates the cognitive implications of being autonomous, Oxford (2003:85) challenges what it means to achieve 'psychological autonomy' because 'it does not look in depth at the details of any sociocultural context'. Oxford reflects on the cultural constraints facing many learners in achieving 'political autonomy' with its emphasis on power and ideology rather than individual development mediated through interaction (2003:85). This is supported by Pennycook (1997:53) who considers that 'Promoting autonomy in language learning [. . .] needs to take into account the cultural contexts of the language learners.' I would expand on Oxford's concerns, arguing that the difficulty with this framework is that the emphasis predominantly lies in the internal-cognitive (Little 2007:18 op. cit.) challenges in psychologically and politically striving for autonomy. It inadequately addresses the socially interactive (Oxford 2003:85) nature of language learning and the relationship between the learner and the interconnecting elements in his environment.

Table 2.2 Autonomy framework 1 (adapted from Benson 1997:19)

Technical learner autonomy	Psychological autonomy	Political autonomy
External implications of being an autonomous learner:	Internal implications of being an autonomous learner:	Internal and external implications of being an autonomous learner:
• Learning outside the educational institution without a teacher. • Learners are obliged to take charge of their own learning. • The challenge – to equip the learners with the necessary skills to be technically autonomous.	• Autonomy as the individual's attitudinal capacity to take responsibility for his learning. • Internal development of the individual towards adopting increased levels of responsibility for his learning.	• Management of the processes and content of learning. • The challenge – creating the conditions where the learner can manage his own learning within the educational context.

Littlewood (1999:74–5) proposes that a supportive, structured context need not interfere with, but rather, encourage autonomy; he cites Ryan (1991), who suggests that the development of autonomy is most effective in an interpersonal environment.

Framework 2 – Littlewood

A further issue with Benson's framework is that the emphasis lies more explicitly with how the individual might become an autonomous *learner*, rather than an autonomous *user* of the target language. This issue is identified by Littlewood (1996:428) who reflects that in the wider literature in 'many of the discussions about language learning, "autonomy" is understood to refer to learner autonomy', whereas he refers to autonomy as 'a capacity for thinking and acting independently that may occur in any situation' (ibid.).

Littlewood considers the ability to communicate and learn independently as significant factors contributing to the personal autonomy of the individual. This view informs his framework for the development of strategies for achieving autonomy as a learner and user of a foreign language, proposing three domains for autonomy in language learning: communication, learning and as a person, summarized in Table 2.3.

Littlewood (1999:74–77) expands his notion of 'autonomy as a learner', introducing the notion of proactive and reactive autonomy thereby connecting the idea of autonomy as self-determination and self-regulation with relatedness and 'people's need to feel [. . .] part of a social network' (1999:74). In this sense

Table 2.3 Autonomy framework 2 (adapted from Littlewood 1996:431)

Autonomy as a communicator	Autonomy as a learner	Autonomy as a person (in a foreign language learning context)
• The ability to use the language creatively – the expression of personal meanings. • The ability to select strategies for communication in specific situations – independently navigating texts and social contexts.	• The ability to work independently (e.g. self-directed learning). • The ability to select suitable learning strategies within and beyond the classroom – supporting language development and extending the communicative range.	• The ability to express personal meaning. • The ability to create personal learning contexts (e.g. interacting beyond the classroom) – seeking opportunities for independent reading, joining target language groups beyond the classroom.

autonomy can be conceptualized as a 'collective experience' (Littlewood 1999:91), extending the concept beyond the 'independent self' (Littlewood 1999:79), embracing the potential of the 'interdependent self' (ibid.) and therefore the individual's ability to realize his potential for autonomy within the construct of the expert-led classroom and VLE. Littlewood's model places greater emphasis on the interrelationship between internal-cognitive thinking and social interaction; however, the framework is problematic considering the view held by Breen and Mann (1997:143) that 'many learners [...] have been socialized into a dependent relationship with the teacher'. It is unclear how the learner might arrive at these enhanced levels of autonomy. Benson (2007:24) argues that models such as Littlewood's overlook the complexity of the relationship between the development of autonomy and the demands of achieving language proficiency.

Nevertheless, in this model there is a clear emphasis on meaningful language use, reminiscent of Kern's (2000:17) reflections on the implications of literacy as it impacts upon language skills. Kern's view supports Littlewood's notion of 'autonomy as a communicator':

> By practising literacy events in a non-native language [...] not just rehearsing reading and writing skills [...] They learn to deal with uncertainties and ambiguities rather than relying on simplistic and rigid form-meaning correspondences. (Kern 2000:17)

Littlewood's 'autonomy as a communicator', with its emphasis on interaction in the target language, has much to recommend it in terms of encouraging communication in English beyond more 'rigid form-meaning correspondences' (ibid.). Yet often students have limited opportunities to use the target language beyond the classroom, as Pica et al. (1996:60) suggest:

> Opportunities for either extensive or wide ranging interaction with NSs is all too infrequent and often simply impossible [...] especially so for learners in foreign language contexts, where classrooms of non native speaking teachers and other L2 learners are the basis for most of their interaction.

The reality of the conventional language classroom makes Littlewood's notion of 'autonomy as a communicator' a challenging goal to achieve.

Framework 3 – Macaro

Like other theorists, Macaro (1997) acknowledges the significance of supporting the learner, identifying the need for long-term learning strategies, and the challenges associated with the decentralization of learning away from the teacher. He reflects that the freedom to learn autonomously includes the way that the individual psychologically engages with the learning process, so that it is not just a matter of external organization. Table 2.4 summarizes Macaro's (1997:170) framework for functional learner autonomy in the foreign language classroom.

Autonomy of language competence

Macaro addresses autonomy relative to language use rather than learning strategies. In a re-evaluation of his framework for functional autonomy, Macaro (2008:50) reflects upon this category suggesting that 'A fundamental precept of autonomy of language competence [...] should be that the learner move gradually towards the competence to generate their own utterances.'

In becoming more linguistically competent, Macaro acknowledges two complications. First, research suggests that learners continue to use formulaic phrases in their transition towards the generation of independent utterances in the target language, so that 'the fluent language speaker is probably making [...] subconscious selections regarding formulas and utterance generation' (ibid.). A second complication is that in the quest for grammatical accuracy, the teacher may overlook the significance of interlanguage in the learner's appropriation of the target language, dampening creativity. Macaro is therefore concerned with how the individual engages with the language on a personal level. This category

Table 2.4 Autonomy framework 3 (adapted from Macaro 1997:170)

Autonomy of language competence	Autonomy of language learning competence	Autonomy of choice and action
• Communication in the target language with a reasonable mastery of the L2 rule system largely without the help of a more competent speaker.	• The internal and external systematic application of strategies, describing the learner's awareness of, and conscious ability to deploy, a range of complementary strategies to complete a task using the target language. • The potential of the individual and the environment in facilitating the application of cognitive and metacognitive learning strategies. • The transference of learning strategies to other contexts.	• The capacity for the individual to be free to make informed choices in the planning and strategizing of their achievement of language learning objectives.

of autonomy resembles Littlewood's view of 'autonomy as a communicator' and the journey towards the expression of personal meanings. Although Littlewood and Macaro make explicit reference to the development of communication in the target language, they make no reference to the 'cognitive dimensions' (Kern 2000:29) and Kern's (2000:16/7) 'expanded notion of literacy'. This perspective incorporates the value of interpretations and reflections on experience, shared understandings about linguistic conventions and the way in which explicit and implicit collaboration makes communication meaningful between individuals through the written or spoken word. Furthermore, Macaro's model makes no distinction between the developmental value of proactive or reactive utterances (Littlewood 1999:75–6). The multiple cognitive dimensions of L2 interaction mediated by a VLE are inadequately served by Littlewood's and Macaro's frameworks for autonomy.

Autonomy of language learning competence

This version of autonomy illustrates the transference of language-learning skills to other situations and the balance between external constraints and the individual's desire for language learning manifested in his 'Cognitive and metacognitive strategic behaviour' (Macaro 2008:55). Rather than linguistic competency, this category is more strategic relative to individual learner autonomy, describing how the student adapts to his learning environment, developing strategies to maximize learning opportunities, making conscious choices about what, when and how to learn. Macaro (1997:171) adds that this also includes developing 'the ability to cope with access to target language sources [. . .] not planned or "mediated" by the teacher.' These notions can be applied to the student's cognitive and metacognitive strategic behaviour (2008:55) in response to the VLE. As I suggested earlier, there seems to be an assumption that the transition from a culture of learner dependency to independence in and out of class is unproblematic.

Autonomy of choice and action

Macaro (1997:171) proposes that learners need opportunities in class to develop their ability to make independent choices. One difficulty with the notion of autonomy of choice and action lies with the view that learners require 'time and psychological space' (Little 1990:9) in which to learn. Furthermore, the individual might be capable of making choices related to his linguistic development and language use, but the challenge lies in providing 'genuine alternatives'(Esch 2009:32), which in the context of the traditional learning environment are beyond the learner's control. Sociocultural constraints and political undercurrents emerge, reminiscent of Benson's political autonomy (1997:19) challenging the students' capacity for 'autonomy of choice and action'. Macaro (2008:60) argues that there 'is no getting away from the fact that individual choice is constrained by society and its institutions', so that expressions of autonomy can be inhibited when teachers are 'insistently interventionist' (Little 1990:9) and when learners typically respond in 'predictable teacher pleasing ways' (Hawisher and Selfe 1991:55). In isolation this view is too simplistic.

Mindful of the notion of interdependence, I would argue that the notion of autonomy of choice and action is characterized by the interplay between contributing environmental stimuli. Macaro (2008:60) sees that ultimately it is freedom of choice that underpins language learner autonomy 'from the smallest classroom task to a lifelong attitude and motivation for learning', arguing that 'autonomy resides in being able to say what you want rather than producing the language of others' (ibid.). His view mirrors Kern's (2000:17) that meaningful use of the target language is more than 'just rehearsing', and reflects Littlewood's (1996:428) view of 'autonomy as a communicator'. Macaro's framework does not overlook the cognitive challenges associated with internalizing and learning a language with the external difficulties in strategizing the journey towards linguistic competence in a socially mediated context. Learning environments might be rich in affordances but tensions emerge from external factors with the potential to overwhelm the individual's cognitive capacity to express his potential to make independent choices.

Framework for autonomy in a VLE

The purpose of this book is to gain insights into the notion of autonomy in a VLE from an evaluation of learners' personal response to a VLE-mediated language development programme. The framework for autonomy in a VLE is designed to examine the construct in practice. Its place as a methodological tool is described in Chapter 4. Attributes of Benson's, Littlewood's and Macaro's frameworks for autonomy have served to inform the development of the framework for autonomy for the more specific context of a VLE.

The framework is divided into two sections: the VLE blended classroom and free-time VLE access to reflect the two components of the VLE learning programme described in this book, known as *EI* (Table 2.5). The notion of VLE-mediated learner autonomy is characterized by students' 'internal-cognitive'

Type of autonomy	Definitions	Context	Example behaviour	Language skills	Descriptors
Poactive and reactive autonomy in the VLE classroom: L2 free expression. Learner autonomy. Explicit interaction – Writing – Speaking Implicit interaction – Reading – Listening	**L2 free expression (VLE classroom):** (a) Student's choice to use L2. (b) Reduced L1. (c) Increased L2 interaction. **Learner autonomy:** (a) Responsibility. (b) Decision-making. (c) Evaluation by the student.	Blended learning (with computers in lab or classroom). Teacher as facilitator and moderator. Self-regulated online/VLE activity. Collaborating with peers. Striving towards common goals.	**Responsibility** – *Proactively* taking the lead, following lesson and links. – *Reactively* following and responding to lesson and links. **Decision** – *Proactively* taking the lead and engaging with peers and lesson. – *Reactively* following direction and interacting with peers and lesson. **Evaluation** – Reflect on lesson. – Use of L2 *proactively* initiated by self. – Use of L2 *reactively* responding to task and others.	Speaking. Listening. Reading. Writing.	Self-directed. Relatedness to others. Interaction. *Proactively* taking the lead in the task. *Reactively* following the lead. Responding to the task and others. Choice. Freedom. Expert support.
Poactive and reactive autonomy during free-time VLE access: L2 free expression. Learner autonomy. Explicit interaction – Writing – Speaking Implicit interaction – Reading – Listening	**L2 free expression:** (a) Student choice of L2. (b) Increased L2 interaction. **Learner autonomy:** (a) Responsibility. (b) Decision-making. (c) Evaluation by the student.	**Free time:** Writing forum posts. Reading forum posts. Reading additional resources. Writing assignments. Discussion (with friends).	Free-time logging into the site. Voluntary use of L2 – posting to the forums. Level 1: *Reactively* responding to 'expert'-generated threads. Level 2: *Reactively* responding directly to peer-generated threads. Level 3: *Proactively* generating own threads. *Proactive* reading of forum posts. *Proactive* engagement with additional resources. *Reactive* post-lesson assignments. *Proactive* discussions about postings to the forums.	Main skills: Writing. Reading. Sub-skill: Speaking. Listening.	Self-directed. Relatedness to others. Interaction. *Proactively* self-directed. *Reactively* task-directed. *Reactively* responding to others. Choice. Freedom. No expert support (except for assignment feedback).

(Little 2007:18) capacity to engage proactively or reactively (Littlewood 1999:75-6) with the VLE in class or in their free-time, incorporating the sense in which learning is cognitively a 'social-interactive' (Oxford 2003:85) experience between the individual and the environment. For example, in VLE-mediated lessons, learners cognitively engage with the class, follow the links and prompts determined by the structure of the lesson, and in so doing formulate their own observations and reflections, manifesting signs of 'reactive autonomy' (Littlewood 1999:75-6). Alternatively, learners might go off-task, charting their own path, exploring alternative online avenues and VLE-mediated resources, suggestive of 'proactive autonomy' (Littlewood 1999:75-6). Free-time use of the VLE could involve the students 'proactively' choosing and strategizing their exploration of VLE-mediated opportunities for language development through reading and populating the student-led forums. On the other hand, learners might 'reactively' read and reflect, thereby implicitly engaging with the structure determined by expert-generated posts and tasks.

The second version of VLE-mediated autonomy is 'L2 free expression', which incorporates the notion of proactive and reactive autonomy (Littlewood 1999:75-6). The structure of the VLE-mediated lesson is moderated by the teacher, triggering classroom interaction, but it is a communicatively collaborative enterprise, reflecting socially interactive relatedness between participants, or 'reactive autonomy' (Littlewood 1999:75-6). In their free time, students can generate their own threads to VLE forums, suggesting an 'internal-cognitive' (2007:18 ibid.) response to the technology and proactive autonomy (Littlewood 1999:75-6) in the online expression of personally held thoughts in the target language. Alternatively, learners might feel better able to express themselves in the target language by 'reactively' following the voices of others, corroborating the view that 'social context and interaction play a vital role in stimulating and shaping the cognitive processes' (Little 2000:17).

Conclusion

The aim of this chapter has been to examine the scope of the concept of autonomy beyond its ubiquitous definition as the 'ability to take charge of one's learning' (Holec 1981:3). I began with an overview of the philosophical complexities of the construct, before considering different versions of autonomy as discussed in the theoretical literature and conflicts between theorists. Examination of this literature led to the development of the notion of ecological autonomy which expands the concept of interdependence between the internal and external dimensions of the construct. Ecological autonomy embraces the individual's cognitive capacity to respond to the fluidity of the socially interactive web of unpredictability, where learners make choices in non-linear ways to the virtual voices of those around them, and where choices are anchored by the structure of a task, mediated by the teacher or the technology. I propose that a VLE lends itself well to the examination of ecological autonomy because it is possible to track and evaluate signs of learner engagement in the form of on-site activity, and to consider this alongside students' personal reflections about the VLE experience. In the next chapter I turn to the literature that relates to the introduction of technology to support second language development.

3
Technology: Virtual Promise or Virtual Reality – the Pedagogical Challenge

Technology can be variously interpreted, but the notion of technology to which I refer in this book is that which Kern (2006:184) describes as 'digital technology', by which he primarily means computers rather than other forms of digitized media, which has been commonly referred to as CALL evolving towards network-based language learning (NBLL). The technology described in this book is a VLE, a technology most effectively described by Dillenbourg et al. (2002:3–4), summarized and illustrated in Box 3.1.

Box 3.1 Characteristics of a VLE (adapted from Dillenbourg et al. 2002)

A VLE can be identified as follows:

- A designed information space.
- Educational interactions occur in the environment turning spaces into places (oral- and text-based).
- Information/social space can vary from text to 3D immersive worlds.
- Students [...] co-construct the virtual space.
- Not restricted to distance education; they also enrich classroom activities (blended learning).
- Integrates heterogeneous technologies and multiple pedagogical approaches.
- Can overlap physical environments (classroom and home).

It is suggested by Lantolf (2003:367) that 'The problem for foreign language learners [...] is that they must ultimately develop the ability to use the language freely and spontaneously without conscious awareness,' with Kessler (2009:81) proposing that 'successful autonomous use of the target language should be the ultimate goal in language instruction'. By virtue of the fact that the student is not yet a master of the target language, the challenge lies in the coalescence between second language acquisition (SLA) and autonomy. The realization of the transition from dependent learner to independent user of the language is held in tension by complex philosophical notions of what it means to be autonomous and theories about SLA, because of the sense in which 'SLA is itself informed by a rich variety of theoretical frameworks and has consistently resisted a single overarching theory', (Kern 2006:187), with Felix (2005:86) considering there to be a tendency for 'learning theories to overlap so that it would be naive to suggest a black and white divide into opposing schools of thought'. The matter is further complicated by overlaying notions of autonomy within the multiplicity of guises of the technological learning environments with which our students engage, from self-access CD-ROMs to collaborative synchronous chat.

The virtual promise of technology in SLA

However complex the strands of the relationship between SLA, autonomy and technology might be, there is an intuitive connection between independent learning and the opportunity for the authentic use of the target language with technology. The literature supports the view that 'educational technology demonstrates its effectiveness as a purveyor of learner autonomy' (Murray 1999:296), enabling students to take control and manage their own learning (White 2006:249), a view corroborated by Lee (2011: 87) who, in her research into student blogging, argues that 'Blogging fosters learner autonomy, as students take charge of making their own decisions as to what, how much and when to publish their work.' Similarly, Villanueva et al. (2010:13) note the parallel relationship between digital literacies and notions of autonomy as the reading of hypertext 'implicates' the individual into making navigational choices about what to do with the information mediated by the link.

With regard to language learning, it is suggested that technology extends opportunities for the learner to read, write and develop intercultural awareness (Fisher et al. 2004:50) providing linguistic opportunities in authentic contexts that encourage the learner to 'strive for autonomy in the target language' (Kessler

2009:79). Villanueva et al. (2010:7) paint a compelling picture of the possibilities for the development of autonomy, created by technology:

> The use of ICT opens up a space for complexity and multiplicity that might help the development of autonomy […] multiplicity of access to authentic documents, multiplicity of access to interaction, the chance to reinforce metacognitive ability through experience with others.

As information computer technology (ICT) tools that are more familiar in other sociocultural contexts find their way into the classroom, the promise and challenge of poly-contextualized teaching and learning become clear (Engestrom et al. 1995, Leander 2002, both cited in Lund 2006). For the students who appear in this book and for students learning English as a foreign language (EFL) worldwide, as English emerges as the lingua franca of the internet, technology has the potential to liberate the language and the learner from the spatial constraints of the classroom. Beyond the classroom, technological social networks are well-populated and have grown exponentially, suggesting that electronic space has the potential to provide a previously unattainable opportunity for linguistic freedom within a rich communicative environment. This notion is reflected in Warschauer's (1996b) study where students indicated that computers had the potential to help them become more independent of conventional educational structures. Warschauer (1997:472) suggests that computer-mediated communication (CMC) has 'finally unleashed the interactive power of text-based communication', encouraging more equal levels of participation, flattering those 'who are traditionally shut out of discussions' (ibid.). Mindful of the view that the autonomous individual has the capacity to plan and strategize his intentions (Wall 2003:308), as the digitalized educational landscape evolves, Warschauer (2002) expands on this view of the construct, suggesting that the notion of autonomy should also include the individual's capacity to be strategically responsive to technological change.

Benson and Chik (2010:63) argue that the ubiquitous presence of 'globalized online spaces' for uploading and generating content, such as *Flickr*, *YouTube*, *FanFiction.Net* and *Twitter* have the potential to stimulate autonomous language development and langue use through online sharing and discussion between participants. In their research into the use of blogs, Sykes, Oskoz and Thorne (2008:532) propose that writing skills can be enhanced 'through meaningful tasks and extended readership'. Similarly, Lee (2011:88) found that blog-mediated asynchronous communication increased students' levels of participation 'they are intended not only for a sole instructor but rather for a broad audience'. It seems therefore that the literature advocates the potential of technology in intensifying the learner's level of engagement with the target language. In terms of SLA, Warschauer (1997, cited in Pachler 2007:220) argues that the mediation of meaning through the written record serves as an 'intellectual amplifier'. The promise of meaningful technological communication on a global scale for the learner is compelling in suggesting the potential of CMC as a tool to mediate learner autonomy and independent use of the target language.

The virtual reality of technology in SLA

Despite these diverse and compelling suggestions about the value of integrating technology into the language-learning classroom, there has been a call for the voice of reason by Hawisher and Selfe (1991:56) in the 'uncritical enthusiasm' shown by those who advocate technology to support learning, and they go on to suggest that 'we take a critical perspective and remain sensitive to the [. . .] use of computers' (ibid.). In a similar vein, Smith (2003:39) cautions against being seduced by the increasing presence of computers in the language classroom, and that assumptions about the similarities between face-to-face and computer-mediated interactions require something of 'a leap of faith' (ibid.) given the differences in the nature of the discourse and interactional patterns. Moreover, research findings into learner experience and CMC are ambiguous and contradictory, and it seems that 'for many of the positive aspects of CMC there is a corresponding negative impact' (Lamy and Hampel 2007c:82). Such concerns are substantiated by the ESRC who, as indicated in Chapter 1, have expressed concern that 'huge technological developments [. . .] have not always delivered their intended benefits to end-users' (PACCIT-ESRC research group 2005:3).

Kreijns et al. (2002:1) hold that these difficulties are attributable to 'taking social interaction in groups for granted and the lack of attention paid to the social psychological dimension of social interaction outside of the task content'. The call for greater objectivity and concerns about the failure of technology to deliver desired learning outcomes indicate that claims about the advantages of technology may have been oversimplified, 'artificially strengthening the apparent causal link between the medium and its pedagogical affordances' (Lamy and Hampel 2007c:84). If, as the literature suggests, electronic space promises a fertile environment within which learners can explore increasing levels of autonomous use of the target language, then it is possible that technology can drive change (Jimenez Raya and Perez Fernandez 2002:64) in students' learning and communicative practices in the target language, but this requires more than the provision of the technology as 'Using a computer does not automatically increase or improve the quality of learner participation' (Lamy and Hampel 2007c:78). In his research looking at MOOs, Schwienhorst (2008:152) found that learners rarely explored the full potential of the 'range and depth' of resources made available to them by their online learning platform. Nevertheless, it is suggested by Stephenson (2001:4) that despite the reported failings of online learning environments, this does not refute the validity of virtual space as an environment for learning nor the potential in reconceptualizing what is pedagogically possible. Yet, the complexity and implications of the relationship between autonomy, technology and language learning are clear, and Chapelle (1997:20) considers that 'The greatest obstacle to the assessment of CALL's efficacy is that still we know rather little about SLA,' compounded further by more recent literature highlighting the complexity of evaluating the effectiveness of technology and SLA. Developments in technology are instigating a 'reassessment of the relationship between teacher, learner and tools for learning', provoking 'new thinking about the role of technology in supporting autonomy' (Esch 2009:30).

In seeking to unravel the 'paradox and promise' (Hawisher and Selfe 1991:62) of the use of technology to support SLA and autonomy it is best to begin by considering the notion that the evolution of technology in the classroom has reflected pedagogical 'shifts in perspective' (Kern and Warschauer 2000:7). In this chapter I demonstrate how developments in technological functionality have been informed by, and adapted to, different pedagogical approaches. This is not to say that developments in functionality have disenfranchised earlier approaches to the use of technology to support SLA. To reflect this, the VLE used by the students who appear in the project described in this book, provided a range of VLE-mediated affordances designed to incorporate different approaches to language development with technology.

Early technological incarnations reflected an online pedagogy where 'the computer substitutes for the teacher and textbook as conveyor of information' (Stephenson 2001:3), reflecting characteristics of 'traditional guided instruction' (Crook 1994:79) of the classroom. It is suggested by Stephenson that by adopting this approach, early potential for learning with technology has been lost (ibid.), which may explain the sense with which there is an 'Inherent tension [...] between the conservation of traditional roles and the destabilization of hierarchy and power' (Kern 1995:470). As technology has become more sophisticated there has been a shift away from the early behaviourist model of CALL (Warschauer and Healey 1998) with the 'computer-as-tutor' (Crook 1994:80) towards interaction with others through and around the computer (Fisher et al. 2004:50), with an increased interest in how learners approach specific communicative situations rather than how well they have acquired linguistic structures (Kern 2000:188).

The difficulty in understanding whether there is a meaningful place for technology in language learning may lie in the application of old questions about effective teaching and learning to new contexts. It is suggested that questions asking whether CALL works or if technology is good for, and leads to, better language learning, confuses tools with methods and outcomes (Ganem Gutierrez 2006:233) and that the evaluation of technologies in SLA has taken a 'simplistic view of the value and role of technology' (ibid.). Ganem Gutierrez goes on to suggest that 'one cannot attribute the success [...] of a task solely to the medium of implementation' (2006:244), and that factors beyond the technology have a role to play. Technology is described by Blake (2008:2) as 'methodologically neutral', with Hutchby (2001:20) suggesting that 'there are no inherent or necessary features of technological artefacts which lead to determinate social consequences'. Kern and Warschauer (2000:2) consider that attention should be redirected towards the practices and contexts within which the technology is used, supporting the suggestion that 'One cannot separate the tool from how it's used or embedded in social interactions'(Blake 2008:132).

Developments in the application of technology to the teaching and learning of foreign languages seem to have been informed by second language learning theories, and in adapting 'current theories to these new realities' (Garrison 2000:4), they have overlooked the fact that while the introduction of technology materially changes the learner's environment, it entails more than 'simply transferring paper based tasks to a computer' (Ganem Gutierrez 2006:244). A simple evaluation of technological 'practices and contexts' (Kern and Warschauer 2000:2) might not provide adequate insight into the effectiveness of technology in supporting SLA. In asking whether early CALL activities lead to better language learning, evaluation criteria in terms of efficacy seem determined by summative outcomes, not entirely surprising considering tight budgets and high set-up costs. This is reflected in the suggestion that 'to justify the investment in a CALL activity, there must be a rationale for why it is implemented via a computer instead of another, less resource-demanding form' (Gonzalez Lloret 2003:86).

With changing and multiple technological contexts for learning, criteria for evaluating CALL practices have moved on to embrace different pedagogical aims. If the effectiveness of the technology were to be considered in the light of the aims of the task, it would then become possible to evaluate the merits associated with the processes of the activity as well as the learning outcomes, allowing an eclectic mix of technological approaches, the new with the old to be embraced. The deployment of technology then becomes a matter of identifying the 'suitability of the particular task design to that medium' (Ganem Gutierrez 2006: 244). In terms of an eclectic approach to technology and SLA, it is suggested by Stickler and Hampel (2007:18) that 'an online language course can work for different approaches: using language communicatively as well as in language practice focusing on form'. As such, there is no right, wrong or improved technological approach, simply the approach that best meets the needs of the learner. To reflect this view and in an attempt to provide a rich learning environment, the design of *EI*, (the VLE used by the students in this book), incorporated affordances that included different approaches to CALL.

In failing to deliver 'their intended benefits' (PACCIT 2005:3), it is possible that developers of CALL applications have underestimated the transformative impact of digital technology, complicated further by the complexity of what it means to be an autonomous learner and become an independent user of the target language.

Theoretical distinctions delineating different approaches to language learning with technology

Kern and Warschauer (2000:2) argue that it is not the computer that brings about improvements in learning, but the practice and context within which the computer is deployed and the pedagogical aims of the task, which in turn has design implications, as Hafner and Miller (2011:82) suggest 'language educators may draw upon the architecture of such spaces in order to design opportunities for autonomous learning in formal contexts'.

I have drawn on the theoretical distinctions made by Warschauer and Healey (1998) to distinguish between the three approaches to CALL, described as 'Structural CALL', 'Communicative CALL' and 'Integrative CALL'.

Structural CALL

Informed by the behaviorist learning model, this mode of CALL featured repetitive language drills, referred to as drill-and-practice. (Warschauer and Healey 1998:57)

Structural CALL dovetails a traditional pedagogical model and mode of learning, which Benson (1997:20) describes as 'positivist' in its approach to the acquisition of knowledge, because the teacher represents knowledge from the perspective of his own reality. However, the onus is on the individual to cognitively process, make sense of and assimilate new information. Indeed Kern and Warschauer (2000:1) reflect that 'CALL has traditionally been associated with self-contained programmed applications such as tutorials, drills' so that the focus of Structural CALL is on linguistic accuracy, form and structure, suggestive of a behaviouristic view of learning. Evans (2009:19) has proposed that this early association between Structural CALL and behaviourist computer-based drills and practice activities has expanded to incorporate a wider range of learning activities. Nevertheless, as Evans explains, as an approach it is still grounded in the notion of the 'computer-as-tutor' (Crook 1994:80) because like the teacher, the technology is the font of knowledge holding 'the key to all linguistic truths' (Hamilton 2009:149). This approach thrives in distance language-learning programmes (Evans 2009:19). I have drawn on Crook's (1994:79) use of the term 'traditional guided instruction', to characterise this mode of teaching and learning which I refer to in this book as 'guided learning.' With learning mediated by CD-ROMs and web-based grammar games and exercises, Structural CALL resources offer little in the way of learner feedback. Sending learners off to the computer room 'to engage with impersonal, decontextualized materials' (Felix 2005:93) seems counterintuitive to the teaching of languages as a means of interacting with others. Chapelle (1997:27) expressed her concern regarding the one-dimensional, non-communicative perspective of this approach to CALL in which 'the task goal is completion of formal grammar exercise' because it addressed the summative learning outcome, rather than the process of learning where learners are periodically 'attending to form while they are working towards a communicative task goal'.

Nevertheless, it can be easy to overlook the transformative nature of Structural CALL with its promise of autonomous learning and the sense in which computer-based language learning potentially liberates the learner, so that instruction need not take place in the classroom with the teacher, nor be dictated by geographical constraints (Garrison 2000:20). This suggests an easy compatibility between technology and self-access which accommodates a view of autonomy as independent learning and the suggestion that 'Outside the normal classroom framework [. . .] self access is in an excellent position to promote the learner centred philosophy' (Jones 1995:228). Materials can be deposited in a VLE for learners to access and respond to in their own time. It is suggested by Jiménez Raya and Perez Fernandez (2002:64) that selection and electronic distribution of materials by the teacher is a practical application of technology, enabling students to make their own decisions about their pace of learning, and providing them with an intermediate step towards full autonomy.

The relationship between autonomy and language learning using technology suggests a decentralization of the focus of learning (Evans 1993:18) away from the teacher. Given the mass of content, information and communicative potential on the internet, the link between autonomy and technology is compelling. In recent years, technology has been hailed as a means by which the learner can be liberated from suppression represented by external forces (Candy 1989:101). Structural CALL provides students with hitherto inaccessible opportunities and choices about engaging with the target language. Affordances corresponding to materials available in distance-learning language programmes and grounded in a more structural approach to CALL were embedded into *EI*, the VLE in this book.

In suggesting that Structural CALL promotes learner autonomy, this fails to acknowledge that students who engage independently with online materials are 'already significantly autonomous' (Blin 2004:381). Furthermore, although the learner has more choice about where and when he engages with the technology, Structural CALL is highly suggestive of Crook's (1994:79) view of 'traditional guided instruction' because the teacher or providers of web-based materials continue to manage the content, 'claiming the role as the primary dispenser of knowledge' (Hawisher 2000:3). Notions of meaningful choice and learner agency remain in question. Nevertheless, the merits of Structural CALL should not be overlooked and we should be mindful of the view held by Kern and Warschauer (2000:2) that the value of practices adopted by Structural CALL should be considered in light of the pedagogical aims of the tasks. As Stickler and Hampel (2007:18) suggest, 'an online language course can work for different approaches: using language communicatively as well as in language practice focusing on form'. A structured approach to CALL is a valid option for students who want independent, guided learning and activities. Although Structural CALL mediates a previously unattainable level of learner independence from the traditional classroom model, autonomy cannot be reduced to learning in isolation, as Stephenson (2001:14) says, 'Providing an opportunity for students is only part of the real challenge – an experience without feedback and reflection is somewhat an empty experience.'

Theoretically, Structural CALL suggests a restrictive view of what it means to be autonomous, with the implication that the freedoms afforded by technology and language development take place out of the classroom. Linguistically, the engagement is between the student and the computer in Structural CALL, overlooking the value of interaction and the fact that language is socially situated. Warschauer and Healey (1998) categorize another view of language learning with technology, which they describe as Communicative CALL.

Communicative CALL

Proponents of communicative CALL stressed that computer-based activities should focus more on using forms than on the forms themselves. (Warschauer and Healey 1998:57)

In defining Communicative CALL, Warschauer and Healey (1998) indicate that, like Structural CALL, this approach corresponds to cognitive theories of learning, with an emphasis on learning as 'a process of discovery, expression, and development' (ibid.). Activities are designed to encourage purposeful interaction between learners, promoting fluency in the target language, with a focus 'not so much on what students did with the machine, but rather what they did with each other while working at the computer' (ibid.). Problem-solving, task-based online interaction between learners mediated by CMC might be considered examples of Communicative CALL. Chapelle (1997:23-7) reflects upon how CALL researchers might draw on the tenets of Interaction hypothesis in the evaluation of computer-mediated communication learning (CMCL) tasks. Chapelle (1997:22) suggests that 'interaction in the target language [...] provides opportunities for learners to (a) comprehend message meaning [...] (b) produce modified output [...] (c) attend to L2 form'. Yet Chapelle (ibid.) goes on to say that 'not just any linguistic production is considered beneficial "comprehensible output" from the interactionist perspective' and that greater understanding is required of the type of activities that address the learner's need to exchange meaning while simultaneously attending to form. The link made by Chapelle between Interaction hypothesis and CMC is supported by others. Lamy and Hampel (2007a:22) suggest that:

> CMCL applications can provide language learners with comprehensible input, but also with a platform for interaction where they can work with text (CALL) or negotiate meaning with peers and a tutor (CMCL). Computers have given learners the opportunity to produce comprehensible output.

For example, discussion forums mediated by a VLE provide learners with the opportunity to construct a response to text-based input. In her research into negotiated interaction in network-based environments, Pelletieri (2000) observed that the nature of students' CMC interactions was significantly affected by task type. In linking the principles of Interaction hypothesis to Communicative CALL activities, Pelletieri (2000) found that goal-orientated, task-based learning (TBL) activities not only fostered the monitoring of their partner's use of language, but also their own, leading to increased levels of negotiation of meaning, linguistic modifications which, in turn, supported comprehension and effective communication between learners. Pelletieri reported that the learners' ability to work towards the achievement of task goals was supported by the 'visual saliency' (Pelletieri 2000:81) of the medium, affording them additional time to reflect upon their use of language. Similarly in her research into the effective design of CALL tasks to promote student interaction, Gonzalez-Lloret found that students produced purposeful language in task-based CALL learning which:

> . . . was typical of negotiation for meaning, where the main aim was the completion of the task, and where language is used with its main communicative purpose in an economical way without paying attention to the production of long accurate constructions. (Gonzalez-Lloret 2003:98)

Although TBL Communicative CALL stimulates a focus on fluency rather than accuracy, two issues emerge. The first is concerned with the pedagogical value of such an approach relative to learner autonomy and the independent use of the target language. The second is linked to the first, and whether learners perceive and attribute value to this communicative, more deconstructed approach to online language development.

Communicative CALL pedagogically encourages reflection suggestive of learner autonomy. In his study of the effects of CMC in an online distance-learning course on learners, Blake (2005:502) found that CMC chat encouraged learners to produce output and, in turn, to monitor their own language (ibid.) thus processing the language 'more deeply' (Swain 2000:99), and encouraging the development of learners' 'mental models through the use of the target language' (Gruba 2004:628–9, cited in Evans 2009:21). Output stimulates feedback, even if, as Blake (2005:508) suggests feedback might come from 'less expert L2 learners', leading to linguistic modification and the subsequent internalization of language. Furthermore if, as is posited, that text-based interaction visually enhances and distances the learner from the discourse (Kern 1995:459), cognitively amplifying (Warschauer 1997:472) their awareness of the language, Blake (2005:508) suggests that this facilitates the process of reflection and the learners' attention is directed towards noticing gaps in their own interlanguage. This view is further supported by Kern and Warschauer (2000:15) who consider that 'the written nature of the discussion allows greater opportunity to attend to and reflect on form and content of communication'. Others consider that CMC slows down the pace of the interaction, affording learners more processing time while reading and typing (Smith 2003:39) and that the 'extra time allowed by text-based online chat might have lowered the learners' cognitive load so that they could allocate their cognitive resources to reviewing and evaluating linguistic forms in their output' (Lai and Zhao 2006:109).

Although the literature reports on the cognitive value of synchronous CMC interaction, theoretically the same principles might be applicable to asynchronous CMC. In terms of autonomy, asynchronous interaction gives learners the opportunity and time to decide whether they want to participate in the discussion. Blake (2005:503) considers that CMC encourages the learner towards directing his own learning environment, highly suggestive of learner agency relative to autonomy. Furthermore, research indicates that CMC encourages learners to take control over their use of the target language in terms of fluency practice and performance anxiety. It is reported that the CMC environment not only generates increased, more evenly distributed learner participation than in face-to face interaction (Smith 2003:38) but that it has the effect of reducing performance anxiety, with Pelletieri (2000:62) suggesting that this results in the production of greater quantities of the target language. Kern (1995:470) reported that in using networked computers for synchronous discussions in class, there was some indication of reduced anxiety, students felt more liberated and able to communicate, furthermore, students who were normally more reticent were more forthcoming in the CMC environment. Nevertheless, there is a trade-off between increased levels of fluency between learners mediated by CMC interaction in the target language and linguistic accuracy. A further effect of more democratic levels of participation between learners is that of the decentralization of learning (Evans 1993:18) so that the teacher 'is no longer able to allocate the floor' (Kern 1995:459), leading to the paradoxical sense that CMC interaction can seem democratic, yet simultaneously anarchic (Kern 1995:470). Theoretically, the pedagogical merits of a task-based communicative approach to CALL are compelling. However, conventions of the guided classroom are de-constructed by such an approach, introducing unsettling changes (ibid.), challenging learners' perceptions about the value of incorporating this technological approach into their language-learning environment.

I return to the suggestion that the difficulty in conceptualizing the value of technological learning environments is that old questions of efficacy and the value of familiar language-learning activities are asked of new learning contexts in which learners are presented with quite different linguistic opportunities. The question therefore re-emerges, as proposed by Kern and Warschauer (2000:2) about how the evaluation of practices in the context of Communicative CALL should be framed in terms of the aims of the task. For example, Pelletieri (2000) found that in encouraging negotiated interaction between learners, tasks most likely to be effective are those which are goal-orientated, with consideration given in their design so that all the participants can make requests to obtain information from one another, and with minimal possible outcomes. Yet, as an approach, this raises questions about autonomous learning because, like Structural CALL, students' use of language is largely determined by the task and guided by the teacher. As Kessler (2009:91) suggests:

> ... it may be equally important to provide students with tasks that do not introduce the power dynamics of the teacher's presence [...]there may be an unseen benefit for the advanced level student in the form of greater output, more opportunities for practice and greater practice.

Research into Structural and Communicative CALL has focused on the summative effect of the technology on student discourse and the task, where use of language might be right or wrong (Structural CALL), or where the learner works towards the fulfilment of communicative goals designed to practise specific linguistic components (Communicative CALL). If the aim is to provide the learner with the opportunity to work towards increased levels of fluency while retaining a degree of attention to specific linguistic forms, then a task-based communicative approach with a 'focus more on using forms than on the forms themselves' (Warschauer and Healey 1998:57) might be appropriate.

With its focus on involvement, support and purposeful student dialogue in the target language, Coomey and Stephenson (2001:49) concur that online learning could be a means by which learner autonomy might be realized. However, caution should be exercised in endeavouring to understand the nature of the relationship between Communicative CALL and autonomous behaviour. Although learners are using the language freely, they are guided in their thinking and use of language towards pre-determined goals in order to successfully accomplish the task. The suggestion is that discovery learning equates to autonomous learning, yet, by design, target linguistic structures are embedded in the activity and goals are pre-determined with information withheld. This raises questions of hierarchy and the 'totality of relationships' (van Lier 2004:3) between participants. Indeed as Godwin-Jones (2011:5) points out, in an LMS-mediated learning programme:

> It is rare that anyone other than the teacher makes the decisions on what is presented in the LMS course Web site, how the materials are organized, and how the learner is expected to progress through the course.

Godwin-Jones' suggestion has clear implications with regard to notions of learner agency and is significant in light of Holec's view that in order to be autonomous, the individual should be capable of taking charge of, and making decisions about, his learning (Holec 1981:7). Indeed, Coomey and Stephenson (2001:40) consider there to be significant differences in terms of autonomy between dialogue that has been shaped by the teacher because of the characteristics of the task, and more student-led conversations emerging from the learners' shared reflections and understanding. As an approach, Communicative CALL represents a controlled view of how language is used, indicating the complexities of the nature of the relationship between technology and autonomous behaviour.

Research suggests that goal-oriented Communicative CALL increases freer use of the target language, by providing 'a learning structure in which control over the learning can be exercised by the learner'(Holec 1981:7) so that students can 'generate original utterances rather than just manipulate prefabricated language' (Warschauer and Healey 1998:57). Communicative CALL is defined by the value of its focus on 'using forms than on the forms themselves' (ibid.). Warschauer and Healey's choice of language 'using forms' suggests that the learner is guided by the task towards the use of specific structures. Tasks that stimulate the generation of original utterances in English, reflect freer thinking and independent L2 manipulation on one level, but the character of the interaction is governed by the aim for targeted freer practice in which 'the goal does not require the participants to converge intellectually' Chapelle (1997:27). If, as research suggests, a task-based CALL approach is an effective means of stimulating negotiated L2 peer interaction, in terms of autonomous response, the significance of structure in stimulating L2 free expression in English in the context of a technological learning environment emerges.

Paradigmatically, Structural and Communicative CALL reflect a cognitive approach to language learning, in which the focus is on the individual making sense of the world around him, but this overlooks the fact that language is inherently a socially situated phenomenon. The social constructivist would suggest that knowledge is constructed through collaboration in authentic contexts. Interaction in the target language between learners, instigated through goal-oriented activities with a focus on specific language items is not authentic interaction, suggesting the view that 'unless learners are able to use the language for real communicative purpose and independently of the teacher, we are unlikely to produce learners who can maximise their potential' (Fisher et al. 2004:51).

And so we turn to the notion of language learning with technology, described by Warschauer and Healey (1998:57) as Integrative CALL.

Integrative CALL

> ... Many teachers were moving away from a cognitive view of communicative teaching to a more social or socio-cognitive view, which placed greater emphasis on language use in authentic social contexts. (Warschauer and Healey 1998:57)

Integrative CALL has been variously interpreted as representing different things 'depending on the constituent features of the integration process'(Evans 2009:24). I have drawn on Warschauer and Healey's (1998) and Evans's (ibid.) view of the ways in which Integrative CALL has been interpreted within the literature, summarized in Box 3.2.

Box 3.2 Characteristics of Integrative CALL

- Multiple use of language skills with technology (reading, writing, listening, speaking).
- Multiple use of technological resources (visual, aural, textual).
- The incorporation of technology into the classroom with students learning to use technological tools as part of the language lesson.
- Collaborative use of technology by students to produce digital texts.
- Blended and collaborative use of technology in the classroom, intertwined with traditional classroom activities, so blurring boundaries between CALL and conventions of the classroom.

These are good descriptors in terms of the ways in which technology might be integrated into a language development programme, whether through free-time access to technology or in a blended environment which Neumeier (2005:164) describes as 'a combination of face-to-face [...] and computer assisted learning in a single teaching and learning environment', such as a classroom or computer room. Blended Integrative CALL illustrates the way in which 'The boundaries between CALL and "conventional" activities in the lesson become blurred' (Evans 2009:25). By focusing on the use of language in authentic social contexts, Integrative CALL draws broadly on social constructivist approaches, which Felix (2005:91) describes as supporting communication and fluency. This approach does not lend itself to the achievement of linguistic accuracy because 'constant corrections of grammar or pronunciation would not only seriously interrupt communication but also compromise the positive aspects of authenticity' (ibid.), sitting in sharp relief to the guided learning environment and challenging learners' expectations and perceptions of a meaningful context for language development.

The integrative, sociocultural approach to CMC embraces the Vygotskyan notion of the mediated mind whereby the individual utilizes and modifies existing knowledge to articulate and convey thinking. L2 oral interaction is mediated by the screen-mediated stimulus shaping 'the ways we interact with the world' (Kern and Warschauer 2000:11). Online CMC constructed text operates as a linguistically productive 'thinking device' (Kitade 2008:64). The interactivity of computer-mediated communication creates a collaborative element to the exchange of ideas and text construction between students. According to sociocultural principles, language is viewed as a socially situated construct where students are identified 'neither as processors of input nor producers of output, but as speakers/listeners in the development process in interaction' (Ohta 2000:51). Other theorists (e.g. Blyth 2009:176) have looked beyond the cognitive stance of sociocultural theory towards the ecological approach in an attempt to better understand the interconnectedness and 'totality of relationships' (van Lier 2004:3) between participants in network-based learning (NBL) and digital learning because it reflects learning as 'non-linear, relational human activity, co-constructed between humans and their environment' (Kramsch 2002:5).

CMC-mediated exchange of thoughts and ideas has the advantage of slowing down interaction, privileging learners with more time to reflect and modify their online contributions. In her study examining the effects of 'nomadic' (Sotillo 2002:16) wireless learning environments on collaborative academic writing, Sotillo reports evidence that 'an audience of critical peers provided scaffolding that stretched each writer's creative limits', suggestive of Vygotsky's ZPD (Zone of Proximal Development) and the view held by Hawisher and Selfe (1991:57) that online discourse creates 'entirely new pedagogical dynamics [...]the creation of written social discourse' and the sense in which it creates a 'more egalitarian sense of authorship' (Blake 2008:134). Furthermore, the change of dynamic mediated by CMC and the socially situated perspective of online writing re-orientates traditional perceptions of writing away from 'the individual mastering his or her craft in isolation, to learning as participation or engagement in a collective activity with participants at various stages of expertise' (Sotillo 2002:17). Moreover, in line with van Lier's notion of the ecological approach (2004), CMC interaction becomes less predictable and learning opportunities are not predetermined but emerge, characterized by the learners' response to events within their learning environment. Nevertheless, managing this level of interactive freedom within a VLE can prove challenging for 'Students accustomed to the direction and structure typical of traditional classrooms' (Piccoli et al. 2001:419).

Yet the merits of a sociocultural approach to CMC need not only be gained by examining online text-based discourse. In her study into students' offline behaviour and the development of metalanguage in asynchronous CMC activities, Kitade (2008:78) found that the 'learners' metalanguage talk did not occur in the online interaction [...] but rather in the offline verbal interaction' (ibid.), concluding that the potential and scope of CMC need not only relate to on-screen interactions but there was also the value in encouraging 'offline talk' (ibid.). In Kitade's study, learners sought assistance from their peers in the construction of replies to their Japanese partners, reiterating findings from Pica et al.'s (1996) study and the merits of peer-based scaffolding.

The construction and exchange of ideas through student participation and collaboration, suggested by Integrative CALL, emerges in Kessler's study (2009) in which students were invited to construct a Wiki, without teacher intervention, collaboratively documenting personal reflections about their course. Kessler had hoped to identify whether, by utilizing the functionality of the Wiki editing tool, learners would work towards the production of a grammatically accurate document. He found that although the project successfully encouraged participation and collaboration in producing the text, with the more competent learners benefiting from the freedom and opportunity to explore language, learners were not attentive to linguistic accuracy. As Stickler and Hampel (2007:18) suggest, 'language learning that focuses on content and communication rather than on form might not be the ideal option for everyone'. Kessler acknowledges that in order for his students to attend to form and accuracy it might be 'more fruitful to provide a variety of collaborative tasks in order to find optimal conditions for particular groups of language learners and their unique needs' (Kessler 2009:91). The construction and selection of successful online tasks depends upon responding to learner needs, choosing the most appropriate technology because 'one tool does not fit all times and places' (Blake 2008:131) and understanding the limitations, implications and parameters of the virtual context.

Kessler's and Kitade's studies indicate that an online environment can provide a stimulus mediated by the technology encouraging peer collaboration. In Kol and Schcolnik's (2008) study, students' reflections and attitudes were examined in light of their use of asynchronous forums which had been incorporated into an advanced course for English for Academic Purposes (EAP). It was hoped that the forums would provide a platform for 'thoughtful communication' (Kol and Schcolnik 2008:52) so that students could write freely and fluently unhindered by the presence of a teacher. Without teacher-led direction the students did not necessarily respond as anticipated to the stimuli mediated by the forum but rather 'they used the forums to react to the ideas, the new information, and the authors' arguments. The texts constituted the stimuli and provided the content, vocabulary, issues and ideas for discussion' (Kol and Schcolnik 2008: 61).

In line with the view posited by Stephenson (2001:14), learning is not a solitary, uniquely intellectual endeavour but a shared experience such that 'The extent to which we can sustain learning over time is a function of the emotional and personal support we gain from others' (ibid.). The students in Kol and Schcolnik's study responded to the opportunity to interact with one another beyond the remit of the task. As students contributed to the forums, Kol and Schcolnik (2008:59) reported signs of reflection and interaction between learners in the students' exchange of opinions, thereby manifesting signs of awareness of one another's online presence in their postings. It is suggested therefore that pedagogically 'these discussions allow for dynamic growth, development and interchange of ideas among students and can therefore play an important role in student learning' (Kol and Schcolnik 2008:49). This view is reminiscent of the notion of ecology and the significance of the 'totality of relationships' (van Lier 2004:3), in which technology becomes 'the tabula rasa which is only given meaning and structure through actors' interpretations and negotiations that the concept of affordances allows us to challenge' (Hutchby 2001:29).

The extent to which the students in Kitade's study flourished was not only restricted to their interactions online but also manifested itself through their interactions with one another alongside the computer, which van Lier (2004:208) would describe as representative of Bronfenbrenner's (1979, 1993) notion that 'education can be characterized as a set of ecosystems, each one nested inside the next'. In Kessler's study, learners responded to the linguistic freedoms afforded by characteristics of the environment, rather than utilizing the editing functions of the Wiki and attending to the detail of their use of language, which suggests that one cannot judge the potential of an application based on its technological functionality. In Kol and Schcolnik's study, rather than following the rubric of the task, students responded to the opportunity to share, exchange and engage with ideas made possible by the 'architecture of electronic spaces' (Hawisher and Selfe 1991:60), yet generated by the stimulus of the task. In their urgency to exchange ideas, the learners were 'more interested in how they attempt to deal with specific communicative situations and with the linguistic, cognitive, social and material resources available to them' (Kern 2006:189). The fluidity and unpredictable character of online text-based interaction suggests the capacity of a VLE to stimulate independent thinking and L2 free expression. The power of Integrative CALL lies in providing learners with an opportunity to interact, collaborate and use the target language for fluency, suggesting a freer, spontaneous, more autonomous use of language, characterized by the ecological notion of an affordance, which describes 'opportunities for meaningful action that the situation affords [. . .] but does not cause or trigger it' (van Lier 2000:252). If, as Pelletieri (2000) found, structured task-based CALL activities encouraged the greatest level of negotiated interactions between learners, albeit with a degree of teacher-led control, then it might also be necessary to provide a structure within which learners might feel capable of engaging in 'thoughtful communication' (Kol and Schcolnik 2008:52). Without a framework for interaction 'simply providing an environment in which students and teachers could interact did not guarantee successful engagement [...] we could see the potential but needed a much more structured approach for facilitating equality of participation' (Mason 2001:69).

Mason's observation about the provision of an effective online learning environment corroborates the view held by Holec (1981:7) that in order to be autonomous there should be a structure within which the learner can exercise his ability to be autonomous. Yet the provision of a predetermined stimulus and structure suggests a degree of external control, even though the direction of the interaction between learners is less carefully managed than in TBL. In striving towards the development of autonomy and second language development, the question remains as to 'where on the continuum between fully directed tasks and complete learner autonomy does good learning lie' (Fisher et al. 2004:57). The association between Integrative CALL, autonomy and social constructivist theories is compelling, with the suggestion that through 'greater emphasis on language use in authentic social contexts' (Warschauer and Healey 1998:57), learners are well placed to learn a second language.

However compelling the suggested relationship between Integrative CALL, autonomy and socio-cultural principles, it is not without its limitations. According to the Vygotskyan notion of the mediated mind, the extent to which learners are capable of participation is largely determined by their knowledge of the language and the extent to which they are dependent on those who might be capable of providing them with the necessary expertise so that 'publicly derived speech completes privately initiated thought' (Lantolf 2000:7). Hawisher and Selfe (1991:56) acknowledge the tension that exists in the integration of technology into the English language writing classroom, suggesting that 'computer technology offers us the chance to transform our writing classes into different kinds of centres for learning'. Yet simultaneously they express concern that without considered attention to the way in which technology is integrated, 'computer use simply reinforces those traditional notions of education that permeate our culture [...] teachers talk, students listen; teachers' contributions are privileged; students respond in predictable teacher pleasing ways' (Hawisher and Selfe 1991:55). According to social constructivist principles, in terms of language development, it is suggested that linguistic awareness and resourcefulness are enhanced. However, the difficulty for the non-native speaker is in precisely articulating his thinking in the target language because he is constrained by his command of the tools he has available to him (Swain and Deters 2007:821). A tension emerges between stimulating learners' active participation, task design and 'social forces [...] teachers and students working together' (Blake 2008:131).

Much has been made in the literature of the role of learners' active participation and the link between learners' use of CMC and the Vygotskyan view of the social construction of knowledge. For instance, Goodfellow and Hewling point to an 'idealised' perception of the learner in this context: 'The online learner is usually idealised as independent and autonomous; participating fully in and benefiting from online discussion with peers in an unthreatening collaborative environment,' (2005:358). The authors argue that collaborative online learning in the target language has promoted 'the valorization of participation' (ibid.) with the effect of demonizing those who choose not to participate, reflected in the pejorative term 'lurker' (ibid.) suggesting that this is because non-participants not only 'fail to do what is best for themselves, but also threaten to undermine the efforts of the community' (ibid.). The positive value of active participation and online contributions are clear but this overlooks the possibility that a silent online presence might denote the learner's implicit participation through actively 'listening', deciding whether and when he or she can explicitly participate, as an indicator of autonomous behaviour. Although participation is the life force of an online community, rather than the 'lurkers' being demonized, they should be afforded greater understanding so that they might feel capable of productive participation and see its value. Felix (2005:88) considers that collaborative success is dependent upon group perceptions of the value of participation, citing the view held by Bandura (1986:448) that 'Perceived collective efficacy will influence what people choose to do as a group, how much effort they put into it, and their staying power when group efforts fail to produce results.' The achievement of a dynamic, collaborative technological working environment is one that requires time, careful planning, design and the selection of the most appropriate tool and approach to meet learners' developmental needs, because 'no one should think that the mere use of technology by itself would create educational change' (Blake 2008:131).

Summary and conclusion

The literature indicates that the increasingly ubiquitous presence of technology from Structural, Communicative and Integrative CALL, each with 'its own appropriate time and place' (Blake 2008:131) offers learners previously inaccessible opportunities to engage intellectually with the language, and liberates the learner from the constraints of the classroom. It is held that 'educational technology demonstrates its effectiveness as a purveyor of learner autonomy', (Murray 1999:296). This implies that humans are not therefore predisposed to behaving autonomously, overlooking the possibility that learners who independently engage with language online are 'already significantly autonomous' (Blin 2004:381). Technology does not instrumentally change a predisposition towards independent behaviour. While explicit participation in the form of text-based or oral interaction is generally acknowledged as the life force of online environments, inactivity through non-contribution need not be an indication of apathy. Non-contribution is a personal response to environmental stimuli and may be a matter of choice. I refer to silent online presence in this study as implicit participation whereby the learner engages by reading or listening, but nevertheless makes a different choice in response to the environmental stimuli.

This book acknowledges that humans are innately autonomous and is not concerned with whether technology can make individuals more autonomous learners and users of language. In light of van Lier's (2004) notion of the significance of the relationship between the individual and the environment, a VLE can provide affordances designed to stimulate language activity with which the learner can choose whether or not to engage. The purpose of this book is to examine:

1. The nature of the relationship between autonomous behaviour and technology by reflecting upon learners' perceptions of the VLE and their use of the technology.
2. The effects of introducing a technological stimulus into the learners' environment on learner behaviour.
3. The 'totality of relationships' (van Lier 2004:3) between participants, and their response to the VLE.
4. The choices learners make in response to the VLE, and their perceptions of the value they attribute to the VLE experience relative to:
   a. Learner autonomy – choosing to engage with the VLE to support language development in class and in their free time.
   b. L2 free expression – exploiting opportunities to use English 'freely and spontaneously' (Lantolf 2003:367).

Mason (2001:69) suggests that 'simply providing an environment in which students and teachers could interact did not guarantee successful engagement [...] we could see the potential but needed a much more structured approach for facilitating equality of participation'. This notion concurs with Holec's (1981:7) view that autonomous behaviour is dependent upon the provision of a structure within which the learner can exercise his right to choose. Though learners might show signs of autonomous behaviour in response to the structure of the VLE, what is more difficult to extrapolate is an understanding of the nature of the relationship between autonomy and technology, and how learner behaviour might be attributable to the technology or whether it is simply a response to screen-mediated stimuli.

Given the philosophical complexity of the construct, how might one capture instances of autonomy in action? In the next chapter, I discuss paradigmatic and practical concerns relative to the examination of the nature of the relationship between autonomy and technology.

4

Shadow Dancing: Autonomy in Action

Working towards understanding the nature of the relationship between autonomy and foreign language learning

Autonomy is the most nebulous of concepts to define, to recognize, to record and to evaluate, so that identifying instances of autonomy might be described as trying to capture shadows dancing. In this chapter I describe the development of three interconnecting tools that facilitate the capture and categorization of ephemeral instances of autonomy in action, mediating insights into the learners' personal response and interaction with the technology, creating a platform from which to work towards a theory about the nature of the relationship between autonomy, foreign language learning and a VLE.

Capturing and evaluating autonomous learner behaviour in response to a VLE: The development of a working definition and a theoretical framework

Analysis of the relationship between autonomy and technology begins with the first of the three tools: a working definition of the autonomous learner and independent user of the target language. The purpose of such a definition is that it should provide a touchstone to which one can return and against which one can question whether an individual might be described as showing signs of autonomous learner behaviour. The following definition, constructed in response to the literature, therefore operates as a frame of reference for the evaluation of the learners' personal response to the VLE

> The autonomous learner and user of the target language shows signs of being capable of taking responsibility for independent thought, action and interaction, grounded within a social structure in response to experience.

Although an invaluable instrument, our definition reveals nothing about the nature of students' response to the VLE, from their classroom engagement with the technology, to their free-time decisions to follow links or read and respond to forum postings. A more targeted tool is therefore required to capture and categorize online learner activity. The second tool is the VLE autonomy framework, shown in Table 4.1 on page 73 and its underlying principles are described in Chapter 2. The framework sets out a clearly defined set of criteria in the form of descriptors to indicate the types of autonomous student behaviour one might expect to observe in the context of a VLE, whether in the blended classroom or in the students' free-time use of the platform. The framework is designed to be used as a reference tool, supported by our working definition of autonomy, with which to monitor, interrogate and categorize instances of autonomous learner and language behaviour in response to the technology.

The ecological approach: The development of a conceptual framework

The VLE autonomy framework and definition of autonomy serve as essential tools in the capture and categorization of evidence of VLE-mediated student activity; however, in isolation, we have no means of knowing whether indications of independent learner behaviour are a response to the technology per se, or whether the students would have produced the same response had the activities been paper-based. Our third tool is conceptual, required to evaluate evidence from a theoretical perspective, and used as an instrument with which to build a theory about the nature of the relationship between autonomy and technology.

Introducing a VLE to the students' learning environment creates a new virtual dynamic, altering the dimensions of their learning experience. Evaluation of autonomy in response to the introduction of the VLE should therefore be considered in light of the context within which the learning takes place. It is of interest to examine the interconnected dynamic of events within a learning environment. The theory underpinning the conceptual framework has been drawn from van Lier's ecological approach (2004). The principles of the ecological approach require closer examination to understand the theory that is underpinning the framework.

Table 4.1 VLE autonomy framework with *EI* – blended learning and free time

Type of autonomy	Definitions	Context	Example behaviour	Language skills	Descriptors
Proactive and reactive autonomy in the VLE classroom: L2 free expression. Learner autonomy. Explicit interaction • Writing • Speaking Implicit interaction • Reading • Listening	**L2 free expression (VLE classroom):** (a) Student choice to use L2. (b) Reduced L1. (c) Increased L2 interaction. **Learner autonomy** (a) Responsibility. (b) Decision-making. (c) Evaluation by the student.	**Blended learning** (with computers in lab or classroom) Teacher as facilitator and moderator. Self-regulated online/VLE activity. Collaborating with peers. Striving towards common goals.	**Responsibility** – *Proactively* taking the lead, following lesson and links. – *Reactively* following and responding to lesson and links. **Decision** – *Proactively* taking the lead and engaging with peers and lesson – *Reactively* following direction and interacting with peers and lesson. **Evaluation** Reflect on lesson. – Use of L2 *proactively* initiated by self. – Use of L2 *reactively* responding to task and others.		Self-directed. Relatedness to others. Interaction. *Proactively* taking the lead in the task. *Reactively* following the lead. Responding to the task and others. Choice. Freedom. Expert support.

Table 4.1 Continued

Type of autonomy	Definitions	Context	Example behaviour	Language skills	Descriptors
Proactive and reactive autonomy during free-time VLE access: L2 free expression. Learner autonomy. Explicit interaction • Writing • Speaking Implicit interaction • Reading • Listening	**L2 free expression:** (a) Student choice of L2. (b) Increased L2 interaction. **Learner autonomy** (a) Responsibility (b) Decision-making. (c) Evaluation by the student.	**Free time:** Writing forum posts. Reading forum posts. Reading additional resources. Writing assignments. Discussion (with friends).	Free-time logging into the site. Voluntary use of L2 – posting to the forums. Level 1: *Reactively* responding to 'expert'-generated threads. Level 2: *Reactively* responding directly to peer-generated threads. Level 3: *Proactively* generating own threads. *Proactive* reading forum posts. *Proactive* engagement with additional resources. *Reactive* post-lesson assignments. *Proactive* discussions about postings to the forums.		Self-directed. Relatedness to others. Interaction. *Proactively* self-directed. *Reactively* task-directed. *Reactively* responding to others. Choice. Freedom. No expert support (except for assignment feedback).

The ecological approach

Ecology as a theoretical approach for research is described by van Lier (2004:3) as a 'contextualised or situated form of research' (van Lier 2004:3) and is concerned with 'complexity and the interrelatedness of processes that combine to produce an environment' (van Lier 2004:4). The ecological perspective visualizes learning as a process of collaboration in which notions of autonomy do not mean individualism but rather 'having authorship of one's actions' (van Lier 2004:8) and 'having the voice that speaks one's words' (ibid.), a view that corresponds to the notion of autonomy as represented by our working definition. The notion of ecology lends itself well to the examination of the impact on the behaviour of learners working together following the introduction of a VLE.

The merits of the ecological approach in working towards understanding the nature of the relationship between autonomy and technology in language learning

It is suggested by Blyth (2009:175) that technology has generated a multiplicity of metaphors such as 'the conduit, the tutor, the tools, the community' by way of conceptualizing its role as a culturally constructed artefact in language learning. This range of metaphorical labels is an indication of the dynamism and pace of change within the technological landscape. Blyth (ibid.) concurs with Warschauer (1999) that the difficulty in adopting these labels is that technology is examined in isolation from the context within which it exists. Given the ubiquitous presence of computers, the effects of technology on human activity should be considered in light of 'the totality of relationships' (van Lier 2004:3) between constituent elements of the environment, for example, the language; the learning; the participants; the classroom. Blyth (ibid.), reflects that, more recently, applied linguists have adopted the notion of ecology as a more appropriate label to express the interconnectedness between factors affecting learners' engagement with technology and learning in an era when social practices mediated by the internet have 'become part of the ecology of human activity' (Warschauer 1999:1). The ecological approach contextualises language as a social activity as shown in Box 4.1.

It is widely suggested that VLEs support social interaction and collaboration but 'these affordances define potential effects not actual ones' (Dillenbourg et al. 2002:10). The realization of the potential for social interaction cannot be assumed as 'the community does not automatically emerge because groups use electronic communication; it takes a lot of time, a lot of interactions. It

> ## Box 4.1 Ecological approach – view of language
>
> - Dynamic, making interaction unpredictable and random.
> - Pedagogically transformative through the coalescence of ideas and language knowledge between learners.
> - Dependent upon, and characterized by, the diversity of learners' perceptions, understanding and interpretations.
> - Defined by, as well as defining, the context within which communication takes place.

requires sharing goals and experiences' (ibid.). The literature reports widely upon the potential of electronic space to support collaborative learning and more dynamic L2 interaction (Arnold and Ducate 2006, Bensousan et al. 2006, Coomey and Stephenson 2001, Gonzalez-Lloret 2003, Kern 1995, Kern and Warschauer 2000, Kessler 2009, Müge Satar and Ozdener 2008, Warschauer 1997, 2002). However, as a pedagogical approach, collaborative learning is deemed effective when learners 'engage in rich interactions when they explain themselves in terms of conceptions and not simply in terms of answers' (ibid.). Relative to the notion of autonomy, how might learners therefore be encouraged to use the language to express themselves freely? Benson (2009:26) suggests that given the right conditions, the individual's innate capacity for autonomy might flourish. The difficulty lies in understanding the nature of the relationship between autonomy and the use of a technological learning environment and in knowing how 'to understand these opportunities and integrate them where they are pedagogically relevant.' (Dillenbourg et al. 2002:12). Three characteristics of the ecological approach emerge (van Lier (2004:4–8) to form the cornerstones of our conceptual framework: affordances, the totality of relationships and language defined by context versus language defining the context.

Affordances – serendipitous opportunities for language development

The first cornerstone is the notion of an 'affordance'. From the ecological perspective, an affordance relates to the view that context provides learners with opportunities for learning and language development mediated by content and materials, described by van Lier (2004:81) as the 'semiotic budget', but significantly it includes the possibility that learners respond to some affordances but not others. The concept is described by van Lier (2004:4) as 'a relationship between an organism (a learner, in our case) and the environment that signals an opportunity for or inhibition of action'.

The notion of affordance embraces the sense of choice and agency integral to the concept of learner autonomy. Interrogation of learners' interaction with the technology reveals which elements of the VLE the students choose to engage with and those they ignore, providing indicators of the characteristics necessary to stimulate autonomous behaviour and revealing something of the nature of the relationship between autonomy and the technology.

Furthermore an affordance need not simply refer to the students' response to content but also to the contributions made by individuals to one another's response to that content. One student's contributions might be perceived, interpreted and picked up by a different student, yet ignored by another. From the ecological perspective, language development becomes a less static 'process of receiving and processing pieces of [. . .] fixed code' (van Lier 2004:90). The notion of the affordance looks beyond the provision of content and includes the multidimensional character of students' interaction with one another as they engage with that content. L2 interaction emerges unpredictably so the affordance reflects the 'active relationship or engagement with the environment in which we find ourselves' (ibid.). The notion of the affordance acknowledges the value of learning opportunities that arise from the exploitation of the unexpected, satisfying the unpredictable quality of spontaneous use of language that might be mediated by the VLE. It becomes possible to interrogate student activity to see whether L2 peer interaction is less controlled, more opportunistic and whether students feel capable of organizing their thinking in order to contribute an 'internal-cognitive' (Little 2007:18) response to the unpredictable web of social interaction in a technologically mediated environment.

It is suggested that 'technology itself does not determine learning outcomes' (Piccoli et al. 2001:408) but rather the endeavours of the people who populate the technological environment and who, by virtue of participation and ad hoc responses, generate their own learning opportunities. If this is the case, then signs of independent behaviour need not necessarily be a response to the technology per se, but to the reaction created by individuals engaging with one another in the context of a technological environment. This leads to the second 'ecological' cornerstone of the conceptual framework, the notion of the 'totality of relationships' (Van Lier 2004:3).

From affordances to the 'Totality of Relationships' (van Lier 2004:3)

As a term, ecology was originally devised to refer to the 'totality of relationships of an organism with all other organisms with which it comes into contact' (van Lier 2004:3). Language is identified as the connecting element not only between people, but also the world. In turn, language learning emerges as a means by which the individual can engage more successfully with his environment (van Lier 2004:4). The notion of 'totality' embraces the multiple ways in which individuals might engage with one another in response to their environment, considering the view that 'the ecological perspective [...] states that we perceive the world always as interactive, reciprocal participants' (van Lier 2004:170).

In this book I am interested in scrutinizing 'the totality of relationships' (ibid.) and the dynamic between learners as they respond to the content and one another following the introduction of a virtual element to their learning context. I am interested in expanding Little's (1990:7) notion of interdependence to explore the possibility of a further dimension of the construct, ecological learner autonomy, where learners proactively or reactively respond to the web of interaction, and the voices of those that surround them anchored within the context of a VLE. In this way it becomes possible to look beyond the identification of instances of independent behaviour so that one might examine the possibility that introducing the VLE alters the contextual dynamic, enhancing the learning experience and relationships between individuals in terms of independent behaviour. Proponents of the ecological approach identify language as the connecting element between individuals and the context within which they exist. Language is the third cornerstone of the conceptual framework.

Language defined by the context versus language defining the context

One might argue that the introduction of a VLE has the potential to encourage learners to feel capable of exploiting their potential capacity to make independent choices about the target language, in terms of the realization, construction and expression of ideas in English, suggesting notions of learner autonomy as well as L2 free expression, as indicated in the VLE autonomy framework. The ecological approach regards context as defining the language, but simultaneously sees language as defining the context within which it exists (van Lier 2004:5), which suggests two outcomes.

On one hand, language choices made by learners might be determined by the context (the structure and direction of VLE blended lessons and free-time resources), raising questions of learner agency. For example, where students are given an expert-generated forum thread students might be said to be responding to the direction indicated by the thread, challenging notions of meaningful choice. Alternatively, students might be responding to the direction initiated by the forum task, but that they create and define the character of the technological context through their individual contributions to the forum, influencing their classmates' thinking and reflected in the development of ideas along the thread. They could be said to have had a hand in shaping their environment. The expression of their own ideas and their choice of language defines the character of the forum postings, revealing something of themselves and setting the tone of the environment for the wider audience. As learners make online judgements based on the views of those who have gone before them, a network of unplanned, interconnected communication emerges. It is suggested by van Lier (2004:41) that analysis of contextual interaction should go beyond the actions that take place, because in class 'things are not always visible and audible in the interaction' but may determine the course of events. This is particularly true online where 'students may leave a trace of their presence [...] Viewing which area has been visited by other students is an indirect mode of interaction' (Dillenbourg et al. 2002:5).

From an ecological perspective, context and language are essential elements in the evaluation of the nature of the relationship between autonomous language and learner behaviour in response to students' use of a VLE. Having captured and categorized the students' explicit (speaking and writing) and implicit (listening and reading) VLE-mediated interaction, one can then apply the principles of the ecological approach embedded within the conceptual framework, making it an essential third tool in working towards the construction of a theory about the nature of the relationship between autonomy and technology in the context of foreign language learning.

Conceptual framework for autonomous learning behaviour in a learning environment: A description

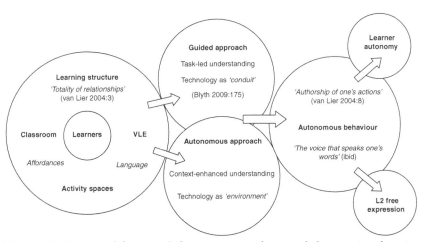

Figure 4.1 Conceptual framework for autonomous learning behaviour in a learning environment

The conceptual framework as illustrated in Figure 4.1 is a visual representation of the notion of autonomous learning behaviour in a technologically mediated learning environment from an ecological perspective. The large circle on the left-hand side represents the learning structure or context, described in ecological terms as activity spaces (van Lier 2004:63) to capture the multiple forms the context might take. The activity spaces are the classroom and the VLE. Within these spaces:

- Affordances avail themselves to the learner, signalling 'an opportunity for or inhibition of action' (van Lier 2004:4).
- Language is the element that connects the relationships between individuals in response to their affordances.
- The concept of the 'totality of relationships' (ibid.) acknowledges the multiple communicative dimensions with which individuals engage with one another within the learning structure or spaces.

The route towards autonomy might be achieved by adopting three pedagogical approaches, represented by the interlocking circles entitled Guided and Autonomous approach and summarized below in Boxes 4.2, 4.3 and 4.4:

Box 4.2 Guided pedagogical approach

Guided Approach reflecting Crook's (1994:79) description of 'Traditional Guided Instruction' as:

a. Teacher-led, didactic approach to learning.
b. Learners are provided with clearly defined affordances where the 'intended use is designed into it' (van Lier 2004:95). They react to the guidance set by the task to arrive at increased levels of understanding. Reactive autonomy (Littlewood 1999:75–6).
c. In a VLE, learner behaviour could be a response to the direction set by the affordance and not the intrinsic characteristics of the technology.
d. The technology acts as the 'conduit' (Blyth 2009:175) for the affordance.
e. The external design and selection of appropriate materials stimulates the learners' personal response to the technology relative to notions of autonomous behaviour and L2 free expression.

Box 4.3 Autonomous pedagogical approach

Autonomous approach reflecting the 'socio-psychological' (Little 1996:203) view of learning where the individual independently constructs knowledge in response to the world as he sees it:

a. Learners respond to multiple stimuli in the context of their learning environment not simply the direction stipulated by the task.
b. Learners determine the direction of activity and adapt behaviour in response to their learning environment. Proactive or reactive autonomy (ibid.) depending on whether the direction is initiated by the learner or the task.
c. Context supports the development of understanding.
d. Introducing the VLE alters the configuration of the learning structure and technology is an element to which the learners respond.
e. The impact of environmental stimuli stimulates autonomous learner behaviour and L2 free expression.

Box 4.4 Eclectic pedagogical approach

Interlocking circles an *eclectic* approach to reflect Little's (1990:7) view that 'As social beings our independence is always balanced by dependence' and that:

a. The student does not know the target language so needs guidance suggested by direction, and the 'presence or absence of the teacher is not the yardstick by which one can judge autonomous learning skills'(Macaro 1997:168).
b. It is a restrictive view to suggest that autonomous behaviour is compromised by structure because learning is a personal experience where the teacher 'cannot control what goes on inside each learner's head' (Little 1990:9).
c. Learners do not exclusively construct knowledge in response to direction but also to the contextual dimensions created by environmental stimuli.
d. Learning is an experience enabled by social interaction which can be in response to direction initiated by others, as well as that which is initiated by the learner.
e. Autonomous learner behaviour and L2 free expression emerge from the *eclectic* blend of both the guided and autonomous approach to learning.

The conceptual framework contextualizes and anchors the analysis of the individual's response to the introduction of the VLE to their learning environment from the theoretical perspective of the ecological approach, making it possible to work towards gaining understanding about the nature of the relationship between autonomy and the use of a VLE in the context of foreign language learning.

Aspects of design and data

This qualitative, heuristic project was conducted as a single, embedded case study. Because of the contemporary nature of the project (Yin 2003:7), it was exploratory in nature, an approach deemed to be effective for the evaluation of 'the subtleties and intricacies of complex social actions' (Denscombe 2003: 35).

The class of students described in this book represented a single case study with eight core students who appear as vignettes to enlighten, enhance and provide deeper 'insights into the single case' (Yin 2003:46). Class data was analysed first before looking in greater detail at the core students' data. Details identified for closer scrutiny were therefore not only pertinent to the core students but the entire class.

Data collection instruments and data sources

Data were collected and examined from two dimensions of the learners' personal response to the VLE. The first dimension was self-report data and the second was observational data.

Self-report data

Online questionnaires were administered before the VLE had been introduced, with follow-on questionnaires in the middle and at the end of the VLE-mediated language development programme. All questionnaires were mediated through the VLE in class and achieved a 100 per cent return rate. Students were asked to reflect on their language learning and VLE-mediated experiences.

Semi-structured interviews gave learners the opportunity to discuss their preferences, attitudes and beliefs about the VLE and were semi-structured so that the students could direct the flow of the conversation, based on their own interpretation of events. Data were triangulated with questionnaire data.

Self-report data enabled the capture of the students' perceptions of the VLE programme, but observational data provided another data source to corroborate what students *said* about lessons and free-time VLE access with what they *did* with the technology.

Observational data

I was predominantly based in the United Kingdom so was unable to be present and observe the students' VLE blended lessons. By necessity observational data was collected virtually by keeping a record and tracking the students' online movements around the platform. The analysis of site records allows the researcher to witness whether students come to class, log into the site in their free time and the affordances they choose to respond to or ignore, creating a 'virtual' observational presence and stimulating further lines of enquiry to follow up in interview. In an online context students may choose not to reply to or to generate forum threads, but this does not necessarily represent inactivity. Tracking explicit written interaction reveals just part of a student's online story, the tracking of a student's implicit interactions reveals their 'silent' on-site choices, for example choosing and following one link over another.

Student assignments following VLE lessons and forum posts can be interrogated for recurring themes in an attempt to capture explicit references to the direction taken in class discussions and topic language, which can be followed up in interview. In the project described in this book, I selected student writing that corresponded to those lessons that were referred to most often in the interviews. Free-time posts can be examined for the development of ideas along the 'post trail' thereby indicating students' implicit interaction (reading) and explicit interaction (writing) if they chose to respond to one another online, raising several lines of enquiry in interview.

Self-report data, supported by the tracking of online learner activity and the analysis of student writing, contributed towards the identification of elements in the VLE with which: students were most likely to engage in their free time, most likely to stimulate L2 interaction and most likely to encourage instances of autonomous behaviour.

Insights into the context, the case study and the learners

The case study group were a class of English language students from the Faculty of Education within a public university in Mexico. The language department has 20 teachers, providing courses to around 1,200 students from the wider community. The language department offers a range of 12 courses at all levels, with students working towards internationally recognized qualifications in English including FCE, CAE and IELTS examinations. The Faculty is technologically well resourced, with over 50 terminals in the computer centre and a further 20 computers in the language laboratory, with Wi-Fi and internet access. Technologically motivated teachers create their own online courses using the Dokeos platform held within the university.

Class profile

Our students were training to be English language teachers and had been studying together for five semesters. They received a total of 30 hours of tuition per week and had the opportunity to extend their language learning online. The class consisted of 8 men and 12 women, aged between 37 and 19 with an average age of 22. Two of the students were also parents. As well as studying full-time, many gave private English classes, with part-time jobs to supplement the family income. Most of the class came from the city and lived at home with their families. A small proportion of students came from outlying towns and villages, living in rented accommodation during the week and travelling home to their families at weekends. Students in the class had been learning English between 2 and 12 years, with the modal average being 8 years, and linguistically their level was between upper-intermediate and advanced. The most commonly cited reasons students gave for learning English were that they liked the language and they felt that English was important if they were to be successful in life. None of the class had visited the United Kingdom, although one student had visited the United States for a short holiday. Although each member of the class had a computer at home, six did not have internet access; however, they regularly visited internet cafés to pick up emails, chat to friends online, do their homework and to participate in the *EI* project. Despite the disparity between students in terms of internet access, all were regular, confident internet users, typically going online to look for information for college, downloading music and social networking. The majority used the computer every day for up to six hours.

The teacher who delivered the blended learning component of the *EI* programme during the students' weekly computer room lesson was a highly motivated teacher and committed to the project because she believed it would support the students' language development beyond the existing syllabus. The students had one *EI* blended lesson each week in the computer room led by their teacher in term time over a period of 8 months.

Core students – overview

The selection process involved: initial discussions with the teacher; the opening questionnaire; insights gained about the students in their first interviews relative to the criteria indicated in Table 4.2.

One of the most important criteria was reliability in terms of how regularly students attended *EI* blended lessons, and whether they visited the VLE in their free time. Regular attendance would inform students' capacity to reflect on their *EI* experiences in interview. While the core students did not necessarily complete all the assignments or reply to all of the forum postings, they submitted a significant amount of work, which was used as data in the analysis.

Table 4.2 Criteria in selecting students as members of the core student group

1. **Access to a computer outside school:** The virtual learning programme provided opportunities for students to interact with the VLE in a classroom environment and their free time. Students needed access to a computer in order to engage with the range of options available within *EI*.
2. **A personal email address:** The learners needed a personal email address to register with the VLE, gain access to the site and receive information about tasks and activities.
3. **Willingness to participate:** The students needed to be willing to participate in the study and talk to the interviewer about their learning experiences with the technology. I discussed the selection criteria with the teacher and asked for guidance.
4. **Reliability:** Reliable attendance in class. A student with a record of poor classroom attendance would have been less likely to choose to engage and contribute to the VLE in class, or submit written work for analysis. This was a point for discussion with the teacher.
5. **Time:** Students needed to be willing to allocate time after class to be interviewed about their experiences with the technology. This was by mutual arrangement, at a time convenient for both parties.
6. **Language level:** Students needed to be at the same level so that they could participate and respond to the VLE content; otherwise their perceptions about the VLE experience would have been overshadowed by difficulties associated with the language in the VLE programme. Language levels were discussed with the teacher. A minimum entry level of IELTS level 4.5 or Upper Intermediate was preferred.
7. **Request:** Students were asked in the opening questionnaire whether they would like to participate as members of the core student group and were aware that they were free to withdraw at any stage.

Core students – profiles (names have been changed to preserve anonymity)

1. Zarita

Zarita was the most mature of the students participating in the project and had been learning English for 12 years. She had decided to become a teacher having been a bilingual secretary. Zarita had three children. Because of the challenges of combining family life and her academic work, she had initially considered an online programme of study, suggesting she was open to exploring the potential of technology.

She regularly used the internet, but preferred to use it from home rather than from the university. She regretted that she did not have as much opportunity as she would have liked to use English, and recognized that she would benefit from the chance to practise her speaking and listening more extensively. She was a hard-working and reliable student, completing all of the assignments and regularly replying to the forum postings.

2. Julia

Julia was 20 years old and had been learning English for 8 years. Academically she was a motivated learner and planned to do a PhD in foreign languages. Julia indicated that she was technologically engaged, using the computer for an extensive range of activities, with work, social networking and music cited as the most common reasons for going online. She spent several hours a day online chatting with native English speakers and valued this arena as a place where she could freely express herself in English, unlike the classroom. Although Julia did not reply to all the posts, or complete all the assignments, she was consistent in her attendance and level of participation in the project.

3. Maribel

Maribel was 23 and had been learning English for 5 years. She considered language learning as a 'hobby', using English as 'code' at home with her younger sister. She spoke French to a high standard. She wanted the opportunity to study abroad in the future. Outside class, she gave private English lessons, and worked as an English-speaking tour guide in the town. Maribel used technology in and out of the university, for a wide range of activities, from work to online social networking. She did not have internet access at home, and used her local cybercafé. She spent several hours a week chatting online with a group of students from Utah who had been on exchange to the university. Maribel contributed and participated regularly with *EI* throughout the project and her classmates valued and commented on her forum postings and contributions in class.

4. Lucia

Lucia was 22. At the time of the study she had been learning English for 3 years. She wanted to become an English teacher to help others to overcome their fear of language learning as she had. She lacked confidence in her ability to communicate in English and felt shy speaking in open class. She regretted the lack of opportunity to practise speaking English in her community. She tried to find opportunities to practise her English outside class by watching films but felt discouraged by the speed of the language. She used technology at home for college work and socialized online with Spanish friends. She did not chat to friends online in English. Towards the end of the intervention, Lucia was instrumental in organizing the class into small groups to meet in the *EI* chat room, with students providing fresh topics for discussion each week. She was one of the most regular contributors to *EI* in terms of her forum posts and completed all of the assignments.

5. Monse

At 19, Monse was one of the youngest students in the class and had been learning English for 8 years. Monse was very shy and found speaking in class intimidating, as she was fearful of error and concerned about what others might think of her. She recognized the need to improve her speaking and she acknowledged that the classroom was the only environment where she could do so because of the lack of opportunity to use English in her home town. Monse found it difficult to write in English. She was particularly anxious about writing online and how long it would take her to produce a good piece of work. Monse did not have a computer at home, and used the computers in the university and at cybercafés. Monse and Lucia were best friends and benefited from sharing concerns about English and working together. During the intervention Monse had a baby. She successfully combined motherhood with her degree course and was a regular, consistent participant in the study.

6. Juan

Juan was 24, and had been learning English formally for only 2 years. He was a resourceful learner, looking extensively for opportunities beyond the classroom to improve his English. He asked his brother to teach him English and had gone to the main square in the local town to ask 'gringos' to translate his favourite songs, and latterly engaged them in conversation. He worked part-time in the local cinema because of his passion for film, watching films in English and noting down new lexical items. He was the most technologically engaged of the class, with his home computer set up in English, not Spanish. He identified with technology, as an academic and a social resource, spending several hours a day online chatting to international friends in English through social networking sites. Juan's online communication skills belied his real-world confidence. He was shy and less forthcoming face-to-face. Juan contributed extensively to the *EI* site, but was more reluctant in formal assignments.

7. Vicente

Vicente was 21 and had been learning English for 9 years. Vicente was the most linguistically inaccurate of the students, most evident in his writing. Despite this, he was a confident communicator in English, taking every opportunity to practise. He always spoke English in class, and his classmates held him in high regard, considering him the most competent student in the group. Vicente's partner was not Mexican, so English was the lingua franca at home. Vicente worked at a local language school in his free time, with future plans to open his own school. Although he was technologically engaged, for academic and social purposes, he used the computer because he had to, rather than because he wanted to. While he actively participated in the *EI* project, he challenged the value of the VLE from the outset.

8. Mateo

Mateo was 19, and one of the youngest students in the class. He had been learning English for 4 years. He was a quiet student and found speaking in open class challenging. He looked up to the students in class he perceived to be the most able. Mateo wanted to study for a PhD. Although he was also learning French, he considered English to be the language of the internet that would provide him with greater life opportunities. He was aware of the lack of opportunities to practise English in his home town, but he read extensively online, especially websites linked to his favourite video games. He was technologically confident, regularly chatting online in English to international friends. Mateo lived in rented accommodation in the town, without internet access. He relied on cybercafés and the university internet throughout the week. He had internet access at weekends in his village. Mateo did not reply to every discussion topic in the forum and did not complete every assignment. However, he attended all the classes and submitted a substantial amount of work for analysis.

Messing about with Moodle: The development of *EI*

The VLE platform

EI was developed on Moodle, a platform that is widely used across the educational community. Moodle is an Open Source Course Management System, accessible from any internet connection. It can be downloaded, installed free of charge and needs to be configured to a server. Moodle enables institutions to provide online content by uploading course materials and activities, set project work and assignments and provides a platform for online discussions. Access was password-protected so that only enrolled students could participate.

EI VLE – modes of delivery and teaching and learning tools

EI was divided into two modes of delivery which were blended learning and free-time access. Three categories of teaching and learning tools were designed for use in the blended and free-time mode: forums, blended learning materials and additional materials. These tools were designed with a primary or secondary mode of delivery in mind. For example, the primary mode for the forums was free-time use, but the secondary mode of delivery was exercised when the popular *Read, Think and Reply* (*RTR*) forum was integrated into six blended lessons. Table 4.3 illustrates the primary and secondary modes of delivery for EI-mediated activities.

Table 4.3 *EI* teaching and learning tools and modes of delivery

Teaching and learning tools	Primary mode of delivery	Secondary mode of delivery
Forums	Free-time	Blended classroom
Blended lessons materials	Blended classroom	Free-time
Additional materials	Free-time	Blended lessons

Defining blended learning and free-time access to *EI*

Blended learning can be variously understood. Driscoll (2002:1) identifies four different interpretations of the concept including:

Box 4.5 Interpretations of blended learning (adapted from Driscoll 2002:1)

1. The blending and use of different technologies for learning.
2. The combination of different pedagogical approaches with or without technology.
3. The combination of technology with face-to-face learning.
4. The integration of technology into the day-to-day learning environment, and classroom tasks.

EI corresponded to the third and fourth of Driscoll's options blending the VLE with traditional face-to-face classroom interaction (Box 4.5). Neumeier advocates that, in developing a blended environment one should consider: accommodating learners' needs; computer skills; their conceptualization of the technology; the integration of the technology in class; and the balance of face-to-face with computer interaction, to create the 'feel' of the course (Neumeier 2005:167–9).

EI was designed to enhance the students' learning environment but the intention was that technological functionality should not overwhelm the language or learning experience, as Warschauer (2002:55) says, 'Technology does not constitute a method, rather, it is a resource that can be used to support a variety of approaches and methods.' The aim in the design of the blended learning strand was that the technology should be integrated and normalized (Bax 2003:23) as a feature of the environment, embedded (ibid.) into the interaction of the classroom.

The *EI* blended approach corresponds to Thorne's (2003:16) definition of blended learning as 'an opportunity to integrate the innovative and technological advances offered by online learning with the interaction and participation offered by the best of traditional learning'. Thorne's definition aptly describes how technology might be exploited to stimulate independence in the classroom and spontaneous L2 peer interaction, where 'autonomy resides in being able to say what you want rather than producing the language of others' (Macaro 2008:60).

Free-time access to *EI* was defined as the students' engagement with the VLE beyond the classroom, for example from their laptop, library computers, internet cafe or at home. In this way one might see whether learners chose to exploit affordances for language development mediated by *EI* in their own time, to examine their reasons for doing so and the value they attributed to their free-time use of the VLE. Examination of learners' free-time *EI*-mediated behaviour might reveal something of the nature of the suggested relationship between autonomy and technology in an EFL context.

EI blended lessons (Appendices 4.1, 4.2, 4.3 – example *EI* lessons)

The pedagogical approach adopted within the blended learning strand reflected the notion of guided learning (Crook 1994:79), in that the latter describes how learners responded to the direction indicated by EI-mediated materials in class. Tables 4.4 and 4.5 provide an overview of each *EI* blended lessons over both stages of the project, with Appendices 4.1, 4.2 and 4.3 providing detailed examples of the content of 3 of the lessons mediated by EI. Blended lessons adopted familiar characteristics of the traditional classroom lessons with screens leading the teacher and learners through the activities in much the same way as a course book unit might. Teaching content was designed in collaboration with the teacher to identify relevant topics for the development of materials for the programme.

EI VLE – approaches to CALL and implications for activities in blended lessons

EI activities were designed with a consideration afforded to the well-documented Structural, Communicative and Integrative approaches to CALL. When asked about their perceptions of CALL, students' conceptualization corresponded to the more behaviourist structural CALL approach. Although Warschauer and Healey described Structural CALL as tending towards 'repetitive language drills' (1998:57), Evans (2009:19) reflects that in recent years this narrow definition has evolved towards a more comprehensive interpretation of the computer-as-tutor, popular in distance language-learning courses.

Although not the mainstay of *EI*, additional activities were incorporated that were grounded in the more traditional notion of the computer-as-tutor and located alongside the content of the blended lesson, to raise awareness in class of extra, free-time opportunities for language development. In terms of exploring

Table 4.4 Stage one: Overview of *EI* blended lessons

Stage 1: Lesson titles	Aim	Language skills	Lesson activities	Additional resources
All about you – Finding out about each other.	Question formation, profile writing for the VLE.	Speaking for fluency and accuracy, listening and writing.	What's the question, form the questions. Interviews and follow-up writing.	
Have your say – Are we scared to let children out to play?	Topical discussion, expression of personal opinion.	Reading for gist, speaking for fluency, listening, writing for the forum.	Speaking, reading, reflection and discussion, individual reading and sharing of ideas, posting personal opinion to *Read, Think and Reply* forum.	Extended reading. Live link to original text.
Making decisions – Teamwork and negotiation.	Problem-solving, language of negotiation	Speaking for fluency, listening, post-lesson writing.	Team work – reaching a team decision, post-lesson assignment.	
Happiness – The greatest thing you can possess.	Reading for gist and detail, exchange of ideas.	Reading, speaking for fluency, listening, writing.	Paired speaking – sharing life experiences, prediction task, reading (newspaper article), discussion leading from article, post-lesson assignment.	
Surviving – Mean what you say, say what you mean: *bored* and *boring*.	Analysis ed/ing adjectives, reading for gist and detail, exchange of ideas.	Vocabulary, speaking for fluency, listening, reading for gist and detail, post-lesson assignment.	Comparing and contrasting adjectives, prediction task, reading for gist and detail – newspaper article reading, post-lesson assignment.	Extended reading. Live link to original article and newspaper website.
International treasures – Teamwork and negotiation.	Discussion and negotiation, Reading for gist and detail, presentation skills, writing.	Speaking, listening, reading, writing.	Prediction task, jigsaw reading, planning and presenting a business presentation, post-lesson assignment.	Live link to further reading from recommended websites.

Table 4.5 Stage two: Overview of *EI* blended lesson

Stage 2: Lesson titles	Aim	Language skills	Lesson activities	Additional resources
Online friendship – Are my online friends real? Topical discussion.	Speaking for fluency, reading for gist, exchange of ideas, writing for the forum.	Speaking, listening, reading and writing.	Prediction, adapted reading from news website, personal response to the reading, individual readings, feedback from individual readings, writing and posting of personal opinion to *Read, Think and Reply* forum.	Live link to original, longer newspaper article. Video resource.
Class and society – Where we fit into society.	Exchange and response to peer opinions.	Speaking, listening, reading, writing.	Topical discussion, prediction task, reading for gist and detail, writing and posting of personal opinion to *Read, Think and Reply* forum.	Video resource.
Texting – Have your say. Topical discussion.	Speaking for fluency, problem solving, exchange of ideas.	Speaking, listening, reading, writing.	Talking about texting, translations: texting vocabulary, reading in text language, reading and exchange of views about texting, posting to *Read, Think and Reply* forum, post-lesson assignment.	Text in English: Live link to 'slang' website. Extended reading, questions, vocabulary resources.
Are you a copy cat? The red hot topic of plagiarism.	Raising awareness about plagiarism, debate and exchange of ideas.	Speaking, listening, reading, writing.	Sharing experiences, teamwork (debate), post-lesson assignment.	Extended reading and questions, adapted from Cambridge University website. Listening and video resources.

Table 4.5 Continued

Stage 2: Lesson titles	Aim	Language skills	Lesson activities	Additional resources
Heroes and icons – Mean what you say, say what you mean.	Vocabulary – similarities and differences in meaning, reading for gist and detail.	Vocabulary, speaking, listening, reading, writing.	Comparing and contrasting lexical items, prediction and jigsaw reading for detail, paired speaking, post-lesson assignment.	Live link to original reading.
Taking responsibility – For our actions. Topical discussion.	Speaking for fluency, exchange of ideas, reading for gist, writing.	Speaking, listening, reading, writing.	Warm up speaking task, read and respond task, individual readings and exchange of ideas, posting to *Read, Think and Reply* forum.	Live link to original text. Extended reading and questions. Listening resources.
Academic institutions – Finding out about academic traditions in Britain.	Reading for gist and detail, speaking for fluency, information search.	Speaking, listening, reading, writing.	Prediction, short reading, gist questions, jigsaw reading, paired and whole-class feedback, internet research task with targeted websites, follow-up report writing for homework.	Reading, optional writing, listening with questions.
Stress-busting – Topical discussion and reading.	Reading for gist and detail, vocabulary, exchange of ideas.	Speaking, listening, reading, writing.	Read and respond to short text, stress-busting questionnaire, reflect and discuss response to questionnaire, reading for detail and questions, vocabulary links, post-lesson assignment.	Link to original text. Video resources.

notions of autonomy in a VLE, in the development of activities this approach was adopted for two reasons:

1. To see whether learners chose to engage with affordances that corresponded more closely with previous CALL experience.
2. To present a robust, pedagogically familiar VLE learning programme. that corresponded with the users' experience of CALL.

Activities for *EI* blended lessons were designed to encourage learners to choose to use English more extensively in class and to extend their engagement with the language beyond the classroom. *EI* tasks were designed to encourage learners to focus 'more on using forms than on the forms themselves' (Warschauer and Healey 1998:57), suggestive of Communicative CALL. The following example (Box 4.6) shows an activity designed to engage learners in lively classroom discussion around the computer, focusing on fluency rather than accuracy:

Box 4.6 Example *EI* blended task – speaking for fluency

Talk to your partner (or in open class)

> It is increasingly suggested that we are living in a 'nanny state' where we are told what to do, how to behave and what choices we should be making about our lives

Who should take responsibility for your good health and well-being and why?

1. You – the individual
2. The government
3. The health professionals
4. All of the above

Click into stage 2 and read a short text about a problem that is reaching mammoth proportions in the developed world.

By design, this task targets the practice of modal verbs of obligation, which might lead one to suggest that *EI* content took a Communicative approach to CALL. Indeed, research has explored the type of tasks most likely to stimulate meaningful L2 interaction and the impact of CMC practices on language development, analysing discourse for indications of language improvement as learners negotiate meaning (Arnold and Ducate 2006, Blake 2005, Chapelle

1997, Ganem Gutierrez 2006, Kessler 2009, Kitade 2008, Kol and Schcolnik 2008, Lai and Zhao 2006, Lamy and Hampel 2007c, Müge Satar and Özdener 2008, Pelletieri 2000, Shekary and Tahririan 2006, Smith 2003, Warschauer 1997). Although the design of many *EI* activities suggests a Communicative approach to CALL, the purpose of this book is not the evaluation of the development of grammatical competence resulting from CMC activities, nor to evaluate the type of computer-mediated tasks most likely to stimulate increased L2 peer interaction, it is to gain insights into the nature of the relationship between autonomy and technology in the context of foreign language learning.

Integrative CALL is described by Warschauer and Healey as 'a more social or socio-cognitive view, which [places] greater emphasis on language use in authentic social contexts' (1998:57). However, in terms of using technology, this can be variously interpreted, 'depending on the constituent features of the integration process' (Evans 2009:24). Evans suggests that Integrative CALL can be understood to reflect the range of language skills deployed by learners as they use the technology, or, when technology-mediated stimuli are visual, textual or aural. In light of the different interpretations of Integrative CALL, the interpretation preferred by Evans is that proposed by Gruba (2004:628–9, cited in Evans 2009:24), when networked computers are used to engage learners in collaborative activities and where they are encouraged to use technology to independently produce 'tangible language/digital outcomes' (ibid.). He proposes a third dimension of Integrative CALL whereby learners collaborate and exploit networked technology in and beyond the classroom. The technology is interwoven into the fabric of the learning experience. The flexibility of a VLE means that it can be integrated into multiple environments, blurring the boundaries between traditional and technology-enhanced activities in class and in students' free time. Table 4.6 shows an Integrative CALL approach in an *EI* lesson where a broader perspective as proposed by Evans is adopted.

EI blended lessons adopted an integrated language skills approach, encouraging students to collaborate through discussion and negotiation and to work towards the construction of a piece of computer-mediated writing in response to the lesson. VLE-mediated lessons were highly visual and enhanced by the functionality of the technology. In an attempt to blur the boundaries between classroom and free-time access to *EI* and to gain insights into links between technology and autonomy, learners were recommended to follow up the lessons by exploring additional *EI* resources and the free-time, *Read Think and Reply* forum was incorporated into several blended lessons.

Table 4.6 Integrative CALL approach to an example *EI* lesson

Stage 1: Warmer – whole-class speaking and listening.	Warm-up discussion questions about the topic. Follow the hyperlink to the second stage.
Stage 2: Texting in English – vocabulary, problem solving, paired speaking and listening.	Task: 'translate' individually hyperlinked English words and phrases in text language. Students use hyperlinks to 'toggle' back and forth to a 'translation' screen. Extension: Translation screen provides a link to an external website, with further examples of text language in English. Follow link to stage three.
Stage 3: Reading for gist, prediction task, paired and whole-class speaking and listening.	Short text describing a problem identified in the British media about the damage text language is doing to writing conventions. Extension: Link to a longer reading Students make prediction about opinion expressed by the British public. Follow link to stage four.
Stage 4: Reading for gist, paired and whole-class speaking and listening.	Students receive short individual texts, to read and exchange ideas from the text with their classmates, check against stage four predictions. Follow the link to stage 5.
Stage 5: Reflection and writing.	*Read, Think and Reply* forum, students write and post their own opinion.
Post-lesson assignment: Reflection and writing.	Student signposted to the assignment from the screen at stage four and *Read, Think and Reply*.

In seeking to gain insights into the choices learners made and their engagement with the technology, the design of VLE content for blended lessons was informed by Warschauer and Healey's (1998:57) distinction between 'Structural CALL', 'Communicative CALL' and 'Integrative CALL.' However, the approach that prevailed is best described as the interpretation of Integrative CALL as suggested by Evans (2009:24).

EI VLE free-time access overview

The free-time strand of *EI* was designed to provide learners with an environment that was rich and varied in resources, providing learners with ample opportunity to engage with English beyond the classroom through the VLE if they so chose. The choices learners make as they engage with language development activities mediated by technology in their free-time provide indicators about the characteristics and types of activity most likely to stimulate independent engagement with the VLE and the target language beyond the classroom.

An extensive body of additional resources were provided at the start of the programme. Digital content can be adapted, added to and changed during an online programme in response to the learners' preferences, unlike traditional paper-based courses. Scrutiny of the characteristics of affordances students are most and least responsive can be used to inform ongoing content development and analysis of notions of autonomy during the learning programme. This is particularly true with free-time activities, because students log into the site of their own volition unlike the blended lessons where they are directed by the teacher to the lesson.

The free-time strand within *EI* gave learners access to a block labelled as 'Your space'. This block provided a series of expert- and student-led forums. Free-time activities also included links to traditional homework tasks with links embedded within VLE blended lessons. Within the 'Your space' block students were provided with links to established foreign language development sites where they had access to practice exercises, an approach that corresponded to their previous experience of CALL.

EI – 'Your space' forums

The 'Your space' block appeared at the top of the opening screen of EI, making it easy for students to locate. The name of the block was a take on a popular social networking site and chosen to reflect its communicative function. 'Your space' provided students with a series of forums and students also had access to a chat facility. Two of the forums (News forum, *Read, Think and Reply* forum) were expert-led. The News forum operated as the *EI* notice board to pass on updates and information about the VLE to the participants. The *RTR* forum proved extremely popular and students were invited to respond in their free time to weekly structured expert-generated discussion threads. Unlike assignments, students received no expert feedback to their forum postings. Photographs, illustrations and rubric on the opening screens of each forum explained the purpose of these virtual spaces to the students, as shown in Box 4.7.

RTR threads provided structured discursive tasks, designed to stretch the students linguistically and to intellectually stimulate L2 free expression of ideas. Table 4.7 provides a list of the weekly free-time expert-generated threads posted to the *RTR* forum, giving an indication of the range of topics to which students were invited to respond to, with an example *RTR* parent thread indicated in Box 4.8.

Box 4.7: *EI* forums and rubric

News forum General news and announcements from *EI*.

The tea room Your place to meet up with friends and students participating in the study to share ideas.

Picture post Use this forum to post photos of you, your friends, your classmates, your travels... or anything that you want to post up. Say something about your photo, and of course comments about classmates' photos are most welcome.

Words to share An online word box. Use this forum to post and share any new English words or phrases that you pick up in class, from friends, or from readings, music, cinema... in fact... anywhere! There may be words or phrases that you have heard but don't understand. Post your 'word queries' here.

RTR Discussion topics will be posted for you each week and you can choose whether you want to *Read, Think and Reply*. This forum will give you something to think about and help you build your writing skills. Before you post a reply, think about what you are going to contribute. Your teacher may use some of the ideas you raise in this forum in the classroom. **Remember to check** this forum regularly for new discussion threads – it's a great way to practise your language.

Learning a language A problem shared is a problem halved!

What do you find challenging about learning English? What points of grammar or vocabulary confuse you? Perhaps you'd like some tips about reading, writing, listening or speaking?

Take the opportunity in this forum to post your language questions to *EI*.

Box 4.8 *RTR* sample thread *RTR* forum: parent thread: 29 February – leap year

It's a leap year – 29 February comes around every four years. If you are on an annual salary, you will get the same pay as in a normal year... for working one extra day, great for your employer, not so great for the employee! In fact this year some workers are being given today as an extra day's holiday.

1. Who should 29 February belong to: the employer or the employee?
2. Who owns time?
3. Should 29 February be awarded as a national holiday?
4. If you were given the 'gift' of one day's time to do as you wished, how would you spend it?

Table 4.7 Topics *Read, Think and Reply* weekly, free-time, expert-generated threads

Stage one: Weekly parent thread	Stage two: Weekly parent thread
I wish more people would take notice of …	New Year's resolutions
The best age to be …	Valentine's day message
Happy times	29 February – leap year
What do you think about …?	Letter writing
Postcard from Cambridge	Film for a friend
Something I'm good at …	Cambridge University
Saying and quotations	It's better to travel than arrive
The next few years …	The most surprising thing …
If you had to choose …	A word or phrase I use too much
Christmas messages	Spring, summer, autumn, winter
	A question of teaching
	The silver screen or the power of the written word
	The first thought that comes to mind
	Daydreaming
	Global chatting
	Chat options
	The long goodbye

The nature of the students' interaction with the *RTR* forum allowed for the examination of issues relating to learner choice, perceptions about language development, online L2 free expression and peer interaction. Expert-generated threads within *RTR* created a context designed to encourage the practice of multiple language skills, the online generation of ideas and the sharing of different viewpoints. Student-led forums created a space where learners could generate threads, post thoughts, experiences and photographs. Student free-time engagement with student-led forums compared to the expert-led *RTR* forum provided a rich context from which to interrogate the significance of structure within the concept of autonomy.

Appendix 4.1 Example: *EI* Blended Lesson (Lesson 9)

Screen 1 (warmer) Txt tlk? 4 better o 4 wrse?

Talk to your partner and consider the following questions

1. Do you text?
2. What is the point of texting?
3. Who do you text most often?
4. Who would you never text?
5. Do you ever find yourself using text language by accident?

Can you text in English? Click to **stage two** and check out the next **task.**

Screen 2 Lost in trnsl8n?

How many of these English texting words and phrases do you know . . . or can you guess?

- Check out the following commonly used words and phrases in English text language.
- In pairs can you translate them?

1. gr8	11. plse	21. np
2. asap	12. soz	22. yw
3. bf and gf	13. tb	23. 2nyt
4. cya	14. imo	24. 2moz
5. l8r	15. ne	25. g2g
6. lol	16. gd	26. ruok
7. m8	17. f9	27. wkd
8. omg	18. brb	28. xlnt
9. ily	19. btw	29. zzzz
10. Thnx	20. kl	

Follow the hyperlink and spend a moment checking to see if your '**translations**' were accurate before moving on to **stage 3**.

If you want more examples of text language in English, try this link http://y2u.co.uk/Knowledge_Information/Technology/RN_Mobile_SMS_Texting_Slang.htm

Screen 3 Text interference

Exam markers have expressed concerns over the use of text messaging language in exam answers.

The proof of its increased usage came when a 13-year-old Scottish schoolgirl handed in an essay written completely in text message shorthand, much to the surprise of her teacher. One extract said:

'My smmr hols wr CWOT. B4, we used 2go2 NY 2C my bro, his GF & thr 3 :- kids FTF. ILNY, it's a gr8 plc.'

Can you translate this extract? If you can mb u r a txt addict? If not click for the translation.

Source: http://news.bbc.co.uk/1/hi/talking_point/2815461.stm

1. Who is concerned about the use of text language?
2. Why has their concern made headline news?

Prediction task: What do you think the consensus of opinion in Britain is on this subject?

1. Do British people think texting is killing off the English language?
2. Do British people think there is a place for texting in the English language?

Click into **stage 4** and find out.

Screen 4 What the general public thought (reading and group discussion)

Individual readings: Available for teacher to print and distribute from the VLE teacher's resources space.

Task 1: You will each receive a different reading posted by people who contributed their opinion to the original discussion. Read your 'opinion' and share the ideas expressed in your text with your partner and classmates.

Task 2: What about you? When you have talked to your classmates, tell us what you think.

Go to **Read, Think and Reply forum, Texting – friend or foe.** Write and post a reply giving your opinion on the topic.

The Forum: Read, Think and Reply (in class) What do you think? Does texting mark the beginning of the end of the English language as we know it?

Free-time resources

By the way . . . If you want to read a longer article after the lesson, that is related to this topic, please take a look at the news story adapted from the BBC that accompanies this lesson, entitled: **Is txt mightier than the word.**

Assignment: Do you think texting is killing off the English language . . . if so, why? Or is there a place for texting in the English language . . . if so, why? Reflect on the classroom discussion and opinions posted by your classmates to the Read, Think and Reply forum. Write an assignment and construct an argument presenting the points for and against text language, concluding with your own point of view.

Appendix 4.2 Example 2: *EI* Blended Lesson (Lesson 6)

Screen 1 From the animal kingdom and the natural world to great works of art, consider three great treasures of the world with your partner to share with your classmates.

A thing of beauty is a joy forever (John Keats)

Click to **stage 1** to reveal two more 'treasures'. How much do you know about them?

Screen 2 What? Where? When? Facts? How? Figures? News stories?

How much do you know about these two 'treasures'? Discuss and share what you know with your classmates.

Terra-cotta Army

Group 1: Find out more about **picture 1** follow the link and read on **stage 3 (1)**.
Group 2: Find out more about **picture 2** follow the link and read on **stage 3 (2)**.

Screen 3 (1) and (2) Jigsaw reading: International treasures

Rubric for group 1 and 2: Read your text and think about any **new and interesting information** you discover about this international treasure (notice the links to the **vocabulary box**)

... and **then** ... share this information with your partner from the other group.

Screen 4 Planning and negotiation

Team tasks

There is funding of £50 million available for which your team have to submit a bid.

1. Prepare a presentation of your funding proposal to the committee, explaining and justifying why the money should be awarded to your group rather than the other.
2. Nominate one member of your team to present your proposal to the class.

Group 1: The Terracotta Army. You are bidding for the money because you plan to mount an international exhibition of the Terracotta Army. You plan to exhibit this international treasure in more that six countries around the world. The exhibition will be shown around the world over a period of two years. Look back at the **Terracotta Army reading** to help you.

Group 2: The Panda. You are bidding for the money because you plan to invest in a new breeding and conservation programme to save your international treasure from extinction. Look back at the **Giant Panda reading** to help you.

(Idea adapted from BBC Radio 4, National Treasures)

Screen 5 Written assignment

Is it possible to put a price on something that is culturally, environmentally and historically precious and to decide which has the most value and is therefore the most worthwhile investment?

Present an argument to explain why or why not.

To support your reasoning, reflect upon the examples of the Terracotta Army and the panda that were discussed in class.

- Open your assignment with an introduction.
- Write three paragraphs within the body of your text, with each paragraph representing a new idea.
- Close your assignment with a conclusion.

Appendix 4.3 Example 3: *EI* Blended Lesson (Lesson 10)

Screen 1 Are you a copycat?

Plagiarism: The unacknowledged use of the work of others as if it were your own original work to gain unfair advantage (definition adapted from: Encarta Dictionary and www.cam.ac.uk/plagiarism).

1. Have you ever copied, imitated or adapted other people's ideas and presented them as your original work?
2. Do you know people who do this and have done this?

Talk to your partner:
It's time to own up now, and we *promise* not to tell anyone . . . your secrets are safe with us!
   Now click into **stage 2** to probe the topic more deeply

Screen 2 Beyond the page

"Dear Mr. Trent: Since you only *pretended* to write this paper, I only *pretended* to grade it!"

Talk to your partner about the following questions:

1. In how many 'arenas' could plagiarism happen? Can you make a list with examples?
2. How can plagiarism manifest itself in education?
3. How common is plagiarism in the education system in your country?
4. How easy do you think it is for teachers and examiners to detect plagiarism?
5. Does plagiarism really matter? Why? Why not?

Now click into **stage 3**.

Screen 3 What would you do?

You and your partner are the judge and the jury, so it's time to think and discuss

Consider the effects of the following examples of plagiarism, and reflect on these two questions.

- Who is the ultimate victim of the crime? Or maybe you feel this is a victimless crime.
- What price will the victim and/or the perpetrator finally pay? Or maybe you feel in some of these examples there is no price to pay.

1. Dan Brown, the author of the Da Vinci Code has twice been accused of plagiarism, and been found innocent on each occasion.
2. Korean singer Lee Hyori was accused of plagiarising a Britney Spears song, resulting in the failure of her song and album.
3. The Vice Chancellor of a University in India resigned from his post after he was found guilty of plagiarising the work of a student.
4. A student studying English as a foreign language is writing an assignment. She cuts and pastes a text directly from the internet, passing the work off as her own.

Examples drawn from: http://en.wikipedia.org/wiki/Plagiarism

For additional reading on this topic you can click into the following **reading** and find out what the newspapers say.

To find out what the University of Cambridge recommends in terms of how to avoid plagiarism you may be interested in this additional resource and further reading.

Free time: Additional resource: Reading 1 – Plagiarism, a step to action
Free time: Additional resource: Reading 1– The vocabulary
Free time: Additional resource: Reading 1– The questions
Free time: Additional resource: Further reading: Plagiarism – A beginner's guide
Free time: Additional resource: Listening – Brains for sale
Free time: Additional resource: Video – Student plagiarism on the rise

5

Learner Reflections about Learning English as a Foreign Language and the Role of Technology

The starting point for the evaluation of the nature of the relationship between autonomy, foreign language learning and technology begins with the learner: their observations and reflections about learning a foreign language and their experiences of learning with technology. The capture of this baseline information represents a rich source of comparative data for consideration alongside their subsequent response to the introduction of their VLE-mediated language development programme.

Students' reflections on aspects of their current EFL learning environment

The notion of the classroom as the 'natural site for learning' (Benson 1997:23) characterizes a traditional view of the guided learning model where the interaction to predominantly takes place between the novice student and expert teacher. The students in this book attributed some value to this approach, raising questions about whether a didactic approach to learning stifles or liberates the individual from 'reliance on others' (Benson and Voller 1997:4). In the context of a technological learning environment, where the boundaries are redefined, one might wonder about the impact of the learners' experiences of the guided learning model on their capacity for autonomous learner behaviour.

Observations about learning English in Mexico made by the students who appear in the context of this book, is of particular interest, because they had been learning English through a period of pedagogical transition from the traditional transmission approach towards the more communicative model favoured by the British Council and private language schools. Their commentary describes their own situation, but is one that in resonates in foreign language classrooms worldwide.

Student perceptions of the pedagogical culture on learning and use of English in a Mexican EFL classroom

Historically, the Mexican language education system has adopted a more transmissive approach to language learning and this was reflected in the students' observations. They reported that there was little expectation or opportunity for them to make independent choices about learning or to interact in the target language. They acknowledged that it was the teacher who managed their learning programme and from whom they sought expert direction and correction. They described a typical language lesson as one in which 'you just learn what the teacher says' (Julia) and said that in 'most of the classes where I have been, the teachers just use the student books and they read the instructions, do the exercise' (Lucia). These are comments that concur with Hawisher and Selfe's (1991:55) view of 'traditional notions of education that permeate our culture [...] teachers talk, students listen; teacher's contributions are privileged, students respond in predictable teacher pleasing ways'.

For many students, speaking the target language was inaccessible beyond the classroom because, as Zarita explained, 'my environment is totally native, really. I really don't have a big opportunity to practise my English language'. Furthermore, students were aware that their exposure to the target language was limited to English lessons during the school day 'I don't know here in Mexico that teachers dedicate to teaching in English, maybe one hour to three hours a week. Then I think that it's very short' (Lucia). They talked with regret about their limited opportunities for meaningful face-to-face interaction in English, identifying the classroom as their target language community 'We only have the classroom to practise and talk in English' (Maribel). Although they acknowledged that using English was important, there was some resistance to do so between learners:

> We *have* to talk in English in the class, because it's the only time we have to practise the English .. . . but most, most of the time we are speaking Spanish (laughs) ... yeah, it's a shame. (Juan)

Juan's observation that the students' resistance is a 'shame' indicates that he sees this as a missed opportunity, which is corroborated by Mateo:

> When we are speaking with our classmates sometimes they are using Spanish or umm laughing ... so I think that it's not a good way to practise ... I think that they don't take it seriously. (Mateo)

The students' target language community was the teacher-led classroom, a controlled environment where 'you just have to say... what the teacher wants to know' (Julia), and the teacher had the ultimate sanction over what was said and how it was constructed. Yet one should not make assumptions about the individual's capacity for independent behaviour within the structure of a guided classroom learning environment. The introduction of a VLE might stimulate students' potential for autonomy in the classroom, as Esch and Zähner (2000:9–10) suggest 'ICTs can be used to activate cognitive and metacognitive language learning strategies.'

Prior to introducing the VLE into these students' learning programme, how did they conceptualize an effective learning environment? These insights serve as a baseline from which to contrast the students' engagement with the target language following the introduction of the VLE, to evaluate their ability to adapt to a different learning environment and to conceptualize the value of such an experience (Esch 1996:36).

Students' perceptions about effective language learning

For these students, in the absence of real-world opportunities to use English extensively, they placed a high level of trust in those whom they considered to be linguistically better qualified than themselves, whether it was their teacher, a native speaker, a workbook or a computer programme. Previous learning experience informed their understanding about how they might learn from their mistakes, in which the teacher not only indicated but corrected linguistic errors. Vicente liked the teacher 'to tell me if this is wrong or right', and felt that '... if someone is correcting me with speaking, I will switch it and I will say "OK this is wrong, now let's deal with it."' The presence of the teacher correcting and providing answers to linguistic conundrums reassured Juan who spoke warmly of being able to ask his teachers for help: 'The teachers... you can ask them about your doubts and worries... and they are always nice with you and they give you the correct answers.'

While the students liked to be corrected, they did not consider this to be the only part of the learning process. There were indications that they felt they could learn from their mistakes. Zarita explained that for her, it was not just a question of the teacher providing her with the correct answer but that 'I need different strategies and I need a bit more time to try to understand a rule.' In line with the constructivist perspective, Zarita was aware that she needed 'time and psychological space' (Little 1990:9) to conceptualize and engage with the 'process and content of learning' (ibid.). These observations suggest a sense of responsibility on the part of the student for their learning, indicating their capacity for autonomous behaviour, but that this does not necessarily preclude the teacher. Julia considered that 'the teacher is good because sometimes they correct your mistakes', so that the teacher's linguistic expertise underpinned students' faith, and they willingly acquiesced to her superior knowledge. This is a view that is reminiscent of the notion that learning is socially situated and presents what might be described as the linear view that in class 'As social beings our independence is always balanced by dependence, our essential condition is one of interdependence' (Little 1990:7).

Classroom interaction and the target language

So what did the students report about classroom interaction and the use of the target language in the guided learning classroom? I look at this from three perspectives: examining the students' views of the teacher/learner relationship in the guided learning classroom; students' reflections on patterns of interaction in the target language in the classroom and their reflections on the strengths and limitations of the guided learning model.

The guided learning view of the teacher/learner relationship

Prior to introducing the VLE, the students indicated in interview that the pedagogical approach and relationship between the teacher and students in the classroom influenced their use of English. They described their appreciation of the teacher's attentiveness to their language activity in class, for example, Monse reported that 'it's important, it's important that the teacher is how do you say ... is ... "pendiente" [hanging on] what the students are doing'. Her comments resonate with Dickinson's (1987a:35) observation that within the didactic model the teacher maintains a degree of control over student interactions in the target language.

Yet tension was detectable between teacher and learner as Mateo described an experience at the start of his university course when the teacher corrected his English 'in the . . . first semester I am writing she came by me and she said, "That's bad and you need to change this" and I think that the teacher is . . . how do you say, 'ponerte la atencion."[paying you attention].' Mateo added that this made him feel that he was failing because 'it's supposed that I know to write in English but I make many errors and I don't like a lot'. The teacher's attention to linguistic accuracy raised Mateo's awareness of the disparity between his teacher's linguistic knowledge compared with his own. Insights emerge into the dynamic between the teacher and the learner in the context of the guided learning model. Although students attributed value to the expertise of the teacher, the classroom was defined by hierarchical and linguistic deference, overlooking the communicative function of language which was 'represented in terms of structures, patterns, words' (Benson 1997:20). This proved problematic for Julia because it left her little room for the expression of independent thought. She described how she felt intellectually stifled 'inside the classroom, you *use* . . . you *just* have to say . . . what the teacher wants to know'. Julia's frustration is an indication that she visualized language 'as a way of re-mediating one's interaction with the world' (Lantolf and Thorne 2006a:5) and that language development was more than a matter of acquiring and perfecting 'new signifiers' (ibid.). Linguistic indicators in the comment Julia makes indicate the level of control she perceived to be exercised by the teacher. Julia's initial selection of the verb 'use' suggests the students used language that was expected of them, but she hesitated, changing her mind to 'just have to' combining an adverb for emphasis alongside a modal verb of obligation and changing the verb from 'use' to 'say'. Classroom use of English emerges more 'drill-like', eliminating a sense of linguistic freedom, rendering the language devoid of meaning; where conventions of classroom behaviour were to 'sit and yes, say yes, yes to everything that the teacher say'. Julia wanted the intellectual freedom to explore English independently rather than defer to choices made for her.

Patterns of interaction in the target language

Student observations suggest that their classroom was defined by notions of hierarchy and linguistic boundaries. It could be argued that this reflects pedagogical traditions in classrooms worldwide. Students individually reported that the language of the classroom was supposed to be English and several said that 'with the teacher it's always in English. But with our classmates it's not usually' (Juan). Monse explained that she spoke in English '*sometimes* outside with the teachers, but in my case, most of the time *only* in the classroom'. Monse's contrastive use of the adverbs 'sometimes' and 'only' suggests the frequency with which the target language was used even with the teacher, and the extent to which she identified using English with the classroom.

Interactions in the target language were guided by the teacher and predominantly limited to the classroom, but the students showed a resistance to using English with their peers: 'your friends ... well if you talk with them in English, they will say you are crazy because you can talk with them in Spanish and then like yeah, yeah, you are crazy' (Julia). Monse who was a shy student was fearful that if she spoke English in open class her peers would tease her: 'I think that if I could make a mistake, everybody is going to laugh at me, and I don't like.' English emerges as the 'working' language of the classroom as determined and encouraged by the teacher, with the students driving the use of Spanish between peers. Yet the default use of Spanish was not welcomed by all the students: 'I like speaking English but when my partner or classmates speak in Spanish so I ... well, I have to answer in Spanish' (Juan). Juan's hesitation followed by his use of the modal verb of obligation heightens the sense with which he felt coerced into using Spanish rather than English. Juan's feelings were reiterated by Vicente who felt that the students should practise speaking more English: 'I just recommend [hesitates] especially just trying to practise and practise, there's no need using Spanish.'

Furthermore, students reported that the balance of use of the target language was weighted in favour of the teacher inhibiting students' potential capacity to exercise control over their learning (Holec 1981:7).

> The teacher talks and talks and the teacher don't give the opportunity for the students to talk and I think that you, as a teacher, you are supposed fluent in English, so you have to give the opportunity to your students to practise as much as possible. (Maribel)

Excessive teacher talking time in the classroom reduced already limited opportunities for students to use English. Julia provided an insight into the effects of excessive teacher talking time on student interactivity in English: 'In fact there are no dynamics; just sit down and listen and listen. I mean you don't do anything.' In a context where the students 'only have the classroom to practise and talk in English' (Maribel), the extent to which they felt able to think and act in the target language as 'free and self determining individuals' (Little 1990:8), was significantly reduced by the norms of classroom behaviour and the conventions of the education system.

In the Kessler (2009) and Kitade (2008) studies it was found that online environments provided a stimulus that encouraged peer collaboration, so that for these students introducing the VLE might reconfigure the communicative dynamic and 'totality of relationships' (van Lier 2004:3) between class members.

Conflicting perceptions – learning and using the target language

The students who appear in this book expressed a diverse range of opinions about the degree of expert-led direction required yet they valued the structure of the guided learning classroom. The teacher alleviated uncertainty and solved linguistic problems. In spite of Vicente's enthusiasm to 'practise and practise', he liked teacher nearby 'to tell me if this is wrong or right or how can you make it better . . . Yeah! It's like showing you, you know, is this OK or not'. Although Mateo explained that his teacher's attention to linguistic accuracy made him feel inadequate, in the next breath he reported that he felt meaningful learning through more formal input was better when provided by the language teacher particularly with 'your grammar . . . I think you need a teacher there'. For Mateo the context for meaningful language learning was characterized by the presence and input of the teacher, even though this had had the effect of making him feel linguistically inadequate. Similarly Julia, who was resistant to saying what the teacher wanted to hear, was happy with the traditional status quo of the classroom where the teacher alleviated students' personal responsibility to seek answers to linguistic challenges: 'The teacher is good because sometimes they correct your mistakes.' The value these students attributed to the presence of their teacher corroborates the view that they are not masters of the language they seek to acquire, so need a teacher (Esch 1996:36). Maribel's concerns that 'the teacher don't give the opportunity for the students to talk' were offset by her observation that meaningful learning was represented by the idea that 'you have to practise grammar and listening and speaking and all the skills. The best way is that [. . .] it would be better if you study at school'. Maribel embeds her list of language systems and skills that the learner 'has to' practise within the framework of the 'school', the notion of duty suggested by the modal verb of obligation. For Maribel, meaningful learning takes place within the construct of the institution as the 'natural site for learning' (Benson 1997:23). Her view that 'it would be better' to learn within this environment suggests that the school is better placed to coordinate and manage language learning, devolving responsibility away from the learner. Yet Maribel also understands the limitations of the guided model in terms of language use. She willingly discards her own understanding about language learned in the classroom for the hard currency of vocabulary that 'you won't learn in the groups' in the formal classroom environment. She differentiates between English learned in class and language that can only be acquired informally from the native speaker:

> I need to learn new vocabulary and there are some words you won't learn in the groups ... With foreign people you learn slangs, idioms phrasal verbs and things like that, and you know it's good because you know that [they] mother tongue is English.

Similarly, Julia disparagingly rejected the formality of language learned in class with the teacher in favour of higher value language acquired online with American friends:

> We used to talk because sometimes I need help with my homework, and I ... I don't know how to say some words and they say 'Oh, not this, is like this, and you don't have to say that word.'

Maribel and Julia's observations indicate that the students conceptualized the value of teacher-led classroom learning as the context for meaningful learning, yet this is offset by an awareness of the communicatively restrictive nature of this environment. Access to up-to-date 'parlance' was limited for these students whose real-world environment was 'totally native' (Zarita), and where the classroom predominantly represented their target language community. Although these students valued direction, their reflections on their own experience of language learning suggests that they also sought independence within the parameters of this structure.

These students acknowledged that the inherent characteristics of their classroom were linguistically challenging on two levels. First, they understood that guided classroom learning made it difficult to reach a level of communicative proficiency where they could interact meaningfully in English, where they could 'join the ideas' (Lucia) and 'be able to express my feelings in another language' (Vicente). The perceived limitations of their guided learning classroom become clear as Zarita described her first experience talking to a group of native speakers the previous summer: 'I didn't realise I could communicate with them. They understood me and I understood them.' Secondly, the students wanted to be able to reproduce the language effectively so that they might 'be as good as the native speakers' (Monse). Embracing the opportunity for authentic 'mother tongue'

(Maribel) practice in English was highly prized, Zarita's description of teaching Spanish to a group of American students captures this: 'They are foreign people and it's more important for me to practise because they have the accent from their country.'

Closer analysis of the students' reflections about their foreign language learning experiences reveals a tension between the virtues and limitations of their learning experiences within a guided learning environment. They acquiesce to the teacher's expertise in the transmission of linguistic knowledge, but as language learners they are aware that the acquisition of linguistic knowledge is just one half of the equation. These students indicated a resistance to the guided learning model when it proved communicatively restrictive, yet the ultimate aim in foreign language education worldwide is to support the learner towards an ability to use the target language with confidence and spontaneously.

Learner confidence in technology

One of the characteristics to emerge as students reflected on their experiences learning in the guided-learning classroom was their faith in the representation of knowledge by the voice of an acknowledged expert, whether this was the teacher or native speaker. They demonstrated similar patterns of confidence in the linguistic expertise of the computer programme. In the absence of a teacher or native speaker, students turned to the computer as an alternative for solving thorny linguistic problems: 'in Valladolid and there's no teacher not near here, I find an internet structure and I find other things. I see the structure and I check it' (Mateo).

Given the limitations of the timetable where the 'teachers dedicate to teaching in English, maybe one hour to three hours a week' (Lucia), the students identified the computer as a viable alternative to the guidance offered in class. Furthermore, the computer was on tap 24 hours a day:

> If I'm having a doubt and I'm online 24 hours a day and I'm having my laptop in there, and I say 'Oh this word ... what's this word, what does this word mean?' And I can go 'It's oh' and that's it, you're done. Or how do I pronounce, how do I say this word? And there are a lot of problems with pronunciation that with the right programme. (Vicente)

Vicente's observation was supported by seven students in their opening questionnaire who selected their favourite websites on the basis of language development, as indicated in Table 5.1.

Table 5.1 Whole-class access and use of technology – opening questionnaire

Home computer	Use technology because they...	Top three uses for technology	Favourite website
18 students out of 21 (18/21)	12/21 – want to 6/21 – have to 3/21 – no answer	2/3 academic	7/21 linked to language development

Two out of three top uses for technology were linked to supporting academic work by four of the eight core students. Students did not question the vagaries of the technologies, indeed, Lucia deferred to the linguistic expertise of Microsoft Office in pointing out her linguistic errors, a function which for many native speakers interferes with the process of writing.

Lucia conceptualized this as a high-tech form of expert error correction which helped her to improve her writing: 'When I'm writing sometimes the computer corrects my mistakes and I realise that I'm wrong ... if I write with a pen, it's more difficult if I make a mistake.' Lucia was happy to exploit the functionality of the computer to produce linguistically accurate English, but made no mention of reflecting upon, or learning from, her errors. This sentiment was replicated by Vicente who acknowledged that writing in English was difficult for him: 'I don't like writing because I know that I have a lot of mistakes.' Technological error correction solved this for him: 'Right now we have a lot of programmes that can help you to correct your mistakes and that's really nice and I love those programmes!'

Mateo was equally persuaded by the linguistic expertise of the computer, but went a step further than Lucia and Vicente. He not only trusted that the computer could accurately identify errors, but that it also provided him with an error correction tool, so that with a 'right click' he could consider his choices: 'When I am writing for example, on the computer, and you see the red lines when you [are] a mistake.... It's helpful because I right click and I can see the options.' Although Mateo was prepared to trust the linguistic options made available to him by the computer, he did not necessarily accept the choices offered to him at face value, and was willing to explore and analyse the options: 'But sometimes I don't know why, so I connect to the internet, check the structure.' Like many of the other students, before introducing the VLE, Mateo's behaviour suggested an innate capacity to take responsibility and to engage in independent thinking, exploiting technology to solve language problems.

Learner confidence in technology – online language practice exercises

The students described their experiences with technology and their beliefs about how it might support their language development in and out of the classroom. Their thoughts about technology were task-based with L2 interaction and engagement limited to interactions between the student and the computer. Neither the technology nor the language were conceptualized as part of the environment within which both exist, (see Figure 5.1). As Table 5.1 shows, of the seven students who favoured websites supporting language development, three expressly mentioned the value of language exercises and activities. Interview data sheds more light on this, indicating the students' deference to the expertise of computer programmes.

Technology has traditionally lent itself to self-access beyond the traditional classroom, with the computer as an 'electronic workbook' (Kern and Warschauer 2000:13), or Structural CALL (Warschauer and Healey 1998:57). The opening questionnaire revealed that 17 students used technology to support their academic work outside class, on the school network and at home (for those with a home computer). At the start of the project, interview data substantiated the view that technology can be an effective means of encouraging learner independence because students can make choices and assume increasing levels of responsibility for their learning. Julia said that with technological language programmes 'they can use it not only inside the classroom, but outside the classroom'. Mateo liked the idea that technology allowed him to take control of his learning, liberating him from the constraints of the classroom, 'because you can consult, you can complete a lesson or unit in your home or in a park, or wherever'. Furthermore, students indicated that they felt encouraged by the range and availability of online language programmes: 'There are a lot of programmes,

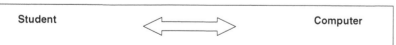

Figure 5.1 Task-based interaction between the learner and the computer

I mean, and especially because of the datas [sic] they have on the internet that you can easily reach' (Vicente).

Students were asked how they felt technology might support their language development. They applied the familiar guided learning model from the classroom to their thinking about a meaningful technological language-learning environment. Zarita's opening questionnaire (see Table 5.2) and interview data indicated that her experience and learning preferences with technology corresponded to the notion of Structural CALL (Warschauer and Healey 1998:57).

Table 5.2 Zarita – access and use of technology – opening questionnaire

Name	Home computer	Use technology because...	Top three uses for technology	Favourite website
Zarita	Yes	Wants to	3/3 academic	Language learning

Zarita's conceptualized the computer as a workbook, and she held the view that 'the activities they need a reason to do, crossword, fill the gaps ... in these ways we are learning'. Her view of language development in a technological context runs parallel to Dickinson's (1989:50) notion of principled learning, represented by activities with a focus on accuracy and detail, rather than fluency and meaning. Yet, significantly, Zarita valued activities with a clearly defined purpose that would help her language development and would be a worthwhile investment of her time. Zarita's thoughts about learning with technology were corroborated by other students:

> Julia: Sometimes I go to the pages where there are readings and then I answer the questions. There is one page called Hot Potato and then you read and then you answer the questions about the reading.
>
> Vicente: There are a lot of problems with pronunciation that with the right programme...

These students had little opportunity in the classroom to engage communicatively in English but they had not conceptualized that the computer could be used to bring the target language alive and in so doing support their language development:

> Lucia: When I'm working and I'm preparing some exercises, that exercise sometimes help me because I realise that I don't know something and I remember that point.
>
> Monse: In the internet you can find a lot of exercise about every topic in English what you like. And you have to download the activity and do it.

Monse and Lucia's observations reflect a view of the 'computer-as-tutor' (Crook 1994:79) and the guided approach of the classroom. In the case of Monse, this is perhaps no surprise when, as indicated in Table 5.3, one considers that with no home computer, and as a language student, Monse used technology because she had to, to meet the academic demands of her course.

Despite the students' exploitation of the communicative potential of the computer using the target language with friends beyond the classroom, pedagogically they only identified with technology in terms of language practice episodes mediated by specifically designed programmes with a focus on accuracy rather than fluency. This corresponds to the Dillenbourg et al. (2002:10) suggestion that 'affordances define potential effects, not actual ones'. Prior to introducing the VLE into their learning programme, the students considered that technology could provide them with linguistic guidance, accessible both in and out of the classroom.

Table 5.3 Monse – access and use of technology – opening questionnaire

Name	Home computer	Use technology because...	Top three uses for technology	Favourite website
Monse	No	Has to	2/3 academic	Language learning

Table 5.4 Maribel – access and use of technology – opening questionnaire

Name	Home computer	Use technology because...	Top three uses for technology	Favourite website
Maribel	No School network Uses cyber café	Wants to	2/3 academic	Google – for information

As Table 5.4 shows, despite not having a home computer, Maribel used technology because she wanted to, going to cyber cafés to access the internet to chat in English.

Furthermore in interview she mentioned several times that she was in regular synchronous and asynchronous correspondence with international friends. She described English as the *lingua franca* 'because it's the only way we can talk, it's like a language we can use and I can't speak Greek'. Maribel exploited technology to use the language communicatively and independently of the classroom, a model suggested in Figure 5.2. Nevertheless her conceptualization of the value of language *use* was divorced from language *development*.

Aim: Focus on fluency in the target language between learners.

Sample contexts: In- or out-of-class use of synchronous chat rooms, asynchronous message boards, email.

Stimulus: Topics and threads posted to the VLE to stimulate discussion, response and communication.

1. Linked to classroom lessons.

2. Interactions independent of classroom activity.

Interactions: Individual responds to contributions that are: synchronous (chat) or asynchronous (message boards, email).

Figure 5.2 Communicative interaction mediated through the computer not face-to-face

When asked about using technology for language development, her attention turned to identifiable language-learning episodes in computer-based language classes, where the learner interacts solely with the technology, rather than communicatively with classmates: 'Sometimes in the English class our teacher takes us to the laboratory of computers and we practise everything for exercises.'

Language learning in the 'laboratory of computers', with students practising 'everything for exercises', indicates that for Maribel technology was not a medium that she could conceptualize as being of value in the development of fluency, considering that 'in my case I haven't done anything in speaking, so I don't think it [technology] will be helpful'. She did not consider L2 online interaction, chatting in English to be a language development opportunity.

Language *development* mediated by technology was defined by explicitly designed learning episodes and language *use* mediated by technology was not perceived to be related to language development. Students' perceptions about language learning with technology seemed to be influenced by their experiences of the guided learning model.

But what of the tensions to emerge as students described the challenges associated with the guided learning model in their pursuit of language and learner independence in the non-technological classroom?

Emerging tensions: Potential for independence in the classroom

According to Holec (1981:7), there should be a structure within which the learner might exercise his potential capacity for autonomy, yet for these students it seemed that the conventions of the classroom suppressed opportunities for independence with Julia complaining that the students 'just have to say . . . what the teacher wants to know.' Conventions of classroom behaviour were further intensified by the dynamic between the teacher and the more confident students who overwhelmed the less confident, 'like you want to talk and talk but the teacher don't listen to you because they are another people in the class and they speak louder than you' (Julia). Students were fearful that the more confident would tease them for making mistakes: 'I think that if I could make a mistake, everybody is going to laugh at me' (Monse). Limited opportunities to use English outside class were compounded in the classroom: 'We *have* to talk in English in the class, because it's the only time we have to practise the English . . . . but most, most of the time we are speaking Spanish [laughs] . . . yeah, it's a shame,' (Juan). Maribel wistfully expressed a sense of the unknown world of English beyond the classroom: 'We only have the classroom to practise and talk in English, and outside we don't know.' A paradoxical sense of opportunity and challenge emerges for these students in seeking to achieve increased levels of linguistic and learner independence within the boundaries of their target language community – the classroom.

For these students, their perceptions about language learning and using the target language before introducing the VLE suggests that they were compliant, had respect for authority and conformed to the traditional pedagogical structure of the classroom. But caution should be exercised in drawing assumptions about their potential for autonomy in the classroom.

Exploring the potential for independence – in the classroom

Students were asked to reflect upon areas of linguistic weakness, Julia exclaimed 'My grammar, my grammar is the worst thing!' In the same breath she correlated this with writing and the stifling of linguistic creativity brought about by a focus on form. She valued the opportunity for self-expression in her writing. Given the right conditions, it seemed that Julia was prepared to set aside her concerns about grammatical accuracy in favour of linguistic freedom:

> I don't like to write essays because of my grammar, *but then* if you ask me to write an essay about your opinion or some kind of topic, then I like because it's my opinion.

Conflict exists for Julia in terms of fluency over accuracy, independent thought over what the teacher tells her to think:

> I think that this is the way I feel about that topic, nobody like has a influence on me, I read about that topic and I say 'OK, I think it's good, or I think it's bad.' Nobody is like saying 'Oh, obey me.'

Her frustration in describing classroom learning is tangible, framing her desire for self-expression with the repetition of the pronoun 'nobody' and the pejorative use of the verb 'obey':

Juan indicated that he valued support from the teacher and the exchange of ideas in classroom discussions. Yet he despaired of his classmates who refused to use the target language: 'It's impossible. We *have to* talk in English in the class, because it's the only time we have to practise the English, but most, most of the time we are speaking Spanish.' Juan's observation reflects the duality of responsibility and interdependence (Little 1990:7) between the teacher and students within the learning structure.

Lucia and Monse reflected that they found it difficult to see the value of classes where learners were not encouraged to take more responsibility for their own learning, where the teachers 'just use the student books and they read the instructions, do the exercise'(Lucia) and 'do the exercise and check' (Monse). Lucia's use of the adverb 'just' suggests that in this context she felt short-changed. Monse agreed, not only echoing her friend's sentiments, but completing the sentence for her. This would suggest a capacity on the part of these learners to take increased levels of responsibility for their learning, described by Holec (1981:3) as an intrinsic characteristic of the autonomous learner.

Similarly Maribel showed a significant level of awareness about the challenges associated with the foreign language learning classroom: 'we are students living in Mexico, so if we don't search the opportunities to talk we only have the classroom to practise and talk in English'. She described her frustration that the teacher 'talks and talks and [. . .] don't give the opportunity for the students to talk', indicating that she wanted increased linguistic independence in English in the classroom.

These learners demonstrated their potential for independence in English beyond the classroom. Mateo not only read extensively in English, but wrote poetry, using English to express more private thoughts: 'sometimes I write in English when it's something that I don't want others to understand, because if it's in English, then they don't understand it and I write it in my notebook'. This serves as an interesting contrast to his experiences writing in English under the supervision of the teacher, where he felt he was 'failing a lot' because of his errors. Mateo felt compromised by the 'tug-of-war' (Riley 2009:46) between his free-style approach to using English and the suffocating constraints of the classroom learning environment.

As a mature student Zarita described how she had felt intimidated joining a class of confident young language students. She felt she needed to be as grammatically capable as her peers. Zarita's attention to form reaped dividends in terms of accuracy, but the language had become divorced from its communicative function. She was unsure whether she could make herself understood to native speakers, showing unmistakable delight in describing her first experience of real-world communication beyond the classroom: 'I didn't realise I could communicate with them. They understood me and I understood them.' At the start of her university education Zarita had embraced and valued the guided learning model as a strategy but became aware that the conventions of the classroom inhibited independent language and learner behaviour.

Unlike many of his classmates, Vicente used English extensively, although he knew this was not always welcomed by his peer group: 'I just start speaking English with them, they feel like "umm like . . . yeah, we know that you know how to speak English" . . . .' His urgency to communicate in English was clear as he explained why he wanted to learn English: 'I like it, I just like it. I want to be able to express my feelings in another language,' indicating his view that language learning was about 'more than acquiring new signifiers [. . .] as a way of re-mediating one's interaction with the world' (Lantolf and Thorne 2006a:5). Nevertheless, it is difficult to reconcile the confidence of Vicente with his sense of defeat with writing:

> To be honest I'm not very good at grammar. I mean whenever it's about structures, yeah, I can handle it. But whenever it's about writing with words and all, I can't spell them, I can say them but whenever it's about writing, no.

The expectations and conventions of the classroom environment overwhelmed his confidence and innate capacity for self-expression and writing in English.

Table 5.5 Summary of student perspectives on their learning environment before introducing EI

Guided learning approach	Positive student perceptions	Negative student perceptions	Students would like	Emergent pedagogical challenge
Classroom				**In class**
High teacher profile: • Focus on accuracy. • Task completion. • Classroom direction. • Error correction.	Expert presence. Guidance. Purposeful. Clearly defined aims.	Communicatively restrictive. Inauthentic use of language. Overly task-led. Resistance to using the target language.	Fewer directed language production tasks. Extended focus on fluency and communication in L2. Increased personal responsibility for learning.	Creating conditions for increased independent behaviour and classroom interaction in the target language. Provision of materials and content to stimulate interaction in the target language.
Classroom and online				**Online**
Attention to accuracy: • Grammar • Pronunciation • Writing • Speaking • Pronunciation. • Language practice exercises.	Expert knowledge. Expert support. Learning from mistakes. Focus on form.	Attention to micro-linguistic detail. Inauthentic use of language. Task-led. De-contextualized. Non-communicative.	Increased opportunity for meaningful interaction in the target language for fluency. • Self-expression. • Ideas and thoughts. • Discussion. • Social interaction.	Harnessing 'out-of-class' online communicative energy in the target language in class and at home. Creating a meaningful VLE context for access in class and at home.

As the students reflected on their experiences learning English before the introduction of the VLE, there were early indications to suggest their potential capacity for increased independence within the framework of the guided learning classroom, summarized in Table 5.5.

This raises questions not only about the nature of autonomy but also whether the right conditions might be created using technology to encourage autonomy, and whether in light of their structured language-learning experiences in the guided learning classroom, learners would consider this to be of value.

Exploring potential for independence – with technology

Before the introduction of the VLE, the students indicated that they predominantly conceptualized language learning with technology in terms of functionality and that online interaction with overseas friends was not 'real' language learning.

Nevertheless, Julia chatted online to American friends, seeing this as an opportunity to *practice* and rehearse the language taught in class in a meaningful context, experiencing online linguistic freedom under the expert eye of the native speaker. Similarly Mateo chatted to overseas friends in his free time. He considered that online communication with friends in English represented an opportunity to communicate in a context in which he could share thoughts and ideas in the target language. Significantly, Mateo identified the potential relationship between CMC and teaching and learning in English: 'Computers is a medium to be communicating with more people, to communicate your ideas, and so to teach and learn.'

Like his classmates, Juan identified with the guided learning approach with technology as an 'electronic workbook' (Kern and Warschauer 2000:13) keenly following up recommendations by his teacher and visiting EFL websites where he practised 'reverse sentences in English'. When asked whether he did anything independently of the classroom to support his language development, Juan described two autonomous learning strategies, distinct from the guided tradition of the classroom. The first was his participation in English-speaking chat rooms:

> I like chatting. . . . it's the rule of the channel, you only have to speak, it's writing, but 'speak' in English . . . every day for two hours, three hours, it depends if I got lots of work, homework.

Juan describes having to 'speak' in English before clarifying that he meant 'writing', suggesting that he was able to use English online. By comparison Julia 'sometimes' practised her English by chatting online, whereas Juan boasted that he chatted daily. Juan specifically chose a chat room where the 'rule' was to use English, looking beyond the limitations of the classroom where his peers resisted using English. The second strategy Juan adopted was to set the default language on his internet browser to English to 'get familiar with English' and 'when I want to know something or, English or news from other parts, I use the internet, I always [in] the internet, looking for something new'. Juan exploited the potential of technology and the opportunities for communicative freedom it afforded him, that were unachievable in the classroom. Juan's observations are reminiscent of the idea that language learning is mediated by the context within which it takes place, and that technology not only represents the tool, but also the learning environment within which communicative activity takes place (Arnold and Ducate 2006:43).

These students exploited technology to achieve increased communicative and learner independence, going beyond the principled tradition of their classroom. Their personal reflections about language learning and their use of technology suggests that autonomous learner and language behaviour is likely to depend on creating the right conditions where independence can thrive, but it is also necessary to 'understand these opportunities and integrate them where they are pedagogically relevant' (Dillenbourg et al. 2002:12) with a transparency of purpose.

Like language learners worldwide, the challenge for these learners was in making the conceptual transition from being language *learners* to independent language *users*. Whether in the classroom or with technology, they were informed by a teacher-led approach to language learning that was driven by the need to achieve accuracy over fluency, the written word over communicative use of language, deferring to the hierarchy and boundaries of language determined by the voice of authority.

Foreign language learners in classrooms around the world have limited opportunities to engage in meaningful face-to-face interaction in the target language. The classroom represents their target language community, language use is functional, and there is a tendency not to go 'beyond their current level of inter-language as the teachers interacted with them' (Swain 2000:99). The students in this book attributed value to the support and purposefulness of the guided approach, despite at the constraints imposed upon them by pedagogical convention. As Benson (2009:25) suggests, 'it is not primarily an individual's "lack of autonomy" but the suppression of their autonomy by educational systems that is the problem'. The view suggested by Benson has a resonance for classrooms around the world.

EI introduced new and unfamiliar electronic spaces, an alternative dynamic, reconfiguring the dimensions of the learning environment in the classroom as well as online access in their free time. Mindful of the students' language learning experience, two issues emerge, which, considered together informs the subsequent discussion in the chapters that follow about the nature of the relationship between autonomy and technology. The first issue is the perceived value students attributed to the VLE and whether they conceptualized the platform as a means by which they might be capable of expressing their capacity to be independent learners and users of English. The second issue is whether the value students attributed to the technology was corroborated by their use of the platform.

6

Perceptions and Reality 1: Students' Response to Using a VLE in Computer Room Lessons

In this chapter I look exclusively at the students' response to *EI* in their weekly computer room lessons. I contrast student perceptions of the value they attributed to the platform with the reality of their online activity in the classroom to see what this might reveal in terms of gaining insights into the nature of the relationship between autonomy and technology in the context of foreign language learning. Table 6.1 summarizes the notion autonomous behaviour relative to L2 free expression and learner autonomy in the context of the VLE classroom.

The term L2 free expression has been applied to indicate where the students chose to use English in class rather than Spanish and includes 'topic language' (Macaro 1997:55 – language identified with the content of the lesson), 'classroom language' (ibid. – classroom management) and L2 naturalistic peer interaction. The term 'learner autonomy' in *EI* lessons has been applied where students showed signs of taking responsibility by making decisions and evaluating their learning experience. The VLE blended learning autonomy framework shows that engagement with the VLE lesson can be described either as proactive or reactive autonomy (Littlewood 1999:75–6 summarized in Chapter 2). Student thinking about language development and technology before the introduction of *EI* is contrasted with instances of learner autonomy and L2 free expression following the introduction of the platform in *EI* lessons. The students' personal response to *EI* has been captured from interview data, supporting questionnaire data as well as the examination of onsite activity data in the form of site records and student writing. Other than self-report data, the ephemeral nature of oral interaction makes it difficult to capture instances of L2 free expression in the classroom. Student writing resulting from *EI* lessons has therefore been scrutinized to see whether this captures the essence of their use of English in the lesson.

Table 6.1 VLE blended learning autonomy framework with *EI*

Type of autonomy	Definitions	Context	Example behaviour	Language skills	Descriptors
Proactive and reactive autonomy in the VLE classroom: L2 free expression. Learner autonomy. Explicit interaction • Writing • Speaking Implicit interaction • Reading • Listening	**L2 free expression (VLE classroom):** (a) Student choice to use L2. (b) Reduced L1. (c) Increased L2 interaction. **Learner autonomy** (a) Responsibility. (b) Decision-making. (c) Evaluation by the student.	**Blended learning** (with computers in lab or classroom). Teacher as facilitator and moderator. Self-regulated online/VLE activity. Collaborating with peers. Striving towards common goals.	**Responsibility** – *Proactively* taking the lead, following lesson and links. – *Reactively* following and responding to lesson and links. **Decision** – *Proactively* taking the lead and engaging with peers and lesson. – *Reactively* following direction and interacting with peers and lesson. **Evaluation** Reflect on lesson. Use of L2 *proactively* initiated by self. Use of L2 *reactively* responding to task and others.		Self-directed. Relatedness to others. Interaction. *Proactively* Taking the lead in the task. *Reactively* Following the lead. Responding to the task and others. Choice. Freedom. Expert support.

L2 free expression – patterns of use of the target language

I hoped to identify differences between the students' use of the target language in the classroom compared with *EI* lessons to see whether they showed signs of interacting with one another more freely and spontaneously in English in response to the blended lessons. Students had seemed deterred by 'opportunities for participation', (Schwartz, cited in Holec 1981:22) in their classroom with limited 'time and psychological space' (Little 1990:9) to use English communicatively. Benson (2009:26) suggests that creating the 'right conditions' enables autonomy to 'flourish'. Creating the 'right conditions' with a VLE necessitates an understanding of 'the opportunities and limitations of the pedagogical approaches within different learning environments [. . .] from the learners' perspective' (White 2006:261) but it also requires an understanding about how opportunities might be integrated so that they are 'pedagogically relevant' (Dillenbourg et al. 2002:12). This suggests that students would be more likely to attribute value to the VLE if they perceived it to address identified needs, corroborating Zarita's observation that she was motivated by technology if activities seemed purposeful.

Patterns of use of the target language in *EI* blended lessons

At the end of the *EI* programme students were asked to report on the language they used with their teacher and classmates in the classroom and in their VLE-mediated lessons. Tables 6.2 and 6.3 show their language choices in the classroom, contrasting responses from the whole class with the sample of core students. Early indications (shown in Tables 6.4 and 6.5) suggest that English was the language of choice in VLE-mediated lessons unlike the classroom.

Table 6.2 Closing questionnaire – language used in the *classroom* – core students

L2 in class between students and teacher	L1 and L2 in class between students and teacher	L1 and L2 between students in class	L1 between students in class
Monse	Zarita	Monse	Juan
Lucia		Lucia	
Juan		Zarita	
Vicente		Vicente	
Maribel		Maribel	
Mateo		Mateo	
Julia		Julia	
7/8	1/8	7/8	1/8

Table 6.3 Closing questionnaire – language used in the *classroom* – whole class (21 students)

	L2 in class between students and teacher	L1 and L2 in class between students and teacher	L1 and L2 between students in class	L1 between students in class
Number of students	18	3	19	2

Table 6.4 Closing questionnaire – language used on *EI* – the VLE core students

L2 used between students in *EI*	L1 and L2 used between students in *EI*
Monse	Zarita
Lucia	
Juan	
Vicente	
Maribel	
Mateo	
Julia	
7/8	1/8

Table 6.5 Closing questionnaire – language used on *EI* – the VLE – whole class (21 students)

	L2 used between students in *EI*	L1 and L2 used between students in *EI*
Number of students	18	3

However, it is unclear whether the students were referring to interactions directly to the VLE site or in *EI* blended lessons, and this question may have been interpreted either way. The operating language of the platform was English, so it would not be unusual for them to use English on the site. Alternatively, students might have provided what they deemed to be the 'right' answers, resulting in a difference in linguistic behaviour between the classroom and *EI* blended lessons.

In a subsequent question students were asked under what conditions they would use Spanish on EI. Responses were wide ranging; students may have replied either with a view to using the VLE online or in the classroom. This ambiguity may have been because of the wording of the question and the preposition 'on'. In Spanish this would be 'en' and taken to mean either *in* the *EI* lessons, or *on* the *EI* site. Examination of the students' replies in Table 6.6 suggests that they interpreted the question both ways. For example, the response 'to write a typical phrase...' suggests online interaction, whereas 'if my classmates misunderstand what I said in eng' suggests that the student is referring to VLE-mediated classroom interaction.

This was followed up in interview to clarify the students' choice of language in *EI* lessons. Maribel explained that she used Spanish when 'I didn't understand a word then, yes... so someone explain me and that's it,' reflecting comments in the questionnaire. However, the students reported that, unlike the classroom, in the *EI* lesson 'it's English, in that lesson it's English' (Julia). Maribel's closing remark, 'and that's it' suggests that she used Spanish for emergencies, substantiated by her closing questionnaire in which she did not report using Spanish. Questionnaire and interview data suggest that students identified English as the language of choice in the *EI* blended environment, unlike the classroom where use of English was largely directed by and to the teacher.

Table 6.6 Closing questionnaire – under what circumstances would you use Spanish on *EI*? (21 students)

Vocabulary	Understanding and being understood	Pedagogy	No circumstances
To say a word that only exist in spanish language.	To clarify about something that I don't understand.	When it is relevant for the topic.	There is not any.
To teach some colloquial expressions.	Just when I didn't understand something.	If it's required.	None. I did not think about it.
May be to write a typical phrase from my country.	If my classmates misunderstand what I said in English.		No response. Four students.
If we are talking about our coloquial vocabulary.	If the other person does not understand me.		
To contrast or compare some words or phrases.	Probably if I don't know how to say a word.		
When contrasting different words with same meaning.			
If I need to explain something really important.			
Ask someone who is from the same country as me.			
To share culture things.			

Students reported increased levels of class-wide L2 interaction in *EI* lessons. Changes in patterns of language behaviour are illustrated in the following extract from an interview with Lucia and Monse:

Researcher:	What's the language of this environment [*EI* blended lessons]?
Lucia:	English
Researcher:	With teacher and students it's . . .
Lucia and Monse (in unison):	English!
Researcher:	Students and students . . .
Lucia and Monse (in unison):	English!

Introducing screen-mediated stimuli seemed to change the 'totality of relationships' (van Lier 2004:3) between constituent elements of the classroom environment, generating increased L2 peer interaction. It could be argued that this supports an expanded view of Little's (1990:7) notion of interdependence, that I have termed the ecological version of learner autonomy, whereby students produce an internal-cognitive (Little 2007:18) response to the interdependent socially interactive (ibid.) network of interaction. Piccoli et al. 2001:408 propose that technology 'does not determine learning outcomes' and VLE-mediated affordances 'define potential effects not actual ones' (Dillenbourg et al. 2002:10). In terms of how the students perceived the value of their use of the VLE relative to notions of learner autonomy and L2 free expression, they may have responded on the basis of their 'understanding of what is valuable and worth doing' (Wall 2003:308), corresponding to self-report concerns about language development opportunities prior to the introduction of *EI*.

Students reported that in *EI* lessons they used English more extensively, although this is not to say they necessarily perceived the platform to be of pedagogical value. They were asked at the end of the programme how they felt that *EI* supported their language development. Its value was predominantly identified as supporting the development of their writing skills, which significantly students linked to increased L2 peer interaction and an alternative classroom dynamic in *EI* lessons.

From the student perspective components of *EI* lessons came together, supporting Bronfenbrenner's (1993:22) notion of 'linkages' between environmental settings:

> I have one vision about that topic, but when I share about that information, I notice that young people have other perspectives, other points of view about that perspective and I try to gather all the point of view about that . . . I listen to them to get just one idea to write. (Zarita)

We can only infer that *EI* discussions were conducted in English, but the volume of student writing produced in response to *EI* lessons corroborates the value students attributed to the *EI* experience and their engagement with the lesson.

Students' reasons for using English in *EI* lessons

Students reflected on their use of English in *EI* lessons compared with the traditional classroom. Three main reasons emerged to suggest why they felt able to use English more freely in their VLE-mediated *EI* lessons.

EI facilitates an exchange of ideas and opinions in the target language

Students considered that the materials, design and structure of the *EI* programme encouraged the expression of independent ideas and opinions, suggesting characteristics from the working definition of autonomy indicated in Chapter 4:

> The autonomous learner and user of the target language shows signs of being capable of taking responsibility for independent thought, action and interaction grounded within a social structure in response to experience.

In their closing questionnaire, 19 of the 21 students responded that discussion in English helped them to develop their own ideas and think of what to say, suggesting cognitive and metacognitive strategies. Their thinking was not externally driven by 'fixed code' (van Lier 2004:90) expectations but rather that 'You can express your own ideas and in the course book you are giving the answer that the book requires' (Juan). Juan valued the notion of being an 'active agent' (Benson and Voller 1997:7) in his learning, contributing ideas of his choice in English. It is unclear whether Juan's L2 interactions extended beyond the teacher to include his peers. Julia felt that they had the opportunity to 'always speaking English in the classroom to this course, it's like a debate of the topics for this course'. Her description of *EI* lessons as being 'like a debate' suggests increased L2 peer interaction, and characteristic of the behaviour and criteria for L2 free expression indicated in the VLE blended learning autonomy framework.

Contribution to classroom debates necessitates listening (implicit interaction), speaking (explicit interaction) and 'evidence of learners contributing to classroom discourse and thereby making a difference to what happens', (Allwright 1988:36), generating 'the seeds of autonomy and individualisation' (ibid.). Lucia contrasts using English in the classroom with *EI* lessons and a sense of intellectual, discursive engagement between peers emerges:

> The teacher gives us the instruction and we complete the exercise and here it's different because it's like a question and all the class have to discuss it and give their own point of view ... It's more interactive.

Lucia's comment describes increased L2 peer interaction facilitated by the teacher and mediated by the technology, albeit using topic-based rather than incidental language (Macaro 1997: 55). Julia's belief that *EI* blended lessons were 'the only time that we have to speak English' indicates that in *EI* lessons learners felt they had more 'time and psychological space' (Little 1990:9) to communicate in English which serves as an interesting contrast with Maribel's description of English in class being 'academic, not something natural like speaking'. Interview data echoes the data from the closing questionnaires with the suggestion that the introduction of the VLE created conditions which stimulated an alternative dynamic, satisfying students' concerns about L2 interaction. From an ecological perspective, and the notion of everything being is related to everything else (van Lier 2004), it could be argued that students cognitively engaged with the web of social interaction in class, reacting to the direction suggested by the activity, but without any certainty where their thinking would lead them.

EI provides a meaningful reason for interaction

Vicente echoed the view that the approach adopted by *EI* lessons was 'personal, you're sharing your own idea'. A sense of choice emerges in terms of ideas, language and participation, resonating with the notion of L2 free expression. For Vicente, *EI* lessons went beyond controlled practice activities, providing a purpose and 'something to talk about' in English where there were no right or wrong answers:

> It's different because ... you're having something to talk about, you're having a purpose of doing an activity ... but when we are in class: "Alright, ask your partner about how often does he umm ... do this ..." You give them a format about using frequency adverbs, and ... "Ask your partner about this," and then that's it, it's over.

By design the discursive nature of VLE lessons meant that outcomes were uncertain and the direction of the interaction was determined by the voices of those who contributed. Vicente's view was reiterated by Lucia and Monse who explained that typically in class they spent five minutes on the activity before gossiping in Spanish. Monse explained that *EI* lessons were cognitively more challenging because they required 'more thinking about the topic of discussion, about the topic, to talk about it'. The 'debate' of *EI* lessons provided 'the opportunity to use the language freely and spontaneously without conscious awareness' (Lantolf 2003:367), challenging students' concerns about the communicative limitations of the classroom. In this sense, for these students *EI* activities had a pedagogical relevance (Dillenbourg et al. 2002:12), echoing the constructivist notion that 'effective learning begins from the learners' active participation in the processes of learning' (Benson 2001:36).

EI provides topics 'that has to do with us'

At the end of the programme 19 of the 21 students said that the choice of topic in *EI* lessons influenced the ease with which they could think of and express ideas in English. This was corroborated in interview with the core students who repeatedly referred to the idea that *EI* topics were interesting, relevant and created the conditions that encouraged them to contribute in English 'because the topics are very interesting, so I feel motivated to speak' (Mateo). The connection between topic and L2 interaction in *EI* lessons was echoed by Vicente who said the topics gave him a greater sense of commitment to the lesson: 'If I'm interested then I will do it happily and I will take more of my time that I have to do it', a view suggesting self-regulation, decision-making and evaluation of the lesson – characteristics of learner autonomy indicated in the VLE blended learning autonomy framework. Vicente's selection of the adverb 'happily' suggests that he did not necessarily feel the need to take up more of his time, implying an element of choice and intrinsic to the idea of autonomy in *EI* lessons. Maribel found L2 self-expression easier when the topics had meaning for her:

> You can express . . . something if you have that experience you can express it, there are some topics . . . that take you a little bit longer . . . if it's politics, then it will be difficult, but if it's something that I am interested in then it will be easier.

When asked in which context she found it easiest to express herself in English, Monse replied, 'Probably *EI* because of the topic' rather than in the classroom. Furthermore Lucia considered that in the classroom 'we are not very . . . like very related to the topic', a view echoed by Julia who reflected that 'in classroom it's different because they are different topics like critical thinking . . . and you don't know anything about it'.

The potential for meaningful choice is constrained if learners are asked to contribute to a discussion in a foreign language on a topic about which they have no life experience. Limited experience makes gathering ideas and subsequent articulation in the target language challenging. The VLE introduced a platform delivering screen-mediated affordances designed to generate 'thoughtful communication' (Kol and Schcolnik 2008:52). Students agreed that the topics for discussion in *EI* lessons were meaningful, stimulating the construction and exchange of ideas in English, so creating the right conditions where autonomy could flourish (Benson 2009:26). It could be argued that the introduction of the VLE altered the classroom dynamic, influencing the sense in which students felt capable of conveying their own opinion, responding to the fluidity and unpredictability of others' views.

The self-report data is compelling but in isolation it is insufficient. I was only able to observe *EI* lessons when I visited the students, and their extensive use of English in these classes may have been a response to my presence so these data could not be deemed trustworthy. In seeking to redress this I scrutinized students' post-lesson assignments and forum posts to see what this revealed about their personal response to the introduction of the VLE in the blended classroom. I compared elements from the students' written work with their self-report data.

Evaluation of learners' assignments and use of the VLE forums

The value of speaking was widely acknowledged by the class, they reported that they needed to speak more English in class and speaking was identified as essential for language development by 18 of the 21 students who considered speaking and communication activities in class to be essential for language development. One of the aims of *EI* lessons was to create conditions in which students could interact more freely in English. Nevertheless when asked which *EI* activities were most helpful in terms of language improvement, only eight of the 21 students selected speaking in blended lessons. Students perceived writing to be of greater pedagogical value in *EI* lessons than speaking (writing posts –12 students; assignments –15 students). In interview, students said they felt encouraged to use English in the VLE classroom and that they spoke more English in the *EI* classroom. Without the presence of the teacher and expert guidance they may not have equated increased L2 peer interaction with meaningful language development. Yet significantly students said that classroom discussions helped them collect their thoughts when writing posts and assignments:

> Zarita: I have one vision about that topic, but when I share about that information, I notice that young people have other perspectives, other points of view about that perspective and I try to gather all the point of view about that ... I listen to them to get just one idea to write.
>
> Vicente: You're having something to talk about; you're having a purpose of doing an activity because you know that you need to write a report ... or something like that.

A synergy emerges between *EI* lessons and follow-up activities as suggested by Bronfenbrenner's (1979, 1993) notion of nested ecosystems where each system 'has its own patterns of operations and relations' (van Lier 2004:208) but are simultaneously linked. Examination of evidence in the form of the students' writing, might therefore offer insights or 'linkages' (Bronfenbrenner 1993:22) into VLE classroom discussions to corroborate students' perceptions of the value of their VLE experience.

Recurring themes following VLE classroom lessons

Recurring themes in student writing may reflect aspects of *EI* classroom discussions. Students referred in their written work to the views expressed by others in class:

- 'I could see the most of my classmates agree' (Maribel – assignment)
- 'I agree with my classmates' (Zarita – post)
- 'I agree with juan' (Mateo – post).

It cannot be ascertained whether class discussions were in English. It is difficult to determine how much English was *spoken* in VLE-mediated lessons, but the volume of posts and assignments illustrate how much English was *written* in response to *EI* lessons. The evidence suggests a surplus of explicit L2 written interaction, corroborating students' perceptions that the value of *EI* lessons lay predominantly in the development of writing skills. Table 6.7 provides a breakdown of assignments and posts in response to *EI* blended lessons. It could be argued that the volume and content of the written work encouraged students to write and that their writing mirrored the turn of classroom events.

Table 6.7 Assignments and associated posts submitted (whole class)

Lesson number	1	3	4	5	6	8	9	10	11	13	14
Assignment number	1	2	3	4	5	6	7	8	9	10	11
Lesson topic	Sizzle	Desert	Happiness	Tiger	Treasure	Class	Texting	Plagiarism	Heroes	University	Stress
Whole class (21)	16	14	14	16	9	18	11	9	15	3	6
Posts	19 Profiles					19 Posts	19 Posts		1 Post (Juan)		

Lessons (with associated posts and no assignments – whole class)

Lesson number	2	7	12
Lesson topic	Children	Online friends	Responsibility
Whole class (21)	4 direct Sent 9 via teacher	4	17

Posts and assignments were scrutinized for recurring themes using two selection criteria:

1. Lessons referred to most often in interview
2. Lessons which stimulated significant written output.

Maribel explained that she took notes during classroom discussions directly onto her computer because it helped with her homework. Six of the eight core students made explicit reference to lesson 9 which was a lesson on the effects of texting on language. Maribel's writing might therefore capture the topics alluded to in the classroom discussion from lesson 9. In the opening paragraph to her assignment Maribel introduces three themes, which correspond to the themes that recurred most often in her classmates' assignments and posts:

- *Texting and context*: 'we have to know when to use it and with whom' (Maribel assignment).
- *Texting and young people*: 'it is appropriated (*sic*) with friends of our same age' (Maribel assignment).
- *Texting and saving time and money*: 'it is [...] a way to save time and money' (Maribel assignment).

Texting and context

In interview, Zarita reflected on lesson 9 and told me the story of her son using text language in his homework school 'I noticed he was texting his assignment and I said, "Enrique, why did you do that? You need to write in a formal way."' Her anecdote reflects the theme of appropriate use and context for text language which appeared in nine posts and nine assignments. Mateo described the lesson as being about 'texting and why we can't use about that', suggesting the way in which the topic was transformed by the students as it evolved cognitively between class members, from the detrimental effects of texting to rules about using text language, the idea emerged in others' writing (Table 6.8).

Texting, young people and fashion

Texting as a fashion appeared in nine posts and six assignments. Vicente laughed as he recalled the lesson, recounting his contribution in class, 'I thought "imagine sending a message like this one to your father, he's not gonna understand it"'. This was replicated in 6 of the 11 assignments illustrated in Table 6.9.

The idea of 'texting and context' evolved to incorporate the notion of boundaries, where texting was fashionable and appropriate between friends,

Table 6.8 Recurring themes – texting and context

Assignment	Post
Teacher will never allow it and students know it. (Maribel)	Not to communicate in formal situations like teachers, firms. (Zarita)
I don't do texting to my teachers or doctors. (Mateo)	Be conscious about 'when to do it and don't do it'. (Maribel)
Only important thing is to notice where and when I should use it. (Monse)	I think that people are aware when they should write or text. (Lucia)
Not to communicate in formal situation. (Zarita)	Texting to my teachers or doctors, because is not polite. (Mateo)
People must be know that the way the usually write when texting someone and that it isn't the correct way of writing. (Ana)	Don´t use it at school or other places or situations. (Paloma)
Almost everybody write in this way in some moment, and write in a formal way when we are writing an essay, an article or other academic way. (Cesar)	It wouldn't be polite or formal texting to a teacher or director. (Adan)
Notice where and when I should use it […] when I'm sending cell phone messages, all of them are written in that way. (Camila)	I think that teachers should pay more attention, students will become more familiar with this type of 'communication' and they won't be worried about the correct spelling of the words. (Luisa)
People are used to writing in this very informal way and when they have to write in a formal way, they don't know how to do it. (Lola)	Is an informal way which we all have used. (Orlando)
I think it is appropriate between friends. (Pablo)	We are not going to write an essay or a formal letter in that way!! (Camila)

Table 6.9 Recurring themes – texting, young people and fashion

Assignment	Post
It is appropriated with friends of our same age. (Maribel)	You are not gonna text to your boss or to your parents like that, because they won´t understand you. (Julia)
Is only a fashionable way to communicate. (Mateo)	We only do texting with our friends. (Julia)
It is a fashionable way to communicate. (Zarita)	You send a message to your mother or father they just don't get it hahaha, it is really funny … have you ever tried it? (Victor)
Texting has become such a common thing to do especially in teenagers. (Juan)	It is a fashionable way to communicate among younger people. (Zarita)
Most of the people who use texting are youngsters. (Pablo)	It is a fashion way that young people use to communicate. (Pablo)
You can save time and text in a fashion way. (Lola)	People only write in this way to be fashionable and save time. (Paloma)
	I think that is a fashion in many parts of the world. (Adan)
	This is just a fashion way of texting for young people. (Luisa)
	The 'texting' is a fashion and one day will finish. (Cesar)

young people or 'teenagers' (Juan), but was inaccessible to the older generation. The discussion progressed towards the notion of the value of texting as a cheap, efficient and easy form of communication between young people with this theme recurring in other posts and assignments.

Interaction was anchored by the task but was mediated by the VLE and the social context, suggesting Little's (1990:7) notion of interdependence. Conceptually, interdependence does not capture the dynamics of autonomous interaction, as learners made judgements and responded in an unpredictable, non-linear fashion to the 'totality of relationships' (van Lier 2004:3) and the voices of those around them, engaging with some and overlooking others. The students' engagement with the target language emerges as a web of L2 interaction in response to the context within which it exists, captured most effectively by the term ecological autonomy.

Texting and saving time

Maribel's assignment mentioned texting as saving time and money. Saving time appeared in eight posts and nine assignments, (see Table 6.10). It might be inferred that the class discussed texting as a means of saving time because of the speed with which young people could communicate. However, Maribel added that texting also saved 'valuable' money, suggesting her personal response to the classroom discussion.

Table 6.10 Recurring themes – texting and saving time

Assignment	Post
To save time and have fun. (Zarita)	To save time. (Zarita)
A way to reduce time … you don't spend too much time on that. (Monse)	In order to do the communication faster. (Monse)
Between friends to save time. (Mateo)	
To save valuable time and money. (Maribel)	To save time. (Mateo)
A way to save time … yes, we save a lot of time. (Juan)	To save time and have fun. (Julia)
If you have a emergency you can text quickly. (Cesar)	People only write in this way to be fashionable and save time. (Paloma)
Texting is just a way to reduce time when writing a message. (Camila)	Some people want to save time. (Susana)
Due to technology and the hurry way of life of our time, we will see this kind of writing as something common more than we do currently. (David)	I think texting is just a way to save time!!! (Camila)
You can save time and text in a fashion way. (Lola)	We should see it as a way to save time and spaces. (Ana)

Writing as a reflection of engagement in class

One might argue that thematic analysis of student writing not only captures the relationship between classroom discussions and student writing, but that it reflects the individual's level of engagement with *EI* lessons, corroborating the value the students attributed to the VLE experience. Mateo explained that when he was less interested his attitude to writing changed 'I do it, but I do it because it's a homework, but not because I enjoy it.' Mateo's explanation reveals how he differentiated between duty and choice, reminiscent of the view that freedom is relative and more a matter of whether the individual is a victim of constraint (Trebbi 2008:35).

The pieces of writing produced by Juan in response to lessons 8 (Class and Society) and 11 (Heroes and Icons) were different stylistically and in length. When asked the reason for this, he was initially reticent 'There are topics that are more interesting for people, that doesn't mean the other topics doesn't interest me.' I asked him why he had contributed two pieces of articulate, innovative writing in response to lesson 11 on Heroes and Icons (see Appendices 6.1, 6.2) compared to his more formulaic piece after lesson 8 on Class and Society(Appendix 6.3). He replied, 'Heroes was more interesting, that's why!' Juan's level of cognitive engagement with the lesson on Heroes and Icons was apparent in his writing, with indications that suggested that his interpretation of the assignment task had been informed by the classroom discussion because parallel themes emerged in his classmates' writing. Furthermore, he also adapted the theme of lesson 11 and generated his own parent thread (Appendix 6.2) for the forum, which was neither part of the lesson or homework. Such a level of activity embodies Littlewood's (1999:75–6) notion of proactive autonomy.

Mateo highly valued Juan's contribution to the classroom discussion in lesson 11. It influenced the way in which he approached his own assignment: 'I remember in the classroom, Juan say that "My hero is my mother" and also I think that my mother is my hero.' Mateo's approach to the assignment after lesson 11 suggests that he engaged with the contributions made by his peers to the lesson, the 'totality of relationships' (van Lier 2004:3) and 'linkages' (Bronfenbrenner 1993:22) between screen-mediated stimuli generating the classroom discussion and the subsequent choices Mateo made in planning his assignment (Appendix 6.4). Significantly, Juan's assignment (Appendix 6.1) makes no explicit reference to his mother, but it reflects Mateo's recollection of Juan's contribution to the discussion. The care with which both students interpreted their assignments suggests their level of intellectual engagement and the dynamic connectivity of ideas that emerged from the classroom discussion.

Heightened level of interest in the VLE lesson stimulated more considered and extensive writing for other learners. Julia selected lesson 8 (Class and Society) as her favourite lesson. She valued 'linkages' (ibid.) between the post-*EI* lesson assignment and forum activity where she could express her views. She produced an extensive assignment as well as generating and posting a parent thread for the forum (Appendix 6.5). Interest in the topic and the class discussion may have stimulated Julia's enthusiasm for writing. However, by contrast her response to the forum (Appendix 6.6) in lesson 7 (Online Friendship) was more perfunctory than her written work following lesson 8 on Class and Society.

The thinking and work contributed by Julia, Mateo and Juan supports the self-report data and the perception that the value of *EI* lessons lay in the classroom discussion, anchored by the task and mediated by the technology. Class discussions stimulated and scaffolded the development of their writing skills. Students reported that *EI* lessons encouraged L2 interaction through the exchange of ideas, providing a meaningful reason to use English in relation to topics that were of interest to them which they followed up in their writing. Each component of their personal response to *EI* lessons was distinct, yet inextricably linked, such that 'everything [was] connected to everything else' (Lantolf 2000:25).

Relative to notions of autonomy indicated in the VLE autonomy framework, learners responded to the communicative freedoms triggered by screen-mediated stimuli, attributing value to *EI* lessons in supporting the development of speaking and writing. Yet caution should be exercised in suggesting that this was necessarily a response to the technology, the nature of the relationship remains unclear.

But what of the notion of learner independence, how capable did the students feel in terms of embracing increased levels of responsibility in *EI* lessons compared with more familiar 'traditional guided instruction' (Crook 1994:79).

Learner autonomy within *EI* VLE blended lessons

On first meeting the students, they indicated a desire to move away from what Hawisher and Selfe describe as 'traditional notions of education that permeate our culture [. . .] teachers talk, students listen; teacher's contributions are privileged, students respond in predictable teacher pleasing ways' (1991:55). Following the introduction of the VLE, it is interesting to consider the value students attributed to VLE-mediated *EI* lessons relative to the notion of learner autonomy indicated in the VLE blended learning autonomy framework.

EI blended lessons and student responsibility – having and relinquishing technological control

EI lessons provided learners with extensive freedoms and increased responsibility. VLE access was mediated through the internet. Students took responsibility for following the *EI* lesson and managing the freedom of the internet in class. An incident occurred during the *EI* programme that successfully captures the students' and the teacher's response to their new-found, VLE-mediated freedom. As a result of a double booking in the computer room, the teacher ran lessons 9 and 10 from the classroom. Internet access was mediated through the teacher's laptop with a projector, whereas in the computer room the students would have had individual computers. They experienced two modes of *EI* blended delivery. *EI* in the classroom more closely resembled the guided learning model because the teacher had technological control. I asked learners which environment they preferred and to reflect upon *having* and *relinquishing* control of the technology.

Learners responded relative to their own development needs. The table below shows the similarities and differences between autonomous decisions and learning outcomes in the computer room and the classroom (Table 6.11).

Table 6.11 Blended classroom 'Learner' autonomy in *EI*

Autonomous decisions	Learning outcomes
EI blended lessons – computer room and classroom	
To contribute and participate in whole class discourse in L2.	Language skills development. Collaboration and exchange of ideas in L2 between all class members.
EI blended lesson – computer room (students controlling the technology)	
To exploit the functionality of the technology. To follow the pace of the lesson with teacher and classmates using the computer. To resist diversion to unrelated internet sites.	Technological multitasking – navigating the *EI* site *and* participating in the lesson in L2. Development of computer skills *with* language skills. Development of online search skills to support contribution to discussion. Prioritizing focus and attention.
EI blended lessons – classroom (teacher controlling the technology)	
To follow the facilitative lead of the teacher. To interact with classmates in response to *EI* materials mediated by the projector and screen.	Coherence and cohesion of L2 interaction and classroom discourse between all class members.

If the findings revealed that the students were able to express their potential for learner autonomy when the teacher had control of the technology, this would suggest that autonomy is more than a matter of 'freedom from mastery exercised over oneself by others'(Ciekanski 2007:112). Signs of autonomous behaviour would not be attributable to the 'medium of implementation' (Ganem Gutierrez 2006:244) but to the students' ability to adapt to 'different learning conditions [...] by conceptualising their learning experience' (Esch 1996:36) and exploiting affordances for learning presented by the technology relative to their 'understanding of what is valuable and worth doing' (Wall 2003:307/8). The class were asked whether they preferred *EI* lessons in the classroom or the computer room (Table 6.12).

There was a strong (though not unanimous) preference for staging *EI* lessons in the computer room rather than the classroom. This view was substantiated by findings from the core students indicated in Table 6.13.

Interview data (Table 6.14) revealed that half the core group of students saw value in both the classroom and computer room. However, closer interrogation

Table 6.12 Mid-course questionnaire 1 preferences: *EI* in the classroom or computer room – whole class (21 students)

Prefer *EI* in class	Prefer *EI* in computer room	A mix of both
2	11	7

Table 6.13 Mid-course questionnaire 1 preferences: *EI* in the classroom or computer room (core students)

Prefer *EI* in class	Prefer *EI* in computer room	A mix of both
Monse	Maribel	Zarita
Lucia	Mateo	Vicente
Juan	Julia	
3	3	2

Table 6.14 Interview data preferences: *EI* in the classroom or computer room (core students)

Prefer *EI* in class	Prefer *EI* in computer room	A mix of both
Lucia	Mateo	Maribel
Vicente	Julia	Zarita
		Juan
		Monse
2	2	4

of the interview data revealed that learners' preferences were based on how they conceptualized each environment as a context for language development which bear closer scrutiny.

Student reflections on *EI* lessons in the computer room

Students described the value they attributed to *EI* lessons where they operated their own computer. I was interested in whether they felt *more* or *less* capable of expressing their potential for autonomy in the computer room in terms of making independent decisions and learning outcomes described in Table 6.15.

Computer room – learner freedom to control pace of learning and language

Students indicated that in the computer room *EI* lessons generated a perceived sense of freedom. Access to individual screens stimulated the range of language skills, with the freedom to choose and make decisions about how they might exploit technological functionality to support their learning. They thought *EI* lessons gave them more time and opportunity to discuss and share ideas in both the computer room and the classroom, because 'we not always have the time to talk plus to express our ideas' (Mateo). Mateo preferred the computer room because 'we have the . . . the free . . . because everyone has a computer'. He felt encouraged to participate, getting ideas from his classmates, the technology facilitated the freedom to 'get information' to support his contribution. The experience helped him plan his assignment:

> I feel motivated to speak . . . to learn or read . . . to compare and share my ideas with my classmate [. . .] The lesson helps for getting to know what I am going to write, but also how to get ideas on how to write, or to get information. (Mateo)

Table 6.15 Learner autonomy – students controlling the technology

Independent decisions	Learning outcomes
To exploit the functionality of the technology.	Technological multitasking – navigating the *EI* site *and* participating in the lesson in L2.
To follow the pace of the lesson with teacher and classmates using the computer.	Development of computer skills *with* language skills.
To resist diversion to unrelated internet sites.	Development of online search skills to support contribution to discussion. Prioritizing focus and attention.

The value Mateo attributed to *EI* computer room lessons exemplifies the descriptors in the VLE blended learning autonomy framework suggesting the 'social and cultural situatedness' (Kern 2006:187) of the classroom and the 'linkages' (Bronfenbrenner 1993:22) between multiple *EI* stimuli. Mateo's observations suggest the possibility of an ecological view of autonomy as he conceptualizes the relationship between elements of the VLE experience as a web of interconnectedness where individuals cognitively engage with one another, with the potential to transform the design intentions of VLE-mediated tasks.

Julia valued the freedom of having her own terminal, stating that 'for me it's easy to be free', keenly feeling the effects of losing control of the technology to the teacher. She wanted to make independent choices about learning and in the computer room she felt capable of technologically multitasking between the screen and the lesson. The main effect of working from the overhead projector was that the pace and nature of the interactions between learners were determined by the teacher, which Julia identified as a hindrance to self-determination because 'when she asks the questions, you think, "Well I need to go back to the previous screen . . . because I don't remember." You cannot do it'. Julia considered the process of learning to be a participative exchange between class members, but with the teacher in control of the technology, the experience became 'passive, just passive, everything is passive. The teacher is talking and talking and nobody's listening'. Julia's concerns mirror a more transmissive approach to language teaching and the view of the passive learner within the expert/novice framework (Packer 1993, cited in Lantolf and Thorne 2006c:276), where 'control and power resides primarily in the teacher' (Lantolf and Thorne 2006c:274).

Computer room – development of language and learning skills

In terms of learning outcomes, some considered that working from individual computers made it easier to mediate the transition between language skills during the lesson, 'when we are in the . . . computer room we have time to write and also express our opinion' (Mateo). Furthermore, Maribel valued the sense that *EI* lessons in the computer room focused the students' attention because they felt encouraged to 'share ideas . . . you are in front of the computers and pay more attention'. She explained the value of having her own screen in facilitating the opportunity for technologically multitasking, taking and saving her notes from the computer room lessons directly to her memory stick.

Maribel's response to her learning environment as she exploited the functionality of the technology suggests both the potential for learner autonomy and the flexibility of students in adapting to 'different learning conditions

[...] by conceptualising their learning experience' (Esch 1996:36). Technology it seems, has the potential to stimulate students' cognitive and metacognitive language-learning strategies thereby supporting the construction of knowledge (Esch and Zähner 2000:9–10).

Computer room – room layout

In the computer room, the terminals were positioned in rows facing the front of the room saving the shyer students their blushes 'because you are not face to face with the others' (Monse), encouraging more equal levels of participation. Lucia liked the idea that her classmates were distracted by the technology by 'just watching the screen'. In the classroom there were no such distractions and 'everyone is paying attention to you', (Lucia). Contrary to Monse and Lucia, Juan thought communication was more difficult in the computer room because 'the computers are blocking the faces'. Julia thought the computer room layout reduced the omnipresence of the teacher because 'I don't like it when the teacher is always behind you telling you what to do, and telling you what not to do'. Juan reported that in class he felt 'like I am being observed, because the teacher is monitoring'.

The value of *EI* lessons in the computer room extended beyond notions of autonomy manifested by external technological control. Suggestions of autonomy in the computer room seem less of a response per se to the technology, but more to the change in dynamic and the interconnectedness between learners created by the technology, making them feel capable of critically engaging with learning as a 'participant in a social milieu' (Esch 2009:33). Students showed their capacity to conceptualize and exploit affordances for language development mediated by the VLE corresponding to their development needs prior to the introduction of EI.

But what of the reasons given by learners for their preference for *EI* lessons in the classroom. Questions emerge as to whether indications of autonomy were directly attributable to the technology or indirectly a response to the alternative dynamic created by the VLE.

Student reflections on *EI* lessons in the classroom

It is too simplistic to suggest that learner preferences for *EI* in the classroom or computer room were a matter of controlling or relinquishing control of the technology. Far from a sense of feeling controlled by *EI* lessons in class, several students believed that using technology in an 'open' classroom environment helped them to address concerns about language development. For these students, autonomy was more than a matter of external organization.

Classroom – meeting identified learning objectives

Zarita described her environment as 'totally native' and despite the students' desire to use more English in the classroom, the tendency was that they reverted to Spanish. Although Zarita liked 'having available the computer for all of us', she found *EI* in the classroom more conducive to the whole-class exchange of ideas 'The activity that we usually do during the class is discuss about the topic . . . in the classroom.' Even though Juan found it difficult to make himself heard in class, it was easier 'to see in real life how your classmates give their own opinions about the topic', and the students spoke more English. Maribel valued *EI* lessons in the classroom and computer room, but echoed Zarita's and Juan's observation explaining 'Of the classroom . . . the overhead projector . . . all of us discuss . . . and give our point of view and discuss.' In class, *EI* lessons seemed to dispel students' inhibitions. They had explicitly identified the value of the VLE as a means by which they might improve their writing, but they valued using more English during in *EI* lessons, corresponding to their pre-intervention concerns about using the target language. This finding should be treated with a degree of caution because of the limitations of self-report data; however, analysis reveals that the students responded more frequently to communicative *EI* affordances. For example, in stage two of the VLE programme the *RTR* forum achieved 1,889 hits, whereas *EI* additional resources that were 'guided' in approach achieved just 118 hits over the same period. Despite the availability of additional resources, learners did not necessarily choose to engage with them, they responded to affordances that corresponded to their concerns about language development, those which they identified as 'valuable and worth doing' (Wall 2003:308) and as Dillenbourg et al. (2002:10) indicate 'affordances define potential effects not actual ones'.

Classroom – group cohesion and collaboration

Sole technological control by the teacher in the *EI* classroom was not necessarily considered by students to be an infringement of their independence and did not devalue their *EI* experience. Many identified this as an effective means of classroom management, reporting that in the computer room 'some students start to chat or doing other things, and they aren't listening to the teacher' (Zarita), whereas in the classroom 'the activity is more guided by the teacher' (ibid.) bringing a sense of cohesion to the group because 'in the classroom only the teacher has the computer and we are all together commencing about the topic' (Monse), thereby encouraging L2 interaction. Furthermore, Lucia emphatically added 'No, no, the point is that umm in the classroom it's more interactive with all the students,' suggesting the 'interdependence'(Little 1990:7) and 'totality of relationships' (van Lier 2004:3) between students in the classroom, implying an ecological view of autonomy as students respond to one another's ideas. By comparison in the computer room Lucia considered that 'it's more individual the work'. The structure of *EI* lessons, in which the teacher moderated rather than directed the interaction enabled learners to make 'a difference to what happens' (Allwright 1988:35) in class, addressing student concerns about the need to use more English. Maribel noted that, unlike the guided learning classroom, in *EI* lessons 'it's easy because you can express your opinion, because if someone says something that can harm you she just stops that person and says "Give respect."'

Students attributed value to the 'coercive nature' (Murray 1999:300) of *EI* in the classroom, revealing difficulties experienced in managing the responsibility and freedom to explore unrelated internet pages in the computer room 'I think that it's a positive thing [the classroom] because when we are in the computer room we are . . . maybe we are checking some other pages and that's why we lost in the class' (Lucia). Lucia acknowledged the challenges associated with increased levels of responsibility in the computer room, suggesting a heightened sense of self-awareness about effective management of a technological learning environment. Similarly, Vicente said he needed the teacher to keep him on track to help him learn more effectively, so that 'you won't to another site or something like that, especially in my case because I seen that one already and I say "Let's skip that one, OK let's go". . .' Although the notion of the teacher exercising control in the classroom seems counter-intuitive to the generic view of autonomy as freedom from external control, at a more complex level of analysis one can argue that learners are 'the creative product of their social context' (Esch 2009:43) and that a nuanced analysis of autonomy needs to account for the social context.

For these students it would appear that they accepted that they might be 'autonomous in one area while dependent in another' (Murray 1999:305). External control of the technology was not necessarily perceived to be detrimental to the value identified by learners of *EI* lessons.

The students' personal response to the value of using a VLE relative to the notion of being an independent learner and user of the target language represents just one dimension of their engagement with the technology. How closely do the students' observations about the value of the VLE correspond to their onsite activity?

EI blended lessons site activity – the classroom and the computer room

Data describing students' movement between different components of *EI* lessons on the site are indicated in Table 6.16 where the number of screen hits to *EI* blended lesson screens in class (column 1) can be compared with the number of screen hits to the same components in their free time (column 2). The third column shows the number of free-time screen hits to the homework screens, related to the corresponding blended lessons, which are shown separately. This gives an indication of how students navigated the site, beyond the demands of checking *EI* homework after class.

Students not only visited homework screens in their free time but revisited screens they had worked with in *EI* lessons, indicative of the notion of nested ecosystems (Bronfenbrenner 1993:22) with *EI* components as the 'linkages and processes taking place between two or more settings'.

Table 6.16 *EI* access – screen hits in class versus free-time hits to the same screens

	Class	Free-time	Free-time homework screens
Stage 1 – Screen hits to *EI* components			
Lesson 1 – All about you	130	28	19
Lesson 2 – Are we scared to let children out to play?	140	77	n/a
Lesson 3 – Decision-making	74	70	91
Lesson 4 – Happiness	125	66	82
Lesson 5 – Surviving	154	65	74
Lesson 6 – International treasures	133	19	35
Totals	756	325	83
Average	126	54.16	63.66
Stage 2 – Screen hits to *EI* components			
Lesson 7 – Online friendship	43	107	n/a
Lesson 8 – Class and society	146	65	98
Lesson 9 – Texting (classroom blended)	0	56	62
Lesson 10 – Plagiarism (classroom blended)	0	35	66
Lesson 11 – Heroes and icons	147	25	91
Lesson 12 – Taking responsibility	124	91	11
Lesson 13 – Academic institutions	79	58	36
Lesson 14 – Stress-busting	89	10	32
Totals	628	447	181
Average	78.5	55.87	56.57

Contrasting learners' free-time response following *EI* classroom lessons with *EI* computer room lessons in Table 6.17 shows that the number of free-time visits by the whole class to the VLE, was not adversely affected by where the lesson had taken place.

Table 6.17 Student interaction with VLE following *EI* classroom lessons and *EI* computer room lessons

Lesson number	Free-time – general	Free-time hits to homework screens	Assignments submitted
Lesson 9	56	62	11
Lesson 10	35	66	9
EI average (stages 1 and 2)	55	58	12

Visits to homework screens in stage 2 increased slightly following the two *EI* lessons in the classroom, but assignment submissions were marginally reduced. Students' perceptions versus the reality of their online activity seem unaffected by the mode of delivery, further suggesting that learner autonomy is more of an internal matter relating to 'the responsibility of the individual as the social agent' (Benson and Voller 1997:5) rather than a matter of who has control of the technology in class.

Interview and questionnaire data may have proved inconclusive but wherever the VLE blended lesson took place, learners showed signs of independent behaviour that corresponded to VLE blended learning autonomy framework. But it remains unclear whether this was a response to the technology or the content provided by the *EI* programme. If learners were responding to screen-mediated content, changes in behaviour would not be solely or directly attributable to the VLE, but would be an indication of their innate capacity for autonomy and an ability to adapt to 'different learning conditions' (Esch 1996:36) that might otherwise be curbed by the conventions of guided learning.

Students made few explicit references to the technology in their interviews, despite acknowledging different patterns of classroom behaviour in *EI* lessons. They willingly relinquished technological control when *EI* lessons were transferred to the classroom, suggesting that autonomous behaviour and the value students attributed to the VLE were not a response to the technology and that the same behaviour could have been achieved using a course book. Yet students refuted the idea that *EI* was simply an electronic workbook, agreeing that the VLE altered their classroom dynamic. This suggests that the technology contributed to their personal response to *EI* lessons, and that a relationship between the technology and independent behaviour could be said to exist, although the nature of the relationship is not clear.

EI: More than an electronic workbook

Most students saw similarities between *EI* and a course book. However, unlike a course book, the VLE introduced flexibility to the classroom, with the freedom not only to navigate around the site but also the opportunity to look further afield to the internet, freedoms that required responsibility, independent decision-making and learner autonomy. Students valued having the responsibility of VLE-mediated access to the internet and the interconnectedness between elements, suggestive of the ecological notion of the 'totality of relationship' (van Lier 2004:3) through the VLE, which was perceived to add value to *EI* lessons.

The value of interactivity within the VLE

Mateo described the value he attributed to interactivity and links between *EI* screens and the internet. He considered this dimension to be the defining characteristic of *EI* because 'it's interactive. The course books I think are some paper, some pictures, but with *EI* you can . . . we have . . . reading, pictures, links to other pages'. Hyperlinks enabled interactivity for learners between *EI* resources, providing additional information related to the lesson 'The links on the pages to where there are the words in text language and also the meaning. I think it's interesting 'cos in a book we can't do it' (Mateo). Vicente reported the value of hyperlinks 'I *love* when you highlight and link from the vocabulary in the reading.' Yet VLE activity reports show that Vicente didn't use these hyperlinks, nevertheless he conceptualized the value and ease with which he could independently explore the language mediated by the technology. As Zarita said, 'it's useful . . . we have available the information . . . it's a very credible . . . because we are seeing in that moment'. Each lesson had four hyperlinked screens representing different stages of the lesson and quantitative data drawn from *EI* site records and illustrated in Table 6.18 which shows a breakdown of the core students' screen hits over the total of 12 *EI* computer room lessons. Quantitative data corroborate the self-report data.

I wanted to examine how students navigated between screens during the lesson and whether they revisited screens after class. If we take Julia as an example, she made a total of 13 hits to screen one, averaging just over one screen

Table 6.18 Core students' interactivity between stages of 12 *EI* blended lessons

Name	Total hits to screen 1 (over 12 lessons)		Hits to screen 2		Hits to screen 3		Hits to screen 4		Hits to homework screens		Hits to additional resources screens	
	Class	Free	Class	Free	Class	Free	Class	Free	Class	Free	Class	Free
Julia	13	6	18	11	26	10	11	7	3	23	8	9
Juan	13	3	13	3	16	4	7	1	2	17	1	11
Zarita	15	12	18	21	22	24	13	17	2	51	13	29
Vicente	14	16	15	23	16	23	11	14	8	21	3	2
Monse	13	11	20	9	20	13	22	17	5	26	6	14
Lucia	16	7	22	11	36	20	30	35	12	65	16	36
Maribel	18	6	24	5	37	8	18	23	8	40	7	13
Mateo	11	6	15	8	20	11	10	7	2	29	5	0
Totals	113	67	145	91	193	113	122	121	42	272	59	114

Average number of class-time hits over 12 *EI* lessons per stage in class

Stage 1	Stage 2	Stage 3	Stage 4	Homework	Additional resources
14.125	18.125	24.125	15.25	5.25	7.375

Average number of free-time hits over 12 *EI* lessons per stage

Stage 1	Stage 2	Stage 3	Stage 4	Homework	Additional resources
8.375	11.375	14.125	15.125	34	14.25

hit to stage one over 12 lessons. By contrast Maribel moved more freely between screens during *EI* lessons. A pattern emerged between students moving back and forth between screens in class. Data in the previous table shows that students not only engaged with *EI* lessons in school, but that they revisited the same screens in their free time.

Movement between *EI* screens in computer room lessons suggests enhanced learner agency, responsibility and notions of learner autonomy (see Table 6.19). Students exploited *EI* hyperlink functionality, navigating the site and independently managing access to *EI* screens and the internet as they deemed necessary to follow the lesson.

In terms of learner autonomy, Julia valued increased levels of responsibility, independence and the feeling that the VLE gave her the freedom to choose:

> The books are completely different because in this one it's up to you, and if you want to read then you read, if you want to discuss with the classmates, you don't have to see every page and like follow certain topics.

Table 6.19 Learner autonomy – decision-making and learning outcomes in *EI*

Autonomous decisions	Learning outcomes
Student controlling the technology (*EI* in the computer room)	
To exploit the functionality of the technology.	Technological multitasking – navigating the *EI* site *and* participating in the lesson in L2.
To follow the pace of the lesson with teacher and classmates using the computer.	Development of computer skills *with* language skills.
To resist diversion to unrelated internet sites.	Development of online search skills to support contribution to discussion. Prioritizing focus and attention.

Interactivity – beyond the VLE to the internet

Exploratory potential extended beyond the hyperlinks embedded within *EI* lessons and resources. Students described that they did not feel constrained by the pre-determined content of the page in *EI* lessons 'You can be limited with the course book and [you] can be available many sources with the internet'(Mateo). Interaction in *EI* lessons was described as more 'dynamic . . . not flat' (Maribel). Access and interconnectedness between the lesson and global resources enhanced the dimensions of the learning experience. Exploitation of the internet emerged when *EI* lessons took place in the classroom when a passing reference to Martin Luther King in the jigsaw reading excited the learners' curiosity. The teacher responded to the students' requests for more information, turning to the internet and finding a video and copy of his speech to share with the class:

> I told her I didn't know about that speech and she said, "No? Wait a minute" She looked at the internet and she showed us about the speech that he gave to, to the USA and then I knew about that. (Zarita)

Lucia believed that internet access mediated by the VLE enhanced the *EI* lesson, transforming class discussions. In terms of learner autonomy, the hyperlinks and the internet mediated by the VLE offered learners the freedom to find out more. The students were not constrained by the direction indicated by the predetermined content of the *EI* lesson, where 'you are giving the answer that the book requires' (Juan). The students saw the value of the functionality and interactivity of the technology liberating them and their teacher from external constraints, rendering the potential of the platform to be greater than the sum of the component parts of each lesson. The notion of interconnectedness emerges. *EI* lessons not only incorporated the multiple stimuli of the classroom, but also the VLE and internet.

This would suggest that the learners' response to *EI* lessons was more than a matter of content and design, but rather it was the 'totality of relationships' (ibid.) and synergy created by the interaction between class members and their use of the technology, with the potential to transform the design intentions of the lesson and stimulate instances of learner autonomy and L2 free expression. The suggestion of an ecological version of autonomy emerges, in which internal-cognitive responses are anchored by the task, mediated by the technology and transformed by the unpredictable web of social interaction.

Yet students made scant reference to the technology in their interviews, which raises questions about the nature of the relationship between autonomy and the technology. Considered in isolation, one might argue that learner perceptions and their online reality was a response to VLE-mediated content and not the inherent characteristics of the technology.

Appendix 6.1 Lesson 11: Assignment by Juan

Heroes and heroines are all around

Task: Identify a hero or icon that is of interest to you. Use the internet and other resources to find information about your hero or icon.

In this world there are real heroes and heroines everywhere. People, who are not known, but they are always doing great things to save, help and protect other ones. They are looking to do simple, but valuable, little things to make this world a better place to life, changing people's life in ways we never imagine.

Maybe you are wondering where this people who I am talking about are. Well just see around and look carefully because you are around by them. Policemen, fire fighters, teachers, friends, single mothers or single fathers, the guy next to you, we don't know, maybe you have brought the help who someone needed in the past and that gave her/him the opportunity to do sometime valuable with her/him life since then.

Do you want a short biography of them? It is impossible. That is what makes heroes and heroines so special. We don't know almost anything about their life but we know that they are outside doing what they do best.

In this case I would have to ask you if you have had a hero or heroin in your life, so maybe you could have one background of that hero or heroin.

And finally I must say that heroes and heroines are not prefect, they cannot save us from everything but they will never let us down. When you feel you world is breaking down and a person appears giving you a friendly hand, you know you have found a hero.

Appendix 6.2 Lesson 11: Independently Generated Parent Thread by Juan

Heroes and heroines

We all have in our minds a definition of what a hero means. We think in a hero like a person who fights for very important causes such as justice, peace, etc. Now imagine that for an inexplicable and out-of-this-world reason something happen to you and you acquire amazing powers.

1. What kind of powers would you like to acquire and why?
2. How would you use your new powers so as to help this world become a better place to live?
3. As all we know, super heroes have got weaknesses. What would be your weak pointand why?
4. Would your identity be known or anonymous? why?

Appendix 6.3 Lesson 8: Assignment and Post – The Class System – By Juan

I think class systems are, without any doubt, a world phenomenon.

People in the past had social classes and that has not changed at all.

Here in Mexico social classes are very clear. Many people can say that social classes are not important and that they don't care about it but the true is that social classes are everywhere in schools, institutions, entertainment sites, etc.

I think every generation has got the same social classes but in a very different way.

There always going to be poor people as well as rich ones, I don't think that has changed and probably will never do.

Class system will always have a place in society even when people don't want. It is something out of our control. That's the way the things are supposed to be. Here in Mexico like in everywhere.

Lesson 8: Forum post – Re: Talking about class (Juan)

Well here in Merida you can see in a very clearly way the division of social classes! In my very personal point of view there are

1. rich people,
2. poor people
3. and the poor people who go pretending be rich people (middle class).

We have both private schools, some of them very expensive, and goverment schools. But there's also schools like mine, which have a cosmopolitan diversity of students! There are rich people, poor people and those ones who think they are rich! Its very interesting see how we can create links between us thanks to what we called Education!

Appendix 6.4 Lesson 11: Hero Assignment by Mateo

My hero

My hero is my mother, I choose her because is a great person and a good mother. She's always helping me and she is there when I need her.

My mother is from Veracruz, she studied until the secondary and she took a commercial career of accountant, because her parents hadn't enough money to pay her studies. So, she started to work early, she worked as a babysitter at evening and in mornings she studied. My mother is woman that everyone respects, maybe because of her personality. Because she is friendly and always try to help everyone. I love her.

She's my hero because she´s always helping me, supporting me when I needed, she´s always telling me advice and tell me the things that are correct. She is my personal hero and with my father are the perfect parents.

I learnt a lot of my family, for example fight for what you want, also the tolerance, honesty, work hard to have the things, never rob, respect, love and be an excellent person.

Appendix 6.5 Lesson 8: Assignment – The Class System by Julia

I'm pretty sure that the class system is part of a global phenomenon, because nowadays we are used to talk about rich and poor countries, rich and poor areas inside those countries, and therefore we tend to judge people by just taking into account what they have rather than for what they really are or represent in the world; class systems is well represented all over the world, cause we will always find economical differences among the countries or families, no matter where we might be.

In my country we can easily notice the class differences in a lot of aspects, as an example, we can notice how a 'pretty last name' can open up a lot of doors and can make a difference in building your relationships with important people, whereas, if your last name is mayan, you can be easily left behind or even ignored; here in Mérida, people who have a Mayan last name are not fairly treated by other people, that happens because that people think that mayan last's names come from small and poor towns, and therefore people that have them are ignorant and poor, when sometimes it is really the other way around.

We can also notice those differences in the north of the city, where we can find beautiful parks, green areas, vigilance, better street lamps, better drainage, etc; whereas in the south we can barely find a clean park with light, or green areas, or at least a cop passing by. The reason of that is that nobody goes there because there is not only a lack of security, but also is because if it rains the streets got flood, because those places doesn't have drainage.

Social divisions can also been seen in night clubs, for example, there are clubs where everybody is allowed to get in (as mambo café), but there are others, such as 'el cielo', where only rich people with a good last name is allowed to get in.So, I think that there is a wide difference among social classes in Merida; just with taking a look we can find them everywhere.

I think that that concept has changed a lot since my grandparent's day, because in those days there weren't much families with 'important last names' and at that time, rich people were the owners of the haciendas and they were from small towns, but as they have disappeared, nowadays rich people is defined by being the owners of the newest car or the biggest business, rather than being from small towns.

As a conclusion, I don't think there is a place for class system in society, because if there would be, then, people wouldn't feel less or more than others, I mean, people would be equal in every sense, and we all could share the same space.

Lesson 8: Independently-generated parent thread – talking about class by Julia

Well, I think that Merida is divided in areas in which there are different kinds of status, for example, in the north there is the 'rich people' and in the south there is 'the poor people', we can see these divisions outside the schools rather than inside them, even the malls represent them in a clearly way, for example if you go to 'la gran plaza' (which is in the north) you will find a 'Sears' there, and any other kind of expensive department stores, but if you go to 'Las Americas' you can find stores in which the prices are suitable for the pockets of the majority of the Yucatecans, I mean, the middle class, this class, the middle one, they belong neither to the north nor to the south, they are just mixed all over the city.

I think that in the schools we will always find people of different social classes, it doesn't matter if you are in a private or public school, or if you are there because of a schoolarship or because of your parents support, the only important thing that should be taken into account is the end, meaning, get an education.

Appendix 6.6 Forum Post: Re: Online Social Networking – by Julia

1. Are social networking sites a sign of the future or just a passing fashion?

    I think that they are a sign of the future, because nowadays it allows us to be in contact with friends who are far away, and you can meet friends from all over the world through them, which I think it's pretty cool and really interesting. That kind of sites are increasing everyday, because there are people who are really shy and they visit that sites to meet people, so I don't think it is just a passing fashion, they will continue increasing instead.

2. Are you worried about being left behind?

    No, I think that I have really good friends, not only in social networking but also at school.

3. Would you rather be anonymous, and not participate?

    I prefer to participate, because in this way people will get to know me better and then we could have a friendship.

4. Would you pay someone to manage your online identity?

    No, I wouldn't do it, cause if you pay somebody it would mean to not have an own life and let somebody else to take the control of your life, which I don't think is fair for the people who are trying to know you.

7

Perceptions and Reality 2: Beyond the Classroom – Students' Free Time Use of the VLE

EI promised the learner more than a platform designed to support computer-mediated blended classroom lessons. *EI* also provided the learners with access to affordances with which to engage in their free time. In this chapter, I look beyond the boundary of the classroom into the more virtual terrain of the students' free-time use of EI. Classroom-mediated, teacher-led use of the platform has a characteristically familiar pedagogical format, but with free-time access, all bets are off with no guarantees that the students will even log on, raising the stakes in exploring the nature of the relationship between autonomy and technology. This chapter explores how these students perceived the value of the VLE as a means by which they might become more independent learners and users of the target language and examines how closely their perceptions corresponded to the reality of their free-time use of the platform.

Student free-time activity and the VLE autonomy framework

The design intentions underpinning *EI* were to provide students with a range of language development resources (affordances) with the potential to stimulate free-time autonomous language and learning behaviour. Results were mixed. VLE-mediated language development activities were of limited interest to the students, receiving just 118 hits in the second phase of the *EI* programme. The discussion forums saw significantly more free-time activity with 1,889 free-time views and 236 free-time posts over the same period. This pattern of online activity supports Dillenbourg et al.'s (2002:9) view that the provision of VLE-mediated affordances might promise potential but this is not the same as actual effects. Content written by students in their free-time in the form of forum posts and assignments along with their personal observations about their free-time engagement with *EI* provide a rich seam of data with which to evaluate notions of learner autonomy and L2 free expression in the context of a VLE.

VLE free-time autonomy framework

By way of foregrounding a discussion based around the students' online activity it is timely to review the VLE *free-time* autonomy framework indicated in Table 7.1.

The first column proposes two types of autonomy, L2 free expression and learner autonomy, defined further as proactive and reactive autonomy, (Littlewood 1999:75). Columns four and six provide examples of behaviour, language skills and descriptors of free-time proactive and reactive autonomy beyond the classroom. Free-time learner autonomy and L2 free expression mediated by *EI* describes the transference of explicit (writing) and implicit (reading) L2 language skills beyond the classroom. Implicit interaction is the activity undertaken by learners who chose 'proactively' to read expert and peer postings or engaged with additional resources embedded within EI. Implicit interaction has the potential to scaffold and stimulate a network of ideas and language, suggesting the sociocultural notion of 'supportive dialogue' (Mitchell and Myles 2004:195) where 'learners are capable of scaffolding one another' (Lantolf 2002:106). The notion of a web of online interconnectedness between students and the idea of an ecological version of autonomy emerges.

A further level of analysis is indicated in column four in terms of the students' personal response to the *EI* free-time component relative to the choices they made about their level of interaction. Learners were considered to have shown signs of explicit L2 free expression by choosing to contribute and engage with the forums in English. Forum postings are divided into three levels, reflecting degrees of proactive and reactive L2 free expression. Students were deemed to have shown signs of learner autonomy by making choices about their level of engagement with VLE-mediated affordances, taking responsibility for their actions and their capacity to evaluate the value of their free-time VLE engagement.

The VLE free-time autonomy framework is a tool to pick out the indicators and counter-indicators in evaluating the students' personal response to their free-time use of the VLE, the choices they made and to determine whether they showed signs of autonomous behaviour.

Table 7.1 VLE free-time autonomy framework for student interaction with EI

Type of autonomy	Definitions	Context	Example behaviour	Language skills	Descriptors
Proactive and reactive autonomy during free-time VLE access: L2 free expression. Learner autonomy. Explicit interaction – Writing – Speaking Implicit interaction – Reading – Listening	**L2 free expression:** (a) Student choice of L2. (b) Increased L2 interaction. **Learner autonomy** (a) Responsibility. (b) Decision-making. (c) Evaluation by the student.	**Free time:** Writing forum posts. Reading forum posts. Reading additional resources. Writing assignments. Discussion (with friends).	Free-time logging into the site. Voluntary use of L2 – posting to the forums. Level 1: *Reactively* responding to 'expert'-generated threads. Level 2: *Reactively* Responding directly to peer-generated threads. Level 3: *Proactively* generating own threads. *Proactive* reading forum posts. *Proactive* engagement with additional resources. *Reactive* post-lesson assignments. *Proactive* discussions about postings to the forums.	*Main skills:* Writing Reading *Sub-skill:* Speaking Listening	Self-directed. Relatedness to others. Interaction *Proactively* self-directed. *Reactively* task directed. *Reactively* responding to others. Choice. Freedom. No expert support (except for assignment feedback).

Free-time mode: Discussion forums

The forums were a dynamic, free-time component, unlike the static provision of additional resources. The defining characteristic of this element of *EI* was that 'it is populated [...] the space becomes inherently social' (Dillenbourg et al. 2002:5). At the start of the *EI* programme the forums were empty spaces to which the students were invited to contribute during the intervention. Four of the five *EI* forums were made available as spaces that were student led, where there was no significant expert presence. Other than initial student curiosity in what *EI* had to offer, activity in the student-led forums was limited. The approach adopted in the expert-led *RTR* forum was different. *RTR* had a low-level 'expert' presence. I generated and posted a weekly discussion thread, unrelated to the *EI* classroom lessons. My 'expert' thread was posted at the weekend, scheduled to arrive in the students' free time. Although the teacher reminded students to check the site, Julia pointed out that 'everyone says "yeah I'm gonna do that later"... then when you are at home you don't have time'. The extent of my contribution did not go beyond the generation of the weekly thread and I never responded to the students' contributions. During stages one and two of the *EI* programme, *RTR* emerged as the most frequently accessed forum. All significant free-time activity was directed here. Learners seemed most likely to exercise their 'ability to take charge' (Holec 1981:7) by responding to communicative affordances with this defined 'learning structure' (ibid.).

For these students, discussion forums, embedded within a language development environment, were a new L2 writing venture. Unlike classroom writing, replies could be formal, informal, long or short, adherence to form was not observed and students posted into a public arena. Students were invited to contribute, but unlike an assignment, they received no expert feedback or correction, exacerbating the difference with the familiarity of the 'traditional guided instruction' (Crook 1994:79). Students were made aware that *EI* assignments and postings were not graded and the course was not certificated. Early in the study this disconcerted Vicente who posted to *RTR*, (Box 7.1), questioning the value of participating in a programme for which there was no apparent purpose and which did not bear the familiar hallmarks of a language learning course.

> **Box 7.1 Early forum posting – Vicente**
>
> ploma or something, could somebody explain it to me. What is the main reason for being part of this course? by Vicente
>
> are they going to give us a diploma or something for our curriculum? Could somebody please explain it to me, hope you can read my message. Have a good day.

Eight students responded to Vicente's post. A recurring theme emerged which was to 'enjoy the experience and see it as an opportunity to learn about online courses!' (Juan).

Although the choices learners made by engaging with the structure of the expert-led forum had the appearance of 'guided' familiarity, they showed their ability not only to 'adapt to different languages and different learning conditions but also to progress in their ability to learn by conceptualizing their learning experience' (Esch 1996:36). A consistent pattern of free-time interaction emerged and students engaged with the *RTR* forum for the duration of the intervention. Patterns of *RTR* behaviour evolved and gathered momentum 'as they pass from figurative hand to hand, and so are shaped and reshaped' (Bijiker and Law 1992:8, cited in Hutchby 2001:140). Quantitative data from site records illustrated the extent of students' free-time proactive and reactive, explicit and implicit engagement. The figures are compelling but they indicate patterns of activity, not the reasons underpinning the activity, nor the value students attributed to their participation.

Students may have felt obliged to respond to the weekly *RTR* posting as a 'homework' task, or felt they were 'helping' the researcher. Learners' responses may have been linked to external demands, rather than as an autonomous expression of cognitive and metacognitive learning strategies and their capacity to reflect and choose whether to participate, raising questions about the extent to which they were the 'active agent' (Benson and Voller 1997:7). Alternatively, learners may have conceptualized free-time participation on the basis of their 'own understanding of what is valuable and worth doing' (Wall 2003:308) and that they could engage more 'freely and spontaneously' (Lantolf 2003:367) with the language, which would correspond with their concerns about the difficulties associated with using the target language.

Language production: Obligation or choice with the free-time component of *English International*?

In striving to gain insights into notions of obligation or choice, it serves us well to begin with the students' free-time forum activity. Table 7.2 indicates the number of free-time threads and return posts to each forum. The most significant level of explicit activity was in the expert-led *RTR* forum.

RTR was also integrated into six VLE lessons. Posts submitted to *RTR* in response to these lessons are described in the table as 'Class-time Posts', to differentiate them from the students' 'Free-time forum posts'. Other than posts submitted in response to *EI* lessons, a regular pattern of free-time posts to *RTR* emerged in stages one and two.

Free-time *EI* participation was predominantly driven by the stimulus of the weekly thread posted to the expert-led forum. As the data in the table shows, students may have replied with such regularity to the *RTR* forum in their free time because the forum was defined by a weekly 'homework' task, compounded by the culture of teacher/learner dependency in a traditional guided learning model. This conundrum about the purpose of the weekly *RTR* thread emerged in Vicente's second interview, 'I'm just replying, but I'm not quite sure, what's this, I don't know why "she" wants us to do this ... is this homework?' Vicente's thoughts were articulated by nine other students. Learners may indeed have perceived the *RTR* thread to be a weekly homework task; but this reveals nothing of the value they may have attributed to their participation. Autonomy emerges as more than a matter of 'freedom from external control' (Benson and Voller 1997:4) in which 'independence is always balanced by dependence' (Little 1990:7). This is significant, considering Holec's (1981:7) view that the autonomous learner has the ability to take charge within a structure where he can exercise that ability, and where, Trebbi (2008:35) argues, autonomy is more a matter of whether the individual is 'a victim of constraint'. How far did the students feel duty-bound to respond online or did they engage freely with the *RTR* forum? Table 7.3 provides a summary of the core students' reflections.

A spectrum emerges relative to perceptions of responsibility, obligation, independent thought and action in response to the structure of the expert-generated *RTR* thread. At one end Lucia and Monse saw the weekly expert thread as homework, dutifully responding, whatever the topic: 'We just reply' (Lucia). In the middle of the spectrum, Maribel located *RTR* posts alongside her assignments in describing the organization of her workload. Yet she considered

Table 7.2 *EI* forums – free-time threads, posts and views

Forum name	Description	Threads generated	Class-time posts	Free-time posts	Class views	Free-time views
Stage 1		(Expert and student)				
Read, think and reply	Posting of discussion topics (including blended lesson threads)	12 (expert threads) 10 (student threads)	11	123 (replies to expert threads) 7 (replies to student threads)	27	920
Learning a language	The challenges of language learning	0	0	0	0	11
Picture post	Photo-sharing forum	1	0	0	0	79
Words to share	Online student word box	1	0	0	0	27
Coffee shop	A place to meet friends	2	0	8	0	301
Stage 2		(Expert and student)				
Read, think and reply	Posting of discussion topics (including blended lesson threads)	22 (expert threads) 5 (student threads)	67	236 (replies to expert threads) 16 (replies to student threads)	117	1889
Learning a language	The challenges of language learning	1	0	0	8	8
Picture post	Photo-sharing site	2	0	0	42	42
Words to share	Online student word box	2	0	0	23	23
Tea shop	A place to meet friends	0	0	0	0	20

Table 7.3 *Read, Think and Reply* – free choice or obligation?

Free choice	Obligation
The forum is not directly for you ... just for other people to read it, but not for you ... writing the assignment I know that I have to post it to you before the deadline. (Julia)	Peer replies: they think it's not important to reply to each other ... maybe because it's not part of our homework. (Lucia)
It's like free choice, but the teacher says you are supposed to do that. Everyone says, 'yeah, I'm gonna do it later' ... then when you are at home you don't have time. (Julia)	I know that I have left some replies and I try to have the time to reply to them. (Monse)
I saw it like something as not obligatory. (Juan)	When I am at home I have my tasks, assignments and *RTR* and then I work, I post it. (Maribel)
NO! Free choice, because not all of us answer them and most of us read them .... (Maribel)	Is this homework, or what's this? (Vicente)
I consider it as homework the assignments but the posts not ... just post our ideas ... our opinions. (Mateo)	I thought it was a kind of obligation for us to do that. (Vicente)
I just reply to the ones that I really like. (Vicente)	Significance of topic... 'no we just reply'. (Lucia)
I think it was free choice ... in my case I wanted to share my ideas. (Zarita)	
Thank god you told me and I can choose, I didn't stop answering you but right now I am answering you because I want to. (Vicente)	

RTR posts as free choice because 'not all of us answer them and most of us read them'. The light and shade of Maribel's phrasing, 'not all of us' alongside 'most of us' offer an insight into her conceptualization of their freedom to choose whether or not to contribute. Furthermore, site records of Maribel's personal response to the VLE indicate her sustained levels of engagement suggesting that free-time interaction with *RTR* was of value to her. Maribel's comment is borne out by the number of 'proactive', yet non-contributory, visits made by the students to view *RTR* shown in Table 7.2. Towards the far end of the spectrum, Julia highlights the juxtaposition of the assignment and forum postings, indicating the difference between the pressures of working to meet assignment deadlines, unlike the forum. Julia's choice of the adverb 'just' implies that in the forum she valued the freedom of writing for others, rather than the critical eye of her teacher.

Vicente's response lay at the opposite end of the spectrum when he learned that contribution to the forums was voluntary. Rather than withdrawing, he became more proactive; not only replying to weekly *RTR* posts, but generating his own threads, increasing his free-time use of English, reaching level three relative to examples of autonomous behaviour on the VLE free-time autonomy framework. He described feeling liberated by the freedom to make meaningful choices, participating because he wanted to rather than out of obligation.

High levels of localized free-time *EI* activity to *RTR* imply the learners' capacity to make independent decisions about levels of participation. However, they responded to expert-generated threads, not one another as Table 7.4 indicates. At first sight, this suggests that they engaged with *EI* in 'predictable teacher pleasing ways' (Hawisher and Selfe 1991:55), reflecting 'traditional notions of education that permeate our culture' (ibid.), and characteristic of the guided learning pedagogical tradition.

Table 7.4 Free-time expert and student threads and responses to *EI* forums

Threads	Stage 1		Stage 2	
	Threads	Replies	Threads	Replies
RTR expert-generated threads	12	123	22	236
RTR student-generated threads	10	7	5	16
Other forums student threads	4	8	5	0

Student behaviour in the forums may have mimicked that of the classroom, yet they received no expert interaction or feedback, nor were they graded for their writing. Indeed the forum was remote from the conventions of the traditional classroom, raising questions about the reasons underpinning their continued engagement with *RTR* and the value they attributed to their participation.

The question of learner agency and meaningful choice emerge: 'It's not a homework BUT it's a kind of homework because you have created engagement a kind of compromise with you and your project' (Vicente). I asked learners why they generally replied 'reactively' to expert-generated threads rather than 'proactively' generating and replying to one another's threads. Their views are summarized in Box 7.2. They acknowledged that they were more responsive to an authority figure, an approach that corresponded to a more transmissive pedagogical culture. Juan was highly proactive onsite, generating a number of his own threads but he despondently described his place in a virtual social order. He believed that he received so few replies to his threads because he was not seen as an expert. He felt 'disappointed and sad because I try to look for topics, interesting topics for young people like us'. Vicente thought his classmates would reply to one another if they were instructed to do so, but that 'I am not an authority there'. Similarly, Lucia reflected that her classmates probably thought it was not as important to reply to one another.

> **Box 7.2 *Read, Think and Reply* – responding to the voice of authority**
>
> - Because ummm ... you are an expert, maybe they see you as an expert doing these kind of things, they think, 'uh, Juan, it's Juan'. (Juan)
> - Maybe because they think that it's not so important to reply to each other. (Lucia)
> - Someway, somehow you are the authority in that case and everybody's replying to you. (Vicente)
> - If you will say 'everybody let's reply to Vicente' I can bet you that everybody is going to do that. (Vicente)
> - You are ... maybe the guide for this programme ... It's an authority. (Zarita)

Comments from the whole class captured in the online questionnaire (Table 7.5) indicate why students chose not to generate independent threads and shed light on where they located themselves relative to the social milieu of the forum.

Table 7.5 Mid-course questionnaire – reasons for not generating threads

Theme 1 – Concern about what others might think
- Because sometimes many students could think that is a waste of time, I don't think so, but many times this discourages me.
- Because I am a bit shy.
- Because if they don't feel like sharing their ideas with their classmates they won't make an effort to write what they really think.

Theme 2 – Difficulty in finding a topic that might interest classmates
- Because sometimes you think that the topic that you want joined, would be not interested in it.
- Because if I dont see that they feel interested in writing these sort of things, I won't encourage them, they need to be curious about.
- Because it is difficult for me to think on a topic that could encourage others to respond.
- Many times I don't know what the preferences are.
- Because they have good ideas and sometimes their much better than mine.

Theme 3 – Leave it to others to take the floor
- Because I know that most of my classmates have written often in the forums.
- Because most of my classmates answered, so I think it's not needed because I know that in the long term they will do it.
- Maybe because I'm a bit selfish that only think of myself and I know that almost all my classmates write in the discussion forums because they are interested, so I trust that they do it and I don't encourage them.
- Because I know they are doing them.
- Maybe because I'm sure they have done them.

Their reasons show the fragility of relationships between class members and the difficulties associated with L2 free expression between peers. Fear of rejection from class members who were 'always together' but who did not feel 'close relations' with one another offers a possible explanation for their reluctance to generate independent threads. Replies to expert threads appeared with relative anonymity because posts appeared in the 'mix' among those of their classmates. Generating new threads exposes the learner within a more public space because the parent thread appears at the top of the screen with the name of the person who started it. *EI* site records corroborate the students' concerns about what their classmates thought of them, an anxiety which is compounded further by their awareness that in the *RTR* forum 'not all of us answer them and most of us read them' (Maribel).

The familiarity of structure mediated by expert-generated threads represented a less intimidating proposition, with little to suggest from the number of postings to this public arena that *RTR* held any fear for them. In this forum students embraced the structure of communicative affordances mediated by the 'architecture of electronic space' (Hawisher and Selfe 1991:1) with the promise of more democratic participation, supporting those 'traditionally shut out of discussions' (Warschauer 1997:472). Littlewood's notion of reactive autonomy opens up the possibility of looking beyond the simplistic view that students replied to a weekly *RTR* homework task. The weekly task created a communicative context for the students to respond to. In evaluating students' personal response in terms of their onsite activity and notions of autonomy, what emerges is the web of interaction as students read and reacted to one another's ideas – the interdependent, cognitive links between ideas expressed by the learners suggesting the possibility of an ecological view of learner autonomy.

Holec (1981:7) argues that the autonomous learner is capable of making decisions about his learning within a defined structure. Site records indicate that students made choices about their free-time use of the VLE, selecting the affordance and level of participation with which they felt most able to engage. Most students contributed to the forums at level one in the VLE free-time autonomy framework, choosing to respond 'reactively' to the structure of the expert-generated thread, stimulating increased L2 output, and meeting the criteria for L2 free expression suggested by the framework. Few students chose to participate 'proactively' at levels two and three and most overlooked the less-defined student-led forums and free-time affordances. This response supports Mason's (2001:69) argument that 'simply providing an environment [...] did not guarantee successful engagement'. *RTR* satisfied the students' desire at the start of the project to use English more extensively beyond the classroom, and they responded to the structure of *RTR* as a space where they could engage communicatively in English in response to a clearly defined task. By contrast, the student-led forums created a less-defined space with no clear reason to engage.

The *explicit* choices learners made in terms of free-time *EI* engagement mirrored the guided learning model as students following the lead from the 'expert'. However, one should not overlook the significance of *implicit* online L2 interaction between students relative to notions of autonomous behaviour, after all 'Not all of us answer them [postings] and most of us read them.' (Maribel)

Implicit interaction within the free-time component of *English International*

Students attributed a high value to reading one another's contributions to *RTR*, (16 of the 21 students indicated that reading classmates' posts encouraged them to contribute). By contrast just five students reported that receiving the weekly expert-generated *RTR* post encouraged them to post back, findings that lend support to the motivational merits of peer interaction referred to in the study by Pica et al. (1996).

Learners implicitly engaged with more threads than they chose to reply to, indicating independence of thought and action suggested by the VLE free-time autonomy framework. Postings did not exist in isolation from one another capturing the notion of the 'totality of relationships' (van Lier 2004:3). A network of implicit and explicit connectedness between technological environmental factors and autonomous behaviour becomes apparent, linking cognitive and social processes between individuals (van Lier 2000:258). The students' decision to log in, read, think and reply to forum threads in their free time, suggests that they identified with the forum as an opportunity to engage with the target language communicatively beyond the classroom which corresponds to concerns expressed prior to the *English International* programme, that their environment was 'totally native' (Zarita).

As the students reflected upon the value of the VLE programme at the end of the project, they not only mentioned the significance of contributing to the forums, but significantly nine of them referred to the importance of reading their classmates' contributions. The number of free-time, non-contributory visits made to the *RTR* forum is an indication of the extent of their implicit interaction (see Table 7.2). Lucia reported that because she knew her message would be read by her classmates, this focused her attention to linguistic accuracy, which made her attend to her grammar and spelling though 'not in what I think' and view shared by Monse, suggesting that the forum cognitively stimulated a freer use of language.

Explicit interaction by posting to the forum left a trail of evidence marking the students' presence and participation and the development of ideas between contributors. Implicit engagement may have left no trace of their on-line presence but 'viewing which area has been visited by other students is an indirect mode of interaction' (Dillenbourg et al. 2002:5). Implicit participation outweighed explicit participation, challenging the argument that students felt duty-bound to participate. Students may have logged in, participating, whether implicitly or explicitly, because they wanted to. Interaction was localized, directed to the structure of the expert-led forum, but their onsite personal response to the VLE suggests that their actions were self-directed.

Interview data corroborate *EI* site records, revealing that learners engaged with their classmates' postings. Lucia expressed surprise as she recollected her classmates' posts following a Valentine's Day thread, 'I can read all my partners' opinions and I didn't know what they think about that date, so when I read it I was like surprised because I didn't know that they thought in that way.' Students cognitively engaged with the language and meaning they wanted to convey because they knew that 'everybody will read it' (Julia), heightening their awareness of the challenges associated with using English publicly and independently of the classroom.

In the technologically mediated community of *RTR* just as 'People do not live their lives in social isolation' (Bandura 1986:449), postings do not exist in isolation. Learners' decisions to engage with the forum represented more than a response to the expert-generated thread, they responded to those who populated the space. Yet their reasons for choosing *RTR*, overlooking other affordances, and their perceptions of the value of their free-time engagement with EI, remain unclear.

RTR threads were designed to be intellectually challenging. Students reported that reading their classmates' posts stimulated and scaffolded the construction of their replies as the following comments indicate:

Maribel: Because of other's writing I thought OK I can express it, so I wrote.
Julia: I see what the other students have replied and then I have replied.
Mateo: If my classmates write a reply to the post, I read, and also I realize my ideas.

Maribel found the reading *and* writing of posts valuable because students shared ideas online 'We are replying and talking about some topics and sharing ideas and it's good because you do realize what other people think about that topic.' A similar pattern emerged when students were asked which posts they would be most likely to read and why, (see Table 7.6). Most students did not specify names, but they mentioned the value of reading one another's postings.

Themes from the interviews reappeared in questionnaire data. Students valued the exchange of ideas, appreciating differences in perspectives on a variety of topics, as well as the opportunity to compare their views with those on the forum. Students said they valued and felt encouraged to post to the forum by

Table 7.6 Mid-course questionnaire 1: Which students' postings would you be most likely to read?

I would read posts written by …	Reason
Maribel, Monse, Zarita, Paloma, Ana and Susana.	I would like to know what they think about the different topics.
Vicente, David, Juan.	David, because he knows a lot of culture.
David, Vicente, Juan.	Vicente writes in an adult way.
Vicente, Juan.	Juan in a funny way.
Classmates.	No reason specified.
No names specified.	They always give their opinions about education or something interesting.
	We share the same culture and their commentaries give an idea about the topic.
	My classmates because I like to know what they think about the topic.
	To check the point of views of others.
	All of them think different so that makes interesting and I always learn something different from all of them.
	The ones that have to do with interesting topics for me.
	ones that catch my attention, because i like reading other people's points of view.
	I think it is important to read all of them because they have interesting opinions.
	Maybe the first one who have the courage to post something for people to discuss about it would be the most interesting for me!
	I often read all the posting because it is interesting for me to know their points of view and compare my ideas with theirs.

reading one another's contributions, suggesting that, relative to the VLE free-time autonomy framework, free-time use of the VLE stimulated autonomous learner behaviour. Moreover, they demonstrated a proactive, implicit response (i.e. choosing to read) to the VLE which stimulated reactive, explicit interaction (i.e. choosing to reply). It could be argued that this supports Little's (1990:7) view that as individuals our independence is balanced by dependence, enhanced by the ecological view connecting cognitive and social processes (van Lier 2000:258), of a socially interactive fluid interrelationship between elements which characterize the dynamics of autonomous learning. In order to gain closer insights into this as a possibility it becomes necessary to scrutinize students' *RTR* posts and threads for signs indicating the relatedness between contributions, in other words the ecological 'totality of relationships'(van Lier 2004:3) between posts.

Forum writing and the wider audience

The longer the 'trail' of posts in a forum thread, the greater the chances of detecting thematic patterns and linguistic motifs. The threads selected for closer scrutiny are those that achieved a high response rate in stages one and two of the *EI* programme.

Typically in non-collaborative classroom writing, output is a private matter between student and teacher. Writing for the forum was not a collaborative writing activity; however, students repeatedly indicated that they were aware that this was a public arena, reading and getting ideas from each other's before constructing their replies, a view corroborated by Lee's (2011:88) research into asynchronous writing through blogs and her suggestion that 'blogs increase students' participation and motivation because they are intended not only for a sole instructor but rather for a broad audience'.

Scrutiny of *RTR* posts should reveal whether the students drew inspiration from one another's work, or whether posts existed in isolation, as they might in an essay. By mapping the trail of thinking between the first and last posts in one of the threads one can evaluate the 'ecological' possibility that ideas evolved along the post trail, corroborating students' reports that online, implicit interaction scaffolded and stimulated explicit L2 interaction. Learners' engagement with the processes associated with conceptualizing and responding to information (Esch and Zähner 2000:9–10) in an online context emerges, suggesting that technology has the potential to activate cognitive and metacognitive learning strategies.

Thematic similarities between posts

Many *RTR* posts were thematically linked, but this may be an indication that students replicated one another's ideas to complete the task rather than thinking independently. In stage one, one parent thread invited the students to consider '*The best age to be . . .*' Maribel opened the discussion with two key ideas: 'Each age is special every stage of our lifes [sic] are important' and 'if you ask me the next year I will tell you that 25'. These ideas can be traced throughout subsequent postings, illustrated in Table 7.7. Students may simply have read Maribel's reply and plagiarized her ideas. Nevertheless, in relation to their personal response to the VLE in terms of autonomous onsite activity they logged into the site in their free time, read and engaged with ideas mediated through the forum, suggesting that proactive, implicit interaction stimulated reactive, explicit L2 interaction, indicated in the VLE free-time autonomy framework. Despite recycling ideas, analysis of posts supports the self-report data that students read one another's writing and the sense that they were not writing in isolation, but for 'an audience of critical peers' (Sotillo 2002:16).

Camila and Mateo made overt references to their classmates in their posts, 'as most of my classmates have said' (Camila), and 'as my classmates have said' (Mateo), substantiating self-report data that students' were aware of one another's

Table 7.7 Thread – '*The Best Age to Be . . .*'

Every age is special	The present is the best age
Every stage of our lifes are important, the best age to me it's now (24 years) . . . . (Maribel)	. . . but if you ask me the next year I will tell you that 25. (Maribel)
Every age in this life is good, you just need to enjoy every moment in it. (Lola)	I think the best age is the time that we are living. (Zarita)
Every stage in your life has some particular characterisctic that makes it unique. (Susana)	I think the best age to be is every age you are in. (Susana)
Each age you live a different stage and you experiment different moments. (Lucia)	I think no exact ideal age but we should enjoy the things which you live in the present. (Cristian)
I think all the years are good in a very different way!! (Juan)	Now I'm 19 and I feel very good and happy, but, as my classmates said, in a year I would say that 20 is the best age and after that 21. (Mateo)
I consider that every age, every stage of our lives are important. (Mateo)	I think that the best age for everyone and to me is the one we are living now. (Paloma)
As most of my classmates have said, I think that there's something special in each single age. (Camila)	

online presence. There is an interconnectedness (Blyth 2009:176) between replies, which is a pattern that appears in other threads.

As Table 7.7 shows, repeated references are made to 'every age' and 'every stage' by Maribel, Lola, Susana, Lucia and Mateo. Although Juan and Camila make different language choices, they repeat ideas expressed by others. The idea that the 'best age' is 'the present' appears in three posts, but Mateo mirrors the way in which Maribel expressed the same idea. Thematically, Julia and Luisa chose infancy.

> Julia: The best age to be is the infancy, I mean the 3 or 4 years old you still being innocent, you don't have to worry about what you are going to wear or what the others will think about you.
>
> Luisa: The early childhood because is when you try a lot of things and you don't care about what is going to happened... play is the only thing that you want to do!

Although expressed differently, Julia and Luisa's ideas of freedom and innocence in the thread run parallel with one another, suggesting a cognitive relatedness between their posts.

Only three students specified an age, with remarkable similarities between ideas which might be an indication of collaboration, but site records shown in Box 7.3 reveal that they posted independently of one another.

Box 7.3 Dates and time (GMT) when students replied to *'The Best Age to Be'*

1. Maribel – Friday, 23 November 2007, 07:54 PM
2. Lola – Saturday, 24 November 2007, 02:47 AM
3. Paloma – Monday, 26 November 2007, 02:29 AM
4. Zarita – Monday, 26 November 2007, 04:25 AM
5. Susana – Tuesday, 27 November 2007, 03:10 AM
6. Lucia – Wednesday, 28 November 2007, 09:59 PM
7. Juan – Thursday, 29 November 2007, 01:28 AM
8. Antonio – Friday, 30 November 2007, 05:34 AM
9. Mateo – Saturday, 1 December 2007, 03:17 PM
10. Maria – Friday, 7 December 2007, 03:08 PM
11. Cristian – Sunday, 16 December 2007, 05:39 PM
12. Julia – Wednesday, 19 December 2007, 07:48 PM
13. Camila – Wednesday, 19 December 2007, 11:34 PM
14. Luisa – Monday, 24 December 2007, 05:32 AM

Julia and Luisa contributed strikingly similar ideas, but they posted five days apart. The same pattern appears throughout the *EI* programme across other posts. In an early *RTR* parent thread (Box 7.4), students were invited to consider:

Box 7.4 *RTR* parent thread – '*If You Had to Choose . . .*'

If you had to choose to be able to do one of the following skills to an exceedingly high standard, which would you choose and why? Choose one and say why you wouldn't choose the others.

1. To sing
2. To paint
3. To write
4. To dance
5. To play a musical instrument
6. To play a sport to a professional standard
7. To think like a philosopher
8. An idea of your own. .or . . . that I haven't considered.

Table 7.8 shows the choices the students made in response to the parent thread. They show surprising thematic and linguistic similarities, not straying from the seven specified skills, with choices evenly distributed, overlooking option eight.

Early in the thread Paloma posted that she had dreamed of being a professional dancer, which re-emerged in Susana's post, suggesting that she may have been influenced by Paloma's post, followed by Maria choosing sport and writing: 'if you decide to work in a professional way'. Although students made different choices, they responded to the idea that music and writing facilitated self-expression. Maribel's and Maria's replies were not only linked thematically by their choosing to play a musical instrument to a high standard, but they both chose the piano, with minimal linguistic variation, changing the verb from 'like' to 'choose' and the omission of 'like' in Maria's post, suggesting that Maria had read Maribel's post.

A pattern emerged between students who chose to explain why they would *not* choose the other skills, with four students saying they did not want to 'think like a philosopher' as indicated in Box 7.5:

Table 7.8 Thread – 'If You Had to Choose ...'

Dance	Writing	Musical instrument	Painting
I think it would be ... to dance, even though I'm not very good. (Ana)	I would like to write about my thought ... it's a good opportunity to express those experiences most importants in your life. (Zarita)	I would choose to play a musical instrument as the guitar. (Julia)	Painting is something that has really caught my attention since I was a child. (Camila)
When I was a child one of my dreams was to be a professional dancer. (Paloma)		I would like to play a musical instrument, like the piano. (Maribel)	I will choose paint ... I used to paint with my mom when I was a child, in my free time. (Lucia)
My golden dream is to dance like a professional. (Susana)	I would choose to write ... it is a way to express myself. (Luisa)	I would choose to play a musical instrument, the piano. (Maria)	
		When you sing you can express your feelings. (Mateo)	
		"To play a musical instrument". I've always admired the ability to transmit feelings and emotions through playing an instrument. (David)	

Box 7.5 I would NOT want to ... think like a philosopher

- I don't want to think like a philosopher because those guys are all just a bit 'off their rockers'. (Lola)
- To think as a philosopher??? no way!!! I could ... lose my mind among all that crazy thoughts!!! (Julia)
- 'Think as a philosopher' doesnt sound interesting for me ... it gets even more complicated when we start to ask ourselves nonsense aspects of life. (Camila)
- Think like a philosopher?? Never!!! my life is quite complicated now, so imagine with a kind of devious mind. (Luisa)

Reasons given were thematically similar, beginning with Lola's powerful choice of the phrasal verb 'to be off their rockers'. Lola's idea seems to have led to Julia's reference to 'crazy thoughts' and the complications associated with a philosopher's concerns over 'nonsense aspects of life' (Camila), concluding with the idea that life is complicated enough without the 'devious mind' (Luisa) of the philosopher. Whether students followed the same or different themes, agreed or disagreed, there is evidence from their personal free-time response to the VLE of their awareness of one another's online presence, responding and transforming ideas in a non-linear way to ideas expressed along the post trail.

Students predominantly responded reactively to expert-generated threads, rather than proactively by generating and responding to their own threads. Although they made few explicit references to one another in their posts closer analysis reveals links between students' contributions, confirming site records and the value they attributed to reading one another's posts in self-report data. Free-time implicit, reactive interaction generated explicit, proactive L2 interaction. This would suggest that the value of *RTR* was in providing a stimulus and reason to use English communicatively beyond the classroom, which corresponded to the students' concerns about their lack of opportunity to use English. Learners not only responded to the stimulus of the task, but to one another so that the forum acquired 'meaning and structure through actors' interpretations' (Hutchby 2001:29).

Ideas evolved along the post trail supporting van Lier's metaphor of ecology because of the 'active relationship or engagement with the environment in which we find ourselves' van Lier (2004:90).

Evolution of student ideas along the 'Post Trail'

Students responded to the weekly *RTR* posts on two levels. First they responded to the task, by contributing similar themes and ideas. On a more subtle and complex level, their thinking evolved along the post trail in response to the parent thread. For example, one parent thread invited students to consider 'I wish more people would take notice of . . .' offering three examples as a model (Box 7.6):

Box 7.6 Idea modelled in the parent thread 'I Wish More People Would Take Notice of . . .'

- The words of wisdom expressed by our children.
- The beauty of the world around them.
- What they already have, not what they wished they had.

The subsequent thread suggests implicit interaction between students, but without explicit reference to one another. However, the following box (Box 7.7) shows the order in which students posted to the site with the different dates and times they posted and the evolution of ideas emerges.

Box 7.7 Tracking the evolution of the theme within a thread

1. Listen to the birds with the sound of the wind against the leaves. (Vicente – Monday, 3 December 2007, 01:38 PM)
2. Take notice of problems such as global warming. (Paloma – Tuesday, 4 December 2007, 11:15 PM)
3. Take care of our world. (Susana – Thursday, 6 December 2007, 03:59 AM)
4. The sound of the tree leaves ... the things that you can feel while the wind is touching you. (Maria – Friday, 7 December 2007, 02:53 PM)
5. There are a lot of children in the world that don't have anything to eat. (Lola – Monday, 10 December 2007, 02:28 PM)
6. Our world ... and its part of the place we live, so we should take care of it. (Maribel – Monday, 10 December 2007, 05:55 PM)
7. Everybody needs to take care of the Earth planet. (Lucia – Monday, 10 December 2007, 11:07 PM)
8. I wish more people would take notice of the world. (Pablo)
9. Problems like contamination, drugs, global warming, *poorness* ... the beauty of the world around them, the beauty of the universe, of their countries and states. (Mateo – Friday, 14 December 2007, 07:07 PM)
10. Global warming, *poverty* and the injustice which are in all the world. (Cristian – Sunday, 16 December 2007, 06:06 PM)
11. I wish more people take notice of the *poverty* of our world ... the tiny things that we can do in order to help people as homeless and abandoned children!!! (Julia – Wednesday, 19 December 2007, 07:30 PM)
12. I wish more people take notice of the violence in the world. They just don't care the damage they make to children. (Camila – Thursday, 20 December 2007, 12:04 AM)
13. Notice the beauty of the world around them. (Luisa – Monday, 24 December 2007, 05:44 AM)

Ideas are reworked, and the theme 'the beauty of the world around them' from the parent thread model metamorphoses from Vicente's simple image, 'listen to the birds with the sound of the wind against the leaves', towards sociological concerns, with 'problems like contamination, drugs, global warming, poorness'(Mateo), and profound reflections about the fragility of the world and the damage caused by man, 'the violence in the world', (Camila). The circle is completed as Luisa returns optimistically to wishing that more people would take 'notice of the beauty of the world around them'. There are signs that students noticed and responded to one another's use of language and linguistic transgressions afforded by the slower pàce of screen-mediated interaction. Cristian notices Mateo's idea of '*poorness*' but makes the correct lexical choice selecting the word '*poverty*', subtly correcting Mateo's linguistic error without humiliation. This is followed up by Julia in the next post, reminiscent of Kessler's (2009) study in which students prioritized the exchange of meaning, but were reluctant to exploit Wiki tools for peer error correction. Tracking the times when students posted supports the self-report data of the value they attributed to the dynamic web of interaction, reading, thinking and responding to one another's ideas; in other words, the importance of the 'totality of relationships' (van Lier 2004:3) mediated by the VLE.

In terms of the students' personal response to the technology relative to the VLE free-time autonomy framework, they made evaluations and decisions, were self-directed and demonstrated an awareness and relatedness with others. They chose to log in, read, reflect and respond to the ideas expressed along the post trail suggesting that implicit L2 peer interaction stimulated explicit L2 free expression in the construction of their own replies.

Data indicate that students resisted proactively generating their own threads, preferring to respond reactively to threads. Patterns of free-time interaction emerged as students' responded to the weekly expert-generated threads mediated by the *RTR* forum, overlooking student-led forums and more structural CALL affordances. Closer investigation revealed that students were doing more than dutifully completing their weekly *RTR* 'homework' task, and that they were not working in isolation from one another as posts were thematically and linguistically interconnected. In so doing, they showed their 'ability to take charge' (Holec 1981:7), proactively logging in to read one another's contributions, choosing whether to respond to the weekly *RTR* thread and one another's thinking.

The notion of reciprocity between autonomy and emergent digital literacies is suggested by Villanueva et al. (2010:12) in the sense that learners make choices about how to proceed (ibid.) in response to digitalized text and links. Benson and Chik (2010:64) have coined the phrase 'globalized online spaces' within which content is predominantly provided by the user rather than the website owner, arguing that these spaces are of interest in foreign language learning as resources for 'authentic communication and autonomous language learning' (ibid.). Both perspectives precisely capture the students' sense of awareness and response to one another's online presence in the context of EI, embedded with all the promise of pedagogical possibility. What remains unclear, however, is the nature of the observed relationship between autonomy and technology.

Site records and the students' contributions to the *RTR* forum provide us with evidence to suggest that learners showed signs of autonomous language and learner behaviour in response to the technology, but how closely does the reality of our students' experience resemble their perceptions of the value they attributed to their free-time use of the platform. In turn what might this reveal about the nature of the relationship between autonomy and technology in the context of learning a foreign language?

Student perceptions of the value of free-time engagement with the *English International* forums

Students were asked to consider which of 14 elements within the site had helped them to improve their language during the intervention. They could select more than one option. Writing assignments and forum posts were the most popular choices. Fifteen students selected assignments; 12 chose writing for the forums and 9 chose reading posts on the site. In terms of the students' personal observational response, Monse's response captured the feeling of the class as she described how she perceived the impact of *EI* on her writing 'I have improved since I am in the project,' concurring with the view that writing skills can be enhanced 'through meaningful tasks and extended readership' (Sykes et al. 2008:532). The writing of assignments and posts was identified as a defining feature of *EI* with regard to language development. Vicente described *EI* 'more as a website for improving, especially writing improvement'. Students valued more formal assignment writing following *EI* lessons, which was more closely aligned to the familiar guided learning model. Writing for the forums was identified as the second most helpful element in terms of language improvement. The recurring theme to emerge from interviews was that 'it [EI] helps us keep in practice ... not only ummm ... school and also at home ... we can do it wherever we are' (Maribel). In interview, the students repeatedly identified *EI* free-time interaction as an opportunity to practise and develop their writing skills. *RTR* created an opportunity for VLE-mediated language development that went beyond 'transferring paper based tasks to a computer' (Ganem Gutierrez 2006:244), corresponding to the learners' concerns before the *EI* programme about wanting to use English more communicatively. In terms of the learners' personal response, they engaged with the pedagogically transparent structure of expert-generated threads mediated by the forum, that provided a platform for learners respond to, by reacting to the voices of those who had gone before them, by writing communicatively for a wider audience, or by reading and reflecting on the web of socially interactive online engagement. The students' personal response reflects the notion and value of 'multiplicity' in online contexts posited by Villanueva et al. (2010:7).

> The use of ICT opens up a space for complexity and multiplicity that might help in the development of autonomy [...] multiplicity of access to interaction, the chance to reinforce metacognitive ability through experience with others, via dialogue.

Vicente lacked confidence in writing, but he explained the value of not writing for accuracy in the forums, 'just writing what I think', without the pressure of achieving good grades, 'I'm not going for a score in that.' Despite flagging up that he 'wasn't into writing', Vicente acknowledged that the site was 'amazingly good for practising'. This was reflected in his level of participation. He was regularly the first to reply to the weekly thread, appreciating the less-guided approach to free-time *RTR* writing because 'you don't have someone beside you saying "this is wrong, that's wrong ... you are not always checking for mistakes"'. The *RTR* forum, as a communicative platform, was identified by Juan as being important because 'when you reply you are giving an opinion at that moment ... the important is how people understand you', suggesting a heightened cognitive awareness and interconnectedness when writing for a public audience. Julia valued the freedom to experiment with language on *RTR*, which she could not with more formal assignments 'You can use the language that you want, like writing crazy things ... writing the assignment, you cannot write like that.' Learners valued having more 'time and psychological space' (Little 1990:9) to write and articulate their thoughts in English. Table 7.9 shows the number of posts made by the core students to *RTR*, including replies and threads generated.

Vicente's level of contribution to *RTR* reflects the extent to which this reluctant writer engaged with *RTR* where he would not be judged or graded for the skill he considered needed most attention. Indeed, Vicente's posts increased between stages one and two, replying to weekly *RTR* threads as well as generating eight of his own, a number matched only by Juan. Vicente made it clear in his final interview that he contributed to *RTR* voluntarily in his free time, with a tangible sense of liberation because he was invited but not obliged to contribute 'Thank god you told me and I can choose, I didn't stop answering you but right now I am answering you because I want to.' Lucia explained that her peers had contributed extensively to the forum and that it had provided a

Table 7.9 Number of postings and threads generated in forums (core students)

Name	Stage 1	Stage 2	Totals	Threads generated	Replies received
Juan	11	25	44	8	7
Maribel	17	20	37	3	3
Lucia	11	24	35	0	0
Vicente	13	21	34	8	1
Julia	15	17	32	0	0
Zarita	10	18	28	1	0
Mateo	11	16	27	0	0
Monse	8	10	18	0	0

good opportunity to practice 'we used to write a lot in the *RTR* . . . and I think that's a great resource to practise'. Free-time forums provided Zarita with an accessible context for writing for fluency beyond the classroom that 'encourage me to follow thinking in English, writing in English. It's another opportunity I had outside of classroom to practise'. Her comment suggests that writing for the forum cognitively facilitated her thinking and writing in English, unhindered by the confines of educational structures because she had 'more time to think my ideas, to reflect in my comments. I am a bit, a bit slower thinking'.

These students repeatedly attributed value to affordances that supported opportunities for L2 free expression, mediated by writing in response to *EI* stimuli, which corresponds to their concerns about the lack of opportunity to use the target language meaningfully in their native context. Voluntary L2 implicit and explicit interaction increased, whether this was a proactive or reactive response indicated in the VLE free-time autonomy framework, suggesting the 'suitability of the particular task to that medium' (Ganem Gutierrez 2006:244). Their choices corresponded to their perceptions of that which was 'valuable and worth doing' (Wall 2003:307/8) in light of their perceived language development needs. This may offer an explanation about why they overlooked structural free-time *EI* additional resources.

Self-report data may not accurately reflect the students' thinking, and they may have provided the 'right' answers but site records corroborate their views. Moreover, writing in response to the VLE emerged as one of the most significant factors to emerge from their *EI* experience. Free-time *EI* postings satisfied a need, identified by the students before the programme to use English more extensively. Their writing corroborates self-report data that they valued the ideas expressed by their peers, through oblique linguistic and thematic references to one another that ran throughout the threads. For these students the forum was a pedagogically new medium, and they identified and responded to the opportunity to practise the target language in a less formal, communicative platform that was different from their classroom, suggesting their ability to adapt cognitively to, and conceptualize the value of, this learning experience (Esch 1996:36).

The notion of autonomy within a VLE is not a simple matter of liberating students from rules and boundaries so they can make their own choices. Patterns of student behaviour emerged during the *EI* programme that corresponded to their concerns about practicing the target language. They chose to overlook structural affordances and favoured opportunities for L2 free expression. It could be argued that their personal response to the VLE was not a manifestation of autonomy because they predominantly responded to expert-generated *RTR* threads but this makes light of the concept of autonomy, obviating one's internal capacity to think and respond autonomously to others within a structured forum or classroom. Students' free-time interaction with the VLE was framed by a series of conditions necessary for autonomy to be achieved: that the learner should be capable of making decisions and taking charge of his learning, and that there should be a structure within which the learner can exercise his potential for autonomy (Holec 1981:7) In the free-time component, autonomy emerged from the learners' personal response to the *RTR* forum. The structure of the weekly *RTR* threads stimulated a pattern of free-time language behaviour unlike the student-led forums, where learners were the sole 'social agent' (Benson and Voller 1997:5) and these forums seemed pedagogically remote and ill-defined. The weekly *RTR* thread anchored a communicative and unpredictable web of interaction, mediated by the technology, leading us towards an ecological view of autonomy. For the students involved in the *EI* programme, everything is connected to everything else, as students cognitively engaged with one another's ideas, decided whether to contribute their opinions, constructed and posted their own replies, they transformed the genesis of ideas from the parent thread and the online discussion.

In the classroom and in their free time, student perceptions of their *EI* experience are corroborated by their online reality, revealing the choices and decisions they made in using the VLE. The value students attributed to their experience of using *EI* corresponds to their concerns about using the language more freely and communicatively in their Spanish-speaking guided learning environment. In the next chapter I return to the main themes that emerged from the literature and consider these in light of the insights about our learners' response to *English International* to see what can be learned about the nature of the relationship between autonomy and the use of a VLE in an EFL context.

8

An Ecological Perspective of Autonomy, Foreign Language Learning and Technology

In earlier chapters, I examined the themes that emerged from the literature and evaluated the students' response to their use of a VLE. With these elements of the puzzle in place, I now construct a case for a theoretical representation of autonomous behaviour and a VLE working towards insights into the nature of the relationship between autonomous learner behaviour and technology.

As the previous two chapters indicate, students showed signs of autonomous behaviour during their *EI* learning programme, such that one might infer that 'educational technology is an effective purveyor of learner autonomy' (Murray 1999:296). Though a compelling proposition, this view draws a simplistic correlation between the tool and the outcome (Ganem Gutierrez 2006:233), failing to address the complexities associated with the notion of autonomy and the impact of introducing a VLE into the students' learning environment. Three significant issues emerge from the evaluation of their classroom and free-time use of *EI* and form the main thrust of this discussion:

1. *Response to direction*: Signs of autonomous behaviour result predominantly from the direction or guidance suggested by the task rather than from the technology. The same effects would be achievable if learners were given the same tasks in a course book instead of a VLE.
2. *Response to the environment*: The introduction of the technology introduced a virtual element in the classroom, extending access to learning into the students' free time. The configuration mediated by the VLE altered the dimensions of interactions between students in class and in their free time. Autonomous learner behaviour was attributable to ecological changes brought about by technology.

3. *Response to direction and the environment*: Students responded to the task mediated by the VLE, but the technology altered the configuration of the learning environment, influencing classroom and free-time interaction between students. Autonomous learning behaviour resulted from the task *and* the environmental changes brought about by the technology.

The discussion of these three main issues is anchored within the theoretical perspective of the ecological approach, the central tenets of which inform and underpin the conceptual framework forming the backdrop to this chapter. By way of framing the discussion that follows, I begin with a review of the principles underpinning the conceptual framework, before reflecting on the complexities of what it means to be an autonomous learner and user of the target language, from this juncture I address the three aforementioned issues in turn.

An ecological representation of the conceptual framework

Language teachers worldwide would no doubt attest to the merits of supporting the individual's capacity to make choices and engage freely and communicatively in the target language. In a technologically supported environment this might be in response to screen-mediated stimuli introduced into a language-learning environment. Holec's (1981:3) view that the student should be capable of taking charge of his learning within a learning structure highlights the role of the student and the significance of the context. This is reflected in the conceptual framework in Figure 8.1, where the learner is located at the centre of the context within which he exists.

In addressing the three main issues, I draw on three elements from the ecological approach: the 'totality of relationships' (van Lier 2004:3), the notion of affordances and language, as they relate to the VLE. Ecologically speaking, context is described as lying 'at the heart of the matter' (van Lier 2004:5). Context immerses the student in language, but also *defines* the language used while paradoxically *being defined by* the language used. This suggests an evolving communicative dynamic, as students respond to stimuli and to one another. Context provides an array of activity spaces, from the VLE classroom to free-time VLE access. As the student becomes more actively engaged with affordances presented within the learning structure, so the affordance grows in relevance and meaning as students respond by using the target language to interact with one another, indeed: 'Perceived collective efficacy will influence what people choose to do as a group, how much effort they put into it' (Bandura 1986:448).

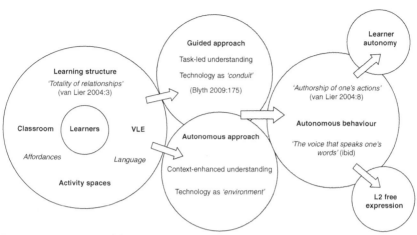

Figure 8.1 Conceptual framework for autonomous learning behaviour in a learning environment

In reflecting upon the students' personal response to their VLE experience, I draw on two contrasting pedagogical stances illustrated in the conceptual framework. The first stance, described as the guided approach, reflects Crook's (1994:79) term 'traditional guided instruction', and the second stance, described as the autonomous approach, is one in which the student is less guided towards the acquisition of knowledge but works independently towards the construction of understanding by psychologically engaging with the processes of learning. Each stance accords a different significance to the factors students respond to in the learning structure so that the interpretation of the task and context in relation to learner behaviour is different. Alternatively the students' response might be an eclectic blend of these contrasting standpoints.

From the guided position, students respond to the characteristics of the task or affordance, when the 'intended use is designed into it' (van Lier 2004:95), for example the introduction of new grammar points, or speaking for fluency. Desired outcomes might be achieved through the selection of appropriate affordances, and their suitability to the medium (Ganem Gutierrez 2006:244), that have been chosen on account of their fitness for purpose by an external agent. In the context of a VLE, the technology might be described as the conduit for the affordance, like the course book or photocopied handout. It is the individuals' response to the affordance mediated by the VLE that stimulates the behaviour rather than the inherent characteristics of the technology.

From the autonomous position, students arrive at new understanding in response to the multiple stimuli that characterize the context within which they find themselves. Introducing new stimuli changes the composition of the environment. Learners adapt their behaviour in response to the reconfigured structure, with an impact upon the language used and the choices they make relative to the affordances for learning and the 'totality of relationships' (van Lier 2004:3) between class members. If the students' personal response to the VLE in terms of their reflections and online activity can be attributed to the reconfigured composition of the learning environment brought about by the technology, a relationship might be thought to exist between the technology and autonomous behaviour.

Alternatively, the students might respond to the design intentions of the affordance suggested by the guided, *as well as* the autonomous approach in which the dimensions of the learning structure are transformed by the introduction of the VLE, so enhancing learner behaviour and language development. This possibility is represented by the overlap between the guided and autonomous circles shown in the conceptual framework.

Notions of autonomy within the conceptual framework

There is a sense in which the student can fulfil his potential for autonomy from both the guided *and* autonomous pedagogical perspectives relative to the conceptual framework. This notion serves to ground an emergent understanding of the nature of the relationship between autonomous learner behaviour and the introduction of the VLE.

Autonomous learning is often identified as representing freedom from control, but this oversimplifies the concept, implying that potential for autonomy is repressed by the constraints of the institution and precludes the sense in which it is possible for the individual to be autonomous in a structured environment, guided by the teacher and the provision of learning materials. This is illustrated as the guided approach towards autonomy in the conceptual framework. Benson (2009:26) suggests that it is the role of the educators to create the right conditions so that the individual's innate capacity for autonomy can thrive. The right conditions might constitute the development and selection of the most appropriate teaching materials for the students, so that autonomy emerges in response to direction stimulated by others, (reactive autonomy, Littlewood 1999:75), rather than the learner initiating the direction of the activity (proactive autonomy, ibid.).

But the autonomous learner does not exist in isolation from his environment. According to the autonomous approach, the individual is the product of the discourse within which he exists, so that 'As social beings our independence is always balanced by dependence, our essential condition is one of interdependence' (Little 1990:7). Creating the right conditions for autonomy is more than a matter of design, it is also one of environmental dimensions and the impact of environmental changes to the learning structure on learner behaviour. I have drawn on van Lier's (2004) metaphor of ecology, and propose an ecological version of learner autonomy, characterized as the learners' internal-cognitive (Little 2007:18) response to external stimuli and the network of voices of those that surround them. An ecological view of autonomy acknowledges the 'totality of relationships' (van Lier 2004:3) and relatedness between multiple elements in a social context, giving 'shape' to the dynamics of autonomous learning and expanding the linear notion of interdependence.

The first of the three issues to emerge from the data is the possibility that signs of autonomous learner behaviour were *not* attributable to the technology, but to the affordances mediated by the technology within the activity spaces provided by the blended VLE classroom and the structure of the free-time VLE environment.

The guided view: Autonomy led by design in the VLE classroom and free-time VLE access

One could argue that students were guided through their VLE-mediated *EI* lessons by the teacher, their choices made by following the direction determined by screen-mediated rubric and hyperlinks. Free-time access to the VLE provided students with access to classroom materials beyond the remit of the classroom, as well as additional stand-alone content supported by hyperlinks between affordances within the VLE and links to the internet. In addition, learners were invited to contribute to expert-led and student-led forums.

Drawing on the theoretical perspective of the ecological approach and in view of the conceptual framework, the possibility emerges that students were guided towards autonomous behaviour in response to the guidance and structure provided by opportunities for language development mediated by the VLE. This leads us to question the impact of the technology on the 'totality of relationships' (ibid.) in the *EI* lessons in the computer room. One could argue that indications of autonomy suggested by the students' personal response to *EI* were more attributable to the content, than the technology, and students responded as they might to a course book.

The guided view: The 'totality of relationships' (ibid.) mediated by the VLE in class and free-time access

Students reported that they used the target language more extensively in their *EI* lessons, describing these classes as being 'like a debate' (Julia). Learner behaviour mirrored the conventions of the traditional classroom. When the teacher conducted two *EI* lessons from her laptop using an overhead projector in the classroom this altered the 'totality of relationships' (van Lier 2004:3) between class members. The teacher adopted her usual place at the front of the class leading the students through the stages of the *EI* lesson; interactions were more linear, guided and mediated predominantly through the teacher. But some students valued the authoritative presence of the teacher, who chaired the discussion, guaranteed fair play, provided cohesion to the group and technologically controlled the pace of the lesson. They liked the 'coercive nature' (Murray 1999:300) of *EI* in the classroom, because the presence of the teacher created the time and space for them to attend to VLE-mediated affordances. This suggests that these students valued learning opportunities created by the design and content of the lesson rather than the advantages afforded by the technology per se.

In their free time, students had access to multiple VLE-mediated resources. Rather than responding to more static Structural CALL[1] resources, students mainly engaged with more dynamic forums, where they were invited to post messages and share ideas for others to read in English. Writing for the forums expanded their readership to 'an audience of critical peers' (Sotillo 2002:16), as Maribel indicated, 'not all of us answer them and most of us read them'. The forums introduced the possibility of virtual L2 interaction between participants, allowing them to expand their use of English beyond the remit of the classroom and providing a new dimension to relationships between classmates. However, one should not necessarily presume there to be a clear correlation between the students' increased free-time use of English and the forums. They seldom generated their own threads, rarely replied to one another and predominantly responded to weekly expert-generated threads posted to the *RTR* forum. Relationships in the forums corresponded to those of the classroom. In virtual space, students' eyes were metaphorically turned to the front in response to expert-led instruction delivered in the form of the weekly posting, manifesting the same behaviour and dynamic between class members as in the VLE blended classroom.

---

[1] Computer-mediated focus on form and accuracy through drills and practice activities with the 'computer-as-tutor' (Crook 1994:80).

But does this mean that the learners' onsite personal response to the VLE in class and in their free time was not autonomous, simply because patterns of behaviour resembled the conventions of the guided, teacher-led learning model. It could be argued that their response to the VLE reflected Littlewood's (1999:75-6) notion of reactive autonomy,[2] as students intellectually engaged with the design intentions of the affordance supported by the facilitative lead provided by the expert. Moreover, the students looked beyond the direction stipulated by the task and engaged with the unpredictable, relatedness of events as they unfolded within the lesson or the forum, suggesting an ecological view of autonomy.

The guided view: Affordances mediated by the VLE in class and free-time access

The concept of an affordance as suggested by van Lier's (2004) ecological approach, not only incorporates the sense in which opportunities exist for learning, but also captures the random sense with which the individual might respond to one opportunity while overlooking another. The ecological approach theorizes that 'Affordances are detected, picked up, and acted upon' (van Lier 2004:91) as they relate to the individual, and depending on whether they are conceptualized as being of value. *EI* computer room lessons were constructed with clearly signposted VLE-mediated design intentions which the students recognized as being 'like a question and all the class have to discuss it and give our own point of view' (Lucia). Lucia's comment indicates that students responded to the transparency of the VLE affordances and felt encouraged to express independently constructed ideas, rather than 'giving the answer that the course book requires' (Juan). In line with the ecological approach, students responded specifically to those elements of *EI* lessons that corresponded to their concerns about their lack of opportunity to use the target language. Nonetheless, by design, they were guided towards an increased use of English, by responding to screen-mediated stimuli as they might, had the same content been provided by a course book. As Hutchby (2001:20) suggests, 'there are no inherent or necessary features of technological artefacts which lead to determinate social consequences'. This challenges the possibility that their behaviour was attributable to the technology, and raises questions about the nature of a relationship between autonomy and technology.

---

[2] Tasks are set by an external agent, learners 'react', cognitively organize resources and work together to reach goals.

In their free-time engagement with the VLE, students responded to the forums and overlooked the more structural 'workbook' affordances. Their choices corresponded to their concerns about their lack of opportunity to use the language more freely. From an ecological stance one can argue that students conceptualized the potential of free-time virtual communication mediated by the forums in terms of their language development needs. But they responded predominantly to the direction provided by the weekly expert-generated threads posted to the *RTR* forum. It could be argued that while students acknowledged their need to use English more extensively beyond the classroom, they needed a structure within which they might explore their capacity to use the language more freely. Student-led forums provided communication spaces that corresponded to their desire to practise the language, but these spaces lacked definition. In contrast, the expert-led forums provided structured affordances that created an opportunity to engage cognitively with ideas, the language and with one another, suggesting reactive autonomy (Littlewood 1999:75–6). The question remains whether the students' increased use of English was a response to the communication spaces created by the technology or whether the technology was simply the conduit for a weekly communicative 'homework' task.

The guided view: Language mediated by the VLE in class and free-time access

Central to the ecological approach is the idea that language is defined by the context within which it exists. But simultaneously, the language used by individuals defines the character of the context. As van Lier (2004:5) says, 'context is not just something that surrounds language, but that in fact defines language, while at the same time being defined *by* it'.

From an ecological perspective, the language classroom provides learners with affordances designed to stimulate engagement with the target language, described as the 'semiotic budget' (van Lier 2004:81). The language of the *EI* blended classroom was determined by the design, structure and direction of the materials provided, that is the semiotic budget. Just as discovery learning elicits a targeted response, students are led towards the generation and free expression of ideas in the target language by the design intentions of the VLE-mediated affordances. Lucia interpreted *EI* lessons as being 'like a question and all the class have to discuss'. In responding to the provision of the VLE-mediated 'question', the language used in class was characterized by the topic and the rubric of the affordance. Students attributed a high value to the topics covered in *EI* lessons, reporting that they were meaningful and relevant in light of their life experience, helping them to construct their ideas and contribute to the lesson.

The 'semiotic budget' (ibid.) afforded by *EI* materials enabled students to feel that they could 'use the language for real communicative purpose' (Fisher et al. 2004:51). The students' use of language might not be said to be directly attributable to the VLE but rather to the language of the VLE classroom, which in turn was defined by the affordances mediated by the technology. By contrast, in the conventional classroom, students had reported that the academic demands of the syllabus rendered topics communicatively inaccessible 'In classroom it's different because they are different topics like critical thinking ... and you don't know anything about it' (Julia).

Students felt more capable of expressing personally constructed topic-based ideas in response to *EI* lessons. However, linguistic behaviour in *EI* lessons was defined by the conventions of the classroom context with learners attending carefully, taking notes and mindful of following up assignments:

Vicente: You are having a purpose of doing an activity because you know that you need to write a report.

Maribel: In my case I can take what they are saying, just to keep in mind and when I am ready to do my task I try to read again.

Students' reflections on and reported increased use of the target language related to the content of their *EI* lesson, rather than the technology. Despite the counter-intuitive sense that students might be capable of autonomous behaviour within the guided construct of the VLE blended classroom, they showed signs of autonomy in their personal response to their experience with the technology. This guided approach towards autonomy suggests that learners can express their potential for autonomy by 'reactively' (Littlewood 1999:75-6) responding to externally created conditions through the selection of appropriate materials supporting them and allowing autonomy to flourish (Benson 2009:26). Teachers worldwide would agree that the reality of classroom management makes it difficult for students to respond 'proactively' (ibid.), because they rarely have a hand in selecting resources and initiating the direction of the activity.

EI students valued the familiar structure of VLE-mediated lessons and the design intentions of affordances. A more spontaneous use of English emerged, anchored by the rubric of the task and conventions of classroom behaviour. From the guided learning perspective, students responded to the affordance rather than the technology, suggesting that autonomous behaviour was not attributable to the technology, rather the technology was the conduit for affordances and subsequent behaviour suggested in the conceptual framework.

In responding to free-time structural affordances, such as a reading comprehension, the construction of the students' replies might be considered to be determined by the questions and the text. By contrast, expert-led parent threads to the *RTR* forum were designed to stimulate internal-cognitive (Little 2007:18) engagement, generating the exchange and development of ideas mediated by online social interaction. Unlike the reading comprehension, responses to the parent thread along the post trail were unpredictable. Learners were invited to freely express their own ideas in English in their own words, and reported that they valued the opportunity for free expression in English. However, one can argue that their use of English was determined by the context, which was defined by the expert-led posting, influencing their choice of register, vocabulary and grammar. The technology was the conduit for the design intentions of the affordance. Learner behaviour would not therefore be directly attributable to the technology.

In examining the nature of the relationship between autonomy and technology, caution should be exercised in suggesting that autonomous behaviour indicated by the students' personal response to the technology was due to the VLE. This overlooks the transformative effects of introducing the VLE into the learning environment and the subsequent impact on learner behaviour.

The autonomous view: Autonomy as a response to the technologically reconfigured dimensions of the learning environment in the VLE blended lesson and free-time access

The possibility emerges that indications of autonomous learner behaviour were attributable to environmental changes brought about by technology, and the suggestion proposed by Shachaf and Hara (2002:2) of 'the reciprocal interdependency between internal processes and the external environment'. Students may have responded to the reconfiguration of their learning environment and the 'totality of relationships' (van Lier 2004:3) created by the VLE-mediated affordances and the language to emerge from *EI* lessons and free-time access.

The autonomous view: The 'totality of relationships' (ibid.) in a VLE blended lesson and free-time access

One can argue that the introduction of the VLE provided a stimulus that changed the configuration of classroom space, reshaping the interdependent network of relationships between class members where learning was 'non-linear

[. . .] co-constructed between humans and their environment' (Kramsch 2002:5). Students were aware that the classroom was the only place where they could practise the target language but widely reported that in the traditional classroom, interactions were hierarchical, with students providing the responses the teacher wanted to hear and where L2 peer interaction was considered 'crazy' (Julia). By contrast they reported more extensive L2 peer interaction in the VLE classroom.

I have previously suggested that students predominantly responded to the lead taken by the teacher rather than the technology in the two *EI* lessons that took place in the classroom. I now adopt a different stance and consider the possibility that learner behaviour was affected by environmental changes created by introducing the VLE to their learning space. Shyer students reported that they felt reluctant to make their voice heard in open class, but that they felt more confident in their VLE-mediated computer room lessons, supporting the value Kitade (2008:78) attributes to offline verbal interaction in blended learning classes.

The presence of the terminals in *EI* computer room lessons created a private space between partners 'because you are not face to face with the others' (Monse). Classmates attended to their own screens instead of 'paying attention to you' (Lucia). Individual terminals reconfigured the communicative dynamic, altering students' response to screen-mediated stimuli and L2 interaction became more accessible for shyer learners than the wide open space of the classroom. The configuration of computer room VLE lessons altered the dynamic of classroom interaction with the decentralization of learning away from the teacher (Evans 1993:18). In the computer room learners did not feel the pressure of the teacher observing and monitoring (Juan) or telling students what to do (Julia). Access to individual terminals altered learners' response to the lesson; they felt they were more actively involved, making their own choices and navigating the direction of L2 peer interaction rather than following the lead of the teacher. In this context it could be argued that changes in the classroom dynamic were not a response to the VLE, but a response to the physical differences between the computer room and classroom.

EI computer room lessons introduced new levels of responsibility, choice and freedom, mediated by hyperlinks embedded within the VLE and with access to the internet. For some, this level of responsibility proved difficult to manage with reports that 'we are checking some other pages and that's why we lost in the class' (Lucia). New freedoms created by the VLE altered the configuration of the classroom, interfering with the pace of the lesson and interaction between learners. Students who preferred *EI* lessons in the classroom said that this was because the distractions of the internet were difficult for them to manage. They preferred the teacher to lead the class from the front. Yet others expressed frustration when their freedom to independently navigate the lesson was withdrawn 'When she asks the questions, you think, well I need go back to the previous screen ... because I don't remember. You cannot do it' (Julia). Technological functionality of the VLE introduced new levels of freedom, enjoyed by many, abused by others, but nonetheless affecting relationships between learners during *EI* lessons, whether in the classroom or computer room.

The VLE reconfigured the temporal and spatial dimensions of learning, not only in the classroom but also by providing free-time online access to additional resources and classroom materials. One could argue that this is unremarkable – after all, students can open their course books at home to look back at the day's lessons. However, as Schwienhorst (2008:167) says 'the CALL environment has many elements that do not have counterparts in the physical classroom'. VLE-mediated functionality not only allowed students to revisit materials, but they could trace the mark left by their classmates, re-reading their thoughts and ideas in response to the six lessons in which the forums had been incorporated in class. This is a dynamic that cannot be replicated by a course book.

The defining characteristic of an online forum is that it provides a context for virtual social discourse, and the ecological notion of 'language as relations between people and the world' (van Lier 2004:4). A clearly defined pattern of behaviour evolved as students engaged in their free time with the VLE. The students:

1. Overlooked the structural affordances.
2. Rarely contributed to the student-led forums.
3. Predominantly replied to the weekly expert-generated thread.
4. Rarely generated their own threads.
5. Implicitly acknowledged one another's contributions.

Lack of explicit learner responsiveness to one another raises questions about how the right conditions might be created to stimulate online social interaction between learners.

I have indicated that students' online behaviour mirrored that of the classroom, as they listened and responded to pre-set tasks. One should be cautious in suggesting that by predominantly responding to the direction of the expert-led thread, students were oblivious to others in virtual space. In terms of explicit written interaction, the voices of those who post can be 'heard', but it is more difficult to observe those who are 'listening', or reading, yet as Maribel reported 'not all of us answer them and most of us read them'. Learners widely reported in interview an awareness of one another's online presence, expressing surprise at their ideas. They were inspired to contribute by one another's postings, which was corroborated by an analysis of student postings and their site records. This supports findings from the Kol and Schcolnik (2008:60) study where students logged into the site and gained a new perspective by reading one another's posts before deciding whether to contribute. Rather than initiating the direction themselves, suggestive of Littlewood's notion of proactive autonomy (1999:75–6) the students' personal, autonomous response to their VLE experience was characterized by a preference for direction indicative of reactive autonomy (Littlewood 1999:75–6).

How might the learners' response to VLE-mediated affordances be conceptualized in light of the autonomous approach?

The autonomous view: Affordances mediated in a VLE blended lesson and free-time access

Technological functionality embedded within *EI* lessons took the students beyond the limitations of the printed page. Students widely reported the value they attributed to improved levels of interactivity in *EI* lessons created by the hyperlinks, describing the VLE as 'dynamic ... not flat' (Maribel) and viewing a conventional course book as 'some paper, some pictures' (Mateo). From their own terminals students were at liberty to move freely between screens and the internet, stimulating an increased perception of learner agency created by the opportunity to check information and consolidate their understanding so that they might contribute to the *EI* lesson. One could argue that these freedoms did not extend far beyond those afforded by the ability to leaf through the course book and that there was nothing significantly different about the VLE. Indeed, the data showed that students rarely strayed, predominantly following the hyperlinked stages of the lesson, overlooking the range of additional affordances embedded within the lesson. Although learners reported that they highly valued the potential promised by hyperlinked connectivity between VLE-mediated affordances, we should be cautious in suggesting that the technological functionality embedded within the affordance significantly altered the configuration of the blended lesson. But significantly students perceived the VLE to promise them choice and freedom 'The books are completely different because in this one it's up to you

[…] you don't have to see every page and like follow every topic' (Julia). Whether they exploited those choices was in itself an expression of free will.

Student perceptions of the value of technological functionality suggest that they believed the VLE to be a dynamic, stimulating learning environment. But like a printed course book, they were constrained by the limitations of the content provided. However, internet access in *EI* lessons increased spontaneity in response to the turn of classroom events. For example, the teacher responded to the students' curiosity following a reading about Rosa Parks, which led to an online search and discussion about Martin Luther King's 'Dream' speech. Internet access took the class beyond the limitations of the screen-mediated rubric, enhancing and transforming the character and direction of the lesson. The potential to go beyond the remit of the printed page excited and motivated the learners:

> I told her I didn't know about that speech and she said, 'No? Wait a minute.' She looked at the internet and she showed us about that speech that he gave to, to the USA and then I knew about that. (Zarita)
>
> You can be limited with the course book and you can be available many sources with the internet. (Mateo)

In terms of autonomy, from an ecological stance, the individual detects, interprets and acts upon affordances within his environment through a process of evaluation and deciding on whether he believes it is worth doing. Given the range of additional resources embedded in the VLE, students were proactively (Littlewood 1999:75–6) selective. They responded to affordances that corresponded to their desire to use English more communicatively that were specific to the technology. Structural VLE affordances embedded within the VLE were not exceptional, like students worldwide, they had access to multiple language development resources at the university. However, uniquely the forums provided a context in which students could not only practise English and express their own ideas, but share their views with a wider audience in English unlike an assignment. The forums provided an environment that signalled an opportunity for proactive or reactive 'action potential' (van Lier 2004:92). Rather than setting the pace in student-led forums, students preferred to be guided by a weekly expert-generated thread, perhaps because they were accustomed to direction in their classroom learning environment. But one could argue that they were proactive, weighing up and choosing to overlook student-led forums after all with access to their own social networking sites there was no identified need and they saw one another every day in class. These learners responded to the VLE-mediated affordances that corresponded most closely to the aspect of language development that concerned them most. Like language learners worldwide they lacked the opportunity for meaningful interaction in the target language in class or in their free time.

The autonomous view: Language mediated in a VLE blended lesson and free-time access

Ecologically it could be argued that the presence of the computer in the VLE classroom altered the communicative dynamic of the learning space. It is possible that the introducing the VLE created the conditions in which learners felt more encouraged to use English, suggestive of Kitade's (2008:78) study where the potential of CMC was considered to include not only online, but also offline interaction as learners engaged with one another *alongside* the computer. One could argue that contextually the presence of the computer transforms the lines of classroom interaction, with implications for the students' use of language. In the teacher-led classroom, student contributions are guided by and directed towards the teacher, who interprets and redirects interaction back to the class. As the teacher brings coherence and cohesion to the lesson, students respond indirectly to their classmates. In the two *EI* lessons that took place in the classroom, students indicated that communicative dimension was 'more guided by the teacher' (Zarita) and 'we are all together commencing about the topic' (Monse).

By contrast, in the computer room the teacher adopts a less dominant position, altering the lines of interaction, facilitating rather than directing the interaction. The configuration of the computer room changed the communicative dynamic. As the teacher stands aside, interactions are peer-led rather than teacher-led. Students interact directly to the ideas and language presented by their classmates rather than mediated through their teacher. In the computer room, the context created by the technology generates an intimacy between student pairings, allowing them time to 'talk and express our ideas' (Mateo). Yet the contextual configuration created by the presence of the technology brought increased responsibility for students to stay on task, impacting upon their use of the language as they worked together around their screens, proving challenging for some and frustrating others. From the perspective of the autonomous approach, indicated by the conceptual framework, the students' use of English during *EI* lessons seems less a response to the inherent functionality of the VLE, and more connected to the changes brought to the learning space by the technology.

According to the ecological approach, it is suggested that the characteristics of the context define the language used, but that the language used also defines the character of the context. One could argue that the students' free-time use of language in the expert-led forum was not only influenced by the direction set by the task but also affected by the context, suggesting a 'reactive' rather than 'proactive' view of autonomy (Littlewood 1999:75–6). Learners' initial call to action was stimulated by the task, but there were indications that the trail of forum-mediated ideas was uniquely characterized by the 'architecture of electronic spaces' (Hawisher and Selfe 1991:60), encouraging a 'more egalitarian sense of authorship' (Blake 2008:134). Unlike classroom interaction, asynchronous communication creates a context where students can write for a wider audience, where everyone has a voice, with the time and space to engage with opinions which help in the development of ideas, as well as revisiting, selecting and re-reading posts. Thematic analysis of students' postings reveals that their thinking was influenced by ideas and language that had gone before, indicating their responsiveness to one another's online presence. The rubric of the tasks stimulated the initial direction learners took, but did not govern the interaction. As Kol and Schcolnik (2008:59) found, learners did not necessarily follow the parent thread as expected. The dynamics of online interaction were anchored and set in motion by the task, but the learners individually and cognitively interpreted the ideas expressed by others, suggesting that the 'totality of relationships' (van Lier 2004:3) shaped the emerging web of interaction.

The second element to consider is that the language used and contributions made by the students characterized and defined the character of the expert-led forum which evolved during the *EI* programme. Expert-led parent threads were designed to challenge the students intellectually, encouraging them to go beyond the construction of formulaic responses, exploring the idea that technology can be used to focus the learners' attention, activating cognitive and metacognitive learning strategies (Esch and Zähner 2000:9–10). Indeed in a different context, forum threads might have been used to generate a formal assignment-style piece of writing. Early in the *EI* programme Maribel contributed a lengthy and formal response to the *RTR* forum. She told me that she had felt self-conscious as she read the more concise, informal posts that followed her posting. Thereafter her posts corresponded to the form and style adopted by her classmates. Constructing a post in English for the forum was a new experience for these learners in terms of language development, but over time an approach to writing emerged that was succinct, informal and defined the character of the space.

Theoretically, one can argue that learners showed signs of autonomous behaviour relative to their personal response to the VLE from two perspectives – the guided and the autonomous approach. Both possibilities point to the ambiguity that has evolved regarding the nature of the relationship between autonomy and technology. There is however a third possibility which is the overlap between the guided and autonomous approaches indicated in the conceptual framework, and described as an eclectic approach.

From the eclectic standpoint the interpretation of students' personal response to their VLE experience in terms of autonomy considers the possibility that autonomous behaviour can emerge from the student's internal-cognitive (Little 2007:18) response to the direction stipulated by the VLE task, however by introducing the technology, the dynamic of the learning environment is reconfigured, changing the 'totality of relationships'(van Lier 2004:3) between class members, the affordances to which they respond to and their use of the target language. This indicates the possibility of an ecological version of learner autonomy, a view that enhances the more linear perspective that 'independence is [...] balanced by dependence' (Little 1990:7) by acknowledging the dynamics of autonomous learning, where ideas are grounded by a task and mediated by the technology but transformed by human interaction.

The eclectic view: The development of autonomous behaviour drawing on guided and autonomous approached in VLE blended lessons and free-time VLE access

The ubiquitous view of autonomy as freedom from control has led to the emergence of a polarized view that independence from the teacher is good, while teacher-led education is bad (Pennycook 1997:43). The external framework of the learning environment might guide the learner, Little (1990:90) argues that one cannot 'control what goes on inside each learner's head' so that autonomy in a classroom is possible, after all: 'the presence or the absence of the teacher is not the yardstick by which one can measure autonomous learning skills' (Macaro 1997:168).

The dichotomy lies in creating the conditions necessary for autonomy to thrive by creating a structure that liberates the learner without abdicating responsibility (Little 1990:7). I propose that for these students, the introduction of the VLE created the necessary conditions for them to explore their potential for autonomy, by providing materials to which they could respond that corresponded to their expectations and experiences of language learning. In so doing, the dimensions of their learning environment were reconfigured by the technology, influencing their response to the activities.

The eclectic view: The 'totality of relationships' (van Lier 2004:3) in a VLE blended lesson and free-time VLE access

I have previously argued that interactions between learners in *EI* lessons were guided by the direction indicated by the affordances mediated by the VLE, raising questions about whether their personal response was attributable to the technology. Yet student reports indicated that they used English more freely in response to the structure of *EI* lessons, showing an inclination towards 'reactive' rather than 'proactive autonomy' (Littlewood 1999:75–6), autonomy and interdependency between internal-cognitive and external, social conditions.

This is not to say that students' responses to one another in *EI* lessons were unaffected by the technology. I have discussed the impact of the technology on the classroom dynamic, introducing heightened levels of responsibility, which motivated some but overly challenged others, illustrating the view that autonomy is 'a highly individual construct' (Murray 1999:301). Some students valued the communicative freedoms created by the transformation from the linear, teacher-led classroom towards a more egalitarian environment where they felt less exposed by the wide-open spaces of the classroom. Others acknowledged that the reconfiguration of the learning environment brought about by the technology proved too great a responsibility, affecting the dynamic between class members, impinging upon the perceived value of the *EI* lesson.

In their free time students responded to affordances designed to stimulate online L2 peer interaction, replying predominantly to expert-generated threads and without explicit reference to one another. The students may simply have reacted to the expert, the task and not the technology. Yet the virtuality of the forum transformed the temporal and spatial dimensions of student writing, and communication, slowing down the pace of the interaction, allowing 'greater opportunity to attend to and reflect on form and content of communication' (Kern and Warschauer 2000:15), creating the necessary 'time and psychological space' (Little 1990:7) to cognitively engage with ideas generated by others.

From the eclectic perspective, the guidance provided by VLE-mediated content created a structure and anchored the task which provided a reason for students to engage with their peers in English. However, the technology reconfigured the 'totality of relationships' (van Lier 2004:3) between elements in the learning environment, affecting the social dynamic in terms of how students engaged with one another and the extent to which they felt capable of learner autonomy and L2 free expression.

The eclectic view: Affordances in a VLE blended lesson and free-time VLE access

An affordance is described as an opportunity that signals 'grounds for activity', (van Lier 2004:5) to which the individual responds according to whether he perceives it to be of value. The students responded to the design intentions of *EI* lessons, followed screen-mediated directions and rarely deviated to explore additional resources. Yet they valued the approach adopted by *EI* lessons, responding to those elements that correspond to their concerns about language development. The students might have responded 'reactively' to the structure of *EI* lessons rather than the technology. But the presence of the technology in VLE-mediated lessons altered the students' response to the content, introducing a new level of interactivity, taking the students beyond the page and creating the perception of a more dynamic, responsive environment.

One might argue that by choosing to log in and engage and interact with the VLE in their free time, students manifested signs of proactive autonomy (Littlewood 1999:75–6). But their online activity was predominantly generated in response to the direction mediated by the expert-generated threads posted to the *RTR* forum. They engaged with both the affordance and the unique characteristics of the forum created by the dynamic of this virtual space where they could read and respond to ideas presented by others, practising the language beyond the classroom. In sum, from an eclectic viewpoint students responded to the structure created by the expert-generated thread, but the virtual configuration of the forum transformed and enhanced their experience.

The VLE created a space within which these learners felt able to explore and contribute their own ideas in response to the guidance provided by the affordance and the voices of others, in other words an ecological perspective of autonomy. Simply examining learners' personal response to the VLE in terms of autonomy fragments the story; it overlooks the impact of the technology on the affordance relative to the reconfiguration of the classroom and the transformation of ideas in the forum thread. An ecological view of autonomy adds shape to the notion of interdependence between the internal, cognitive and external, social dimensions of the construct by acknowledging the sense that everything is connected to everything else (Lantolf 2000:25). Ecological autonomy emerges as a socially interactive web of individually constructed ideas stimulated and anchored by VLE-mediated affordances.

The eclectic view: Language in a VLE blended lesson and free-time VLE access

From an ecological perspective context is described as lying 'at the heart of the matter' (van Lier 2004:5) where the learner is immersed in language and where language defines and is defined by the context within which it exists. On one level the students' VLE-mediated use of language reflected the semiotic budget determined by the structure of *EI* lessons and the expert-generated *RTR* threads, but to suggest that their language was governed entirely by the direction indicated by the VLE-mediated materials would be a simplistic representation of student behaviour in response to the technology. Closer analysis indicates a more profound level of linguistic engagement characterized by the configuration of the space in response to the structure provided by VLE lessons and students' free-time access to the site. The dual value of the guided task supported by the characteristics of virtual space is expressed by Sykes et al.(2008:532) who propose that language development might be enhanced 'through meaningful tasks and extended readership'. An ecological view of autonomy connects the cognitive with the social processes of interaction where language and learning are seen as constituting a relationship between learners within their environment (van Lier 2000:258). Ecological autonomy embraces the unpredictability of interaction between participants in a social context, in which individual elements are not considered in isolation but as contributory factors to the wider discourse in the classroom or online.

Towards a theoretical representation of the relationship between autonomy and virtual language learning

The difficulty in identifying how technology might be exploited in order to encourage autonomous learner behaviour is two-fold, considering that Hawisher and Selfe (2000:56) caution against the 'uncritical enthusiasm' regarding the relationship between technology and autonomy, and concerns expressed by

PACCIT (2005:3) that 'huge technological developments [...] have not always delivered their intended benefits to end-users'.

The first difficulty lies in capturing the essence of what autonomy represents, and therefore understanding what is required so that we might create the conditions to stimulate such behaviour. The second problem relates to understanding the impact of technology on the dynamic of the learning environment taking into account the view that students do not simply respond *to* the materials with which they are provided, but also to the effect *of* those materials on the environment because they are 'the creative products of their social discourse' (Esch 2009:43). Technological functionality creates opportunities for us to observe and scrutinize the intangible, in so doing it becomes possible to gain more profound insights into the construct and to examine the nature of the relationship between autonomy and technology.

I propose a theoretical representation of the relationship between autonomy and virtual language learning that is divided into two parts. The first part draws on Little's (1990:7) view that 'independence is always balanced by dependence' and that 'there must be a learning structure in which control over the learning can be exercised by the learner' (Holec 1981:7). The provision of a well-resourced technological environment mediates the potential for 'proactive' or 'reactive' autonomy (Littlewood 1999:74–7) but this is no guarantee of success and may not stimulate autonomous behaviour (Mason 2001). The relationship between autonomy and virtual learning is more profound than the provision of pedagogically well-considered tasks mediated by a technological platform. The design intentions of VLE content are clearly an important element, but considered in isolation reveal little about the nature of the impact of the technology on the learner's 'psychological relation to the process and content of learning' (Little 1990:7), failing to address the effect of introducing the VLE on 'the practices and contexts within which the technology is used' (Kern and Warschauer 2000:2). Introducing technology materially transforms the configuration of the learners' environment, leading to the second component of my theory about autonomy and virtual learning.

The second part of my theoretical representation asserts that the VLE introduces a virtual element that is singular to a technological context. The virtual element transforms the configuration of the learning environment, affecting how students respond to one another, altering the dimensions of affordances for learning, and influencing learners' use of language. Students' might respond *proactively* to learning opportunities mediated by the VLE or *reactively* to the direction stipulated by the activity. But it is the virtual element that takes the learner beyond the rubric of the task, enhancing and adding a dimension beyond that which is provided by the printed page. The virtual element highlights the possibility of an ecological version of learner autonomy, characterized by the significance of the idea of 'the totality of relationships' expanding the notion of interdependency between internal-cognitive and social-interactive (Little 2007:18) elements in a blended or free-time virtual learning context. The dynamics of learning are set in motion and grounded by the affordance, stimulating autonomy that emerges as a responsive state, and defined as an unpredictable web of human interaction, as ideas are transformed and passed between those engaged with the activity.

I propose that autonomous learner behaviour in a VLE emerges from the effective coalescence of a clearly defined structure that by design exploits the virtual dynamic, visualizing the learner as 'physically, socially and mentally moving around a multidimensional semiotic space' (van Lier 2004:93).

9

Looking Back, Thinking Forwards

Technology presents learners with web of world-wide proportions to explore, with a tantalizing, infinite range of pedagogical alternatives mediating access to the target language in authentic situations, taking learners beyond the confines of their classroom and their course book so that they might take charge of their learning and use the target language spontaneously. Although the focus of this book relates to notions of autonomy, foreign language learning and technology with English as the target language, insights emerging from the discussion have implications not only for other foreign languages but other academic disciplines. Web 2.0 technologies, such as the VLE described in this book, promise the potential for independent and autonomous learning if one considers the following distinction:

> Independence means to do for yourself, to not rely on others for personal nourishment and support. Autonomy in contrast, means to act freely, with a sense of volition and choice. It is thus possible for a person to be independent and autonomous (i.e. to freely not rely on others). (Deci and Flaste (1996:89)

Technology creates a context where the individual can make choices and 'chart his own course through life [. . .] according to his own understanding of what is valuable and worth doing' (Wall 2003:307–8). The notion of a relationship between autonomy and technology is indeed intuitive, but what of its dimensions and characteristics and how might such a relationship be nurtured in terms of design and pedagogy so that learners might be supported towards taking charge of their learning and work towards the ability to use the target language spontaneously.

A review of the problem: Understanding the nature of the relationship between autonomy and virtual language learning

Conceptually, autonomy is a complex and multidimensional notion and theorists warn against the 'uncritical enthusiasm' (Hawisher and Selfe 2000:56) for educational technologies. Esch (2009:31) argues that the 'mainstreaming' of autonomy into educational practice has distorted what it means to be autonomous. Despite the multiplicity of computer-mediated language educational programmes, the ESRC research group PACCIT, have expressed concern that 'huge technological developments [. . .] have not always delivered their intended benefits'.[1]

If we are to exploit technology so that our learners might realize their capacity for autonomy, simply creating a platform packed with teaching and learning activities and technological functionality is no guarantee of success (Mason 2001:69). In our desire to partner autonomy, technology and language learning there has been a tendency to overlook the interdependence between the internal and external dimensions of autonomy as well as the sense that autonomy is relative to the socio-cultural context within which the individual and the technology exists.

From this perspective, it is not only that the learner should have the ability to take charge of his learning (Holec 1981:7) but that the learning structure should be so constructed to enable the learner to exercise his capacity to take charge of his learning (ibid.). There are clear implications for the effective design and integration of technology in language learning in promoting learner autonomy and L2 free expression. We not only need to understand how the students conceptualize the value of technology relative to notions of autonomy but consider how their perceptions correspond to the reality of their online activity. In so doing it becomes possible to gain more profound insights into the nature of the relationship between autonomy and language learning in a VLE which in turn has the potential to inform the development of content, platform design and technological functionality so that they might then deliver their 'intended benefits' (ibid.)

Questions and answers

What conclusions might be drawn about these students' perceptions and the ensuing reality of their use of a VLE and what might this reveal about the nature

---

[1] www.esrcsocietytoday retrieved May 2010.

of the relationship between autonomy, language learning and technology? In the commentary that follows the concept of autonomy is based upon the following definition of the construct, presented in Chapter 4:

> The autonomous learner and user of the target language shows signs of being capable of taking responsibility for independent thought, action and interaction grounded within a social structure in response to experience.

Student perceptions and reality in the VLE blended classroom

Students widely reported that they perceived the value of VLE blended lessons in terms of improving and creating opportunities for L2 interaction, independent thought and action in response to one another's contributions within the structure of the lesson. Their views corresponded with their concerns that they had limited opportunities to use English outside the classroom and that their classroom represented their target language community. Yet they expressed a reluctance to use English in class, except with the teacher, and only fleetingly with one another, reporting that they felt inhibited by the external constraints of the syllabus and the more transmissive teaching style of their learning environment.

The introduction of the VLE brought increased levels of responsibility associated with managing the navigation of the site. Initially students were concerned that they might be distracted by other VLE screens and their direct link to the internet, indicating a sensitivity to the differences brought to their learning environment by the technology and demonstrating the students' potential for embracing increased levels of responsibility, reflecting their capacity for 'proactive' autonomous behaviour (Littlewood 1999:75).

Technologically, students valued the added dimension the technology brought to their lessons. Hyperlinks embedded into the VLE between the stages of the lesson guided and helped maintain pace, facilitating the opportunity to move easily between screens to check information. The experience was enriched further as students reflected on the value of using the internet to find more information about topics covered in the lesson leading into lively classroom discussions. Technology introduced a virtual dimension, extending the boundaries of the lesson beyond the dimensions of the 'page' to the world-wide web. Technology emerges as a component with the potential to enhance the notion of interdependence (Little 1990:7) between internal and external dimensions of autonomy, giving shape to the construct so that autonomy might be conceptualized as a web of interactivity.

Although self-report data make it difficult to corroborate with any degree of certainty the reality of these students' response to the VLE and reported instances of autonomous learner behaviour and increased L2 interaction, analyses of supporting data sources indicate this to be the case. Assignments and forum posts shared thematic and linguistic links and notes taken on a student's laptop in *EI* lessons re-emerged in the ideas and linguistic motifs expressed in her writing as well as her classmates' writing. Site records reveal something of the dynamic of the online activity in class. Students responded to increased levels of responsibility, choosing to stay on track and follow the flow of the lesson, corroborating the self-report data. Students claimed that VLE blended lessons enhanced their learning experience, bringing a new dimension to their classroom.

The students' personal response to the VLE is suggestive of Littlewood's (1999:75–6) notion of proactive and reactive autonomy in terms of taking responsibility for independent thought, action and interaction grounded within a social structure in response to their VLE blended-lesson experience. It could be argued that indications of autonomy were a response to the technologically enhanced dynamic of the learning environment. Alternatively, students may simply have responded to the direction suggested by the screen-mediated stimuli, and that the same materials mediated through a course book would have generated the same response.

However, one should not overlook the interconnectedness between elements in the technologically mediated learning environment and the impact of the 'totality of relationships' (van Lier 2004:3) on the dynamic of the learning environment. Evaluation of learners' personal response to the VLE revealed the communicative dynamic to be anchored by the direction indicated by the VLE-mediated affordance, stimulating a trail of internal-cognitive thinking in a socially interactive context. Topics were transformed by students weaving their opinions into the debate and the notion of an ecological view of autonomy emerges, defined by the interdependent, but unpredictable exchange of ideas between contributors.

Student perceptions and reality in the free-time strand

The free-time VLE strand presented students with a new language-learning context with which to engage. They perceived that the value of their free-time participation with *EI* was that it provided an opportunity for independent writing practice. This conjures up an image of students seeking out opportunities for extra writing 'homework', but this simplifies their conceptualization of the value of free-time writing in response to the VLE on three levels:

Level 1: In writing for the forums students valued their right to choose whether or not to participate and that they were not judged for their contribution in terms of 'going for a mark' (Vicente). Yet the value students attributed to writing for the forums extended beyond the freedom to write online in English, liberated from the watchful eye of the teacher.

Level 2: Students showed an awareness of the differences between the challenges associated with constructing an assignment written for their teacher that exists in isolation, and writing for the public arena of virtual space. Students made proactive choices (Littlewood 1999:75–6) about their level of participation and whether they wanted to contribute to the ideas emanating from responses to the parent thread, suggestive of reactive autonomy (ibid.). They reported that they were attentive to matters of accuracy, reflecting the view proposed by Warschauer (1997:472) that permanence of the written record serves as a 'cognitive amplifier'. With one eye on their virtual audience, students indicated that writing online encouraged them to self-evaluate and take responsibility for their written output.

Level 3: Students who had reported that they were less confident speaking in class, showed signs of engaging with online discourse, constructing an argument and expressing themselves more 'freely and spontaneously'(Lantolf 2003:367), threading their ideas into the online discussion.

A compelling picture of autonomy emerges in terms of learner perceptions but what of the reality? Free-time, online activity was localized. The students ignored structural free-time learning tasks and student-led forums in favour of the expert-led *RTR* forum. On a superficial level, one could argue they were simply responding to direction but this would suggest that the presence of the expert undermines an individual's capacity for autonomy, overlooking Littlewood's (1999:75–6) notion of reactive autonomy, where students show their ability to organize resources and work with others to achieve the goals of a given task. On a more profound level, it is a view that overlooks the ecological dynamic of the virtual context and the 'totality of relationships' (van Lier 2004:3) observable in the reality of the online interplay between learners. In writing for the forum, students not only responded to the theme suggested by the parent thread, but also to the 'voices' of those who had gone before them.

In light of the suggestion that autonomy is not considered to be a 'steady state' and that the learner 'is likely to be autonomous in one situation but not in another' (Pemberton 1996:4), the reality of these students' free-time online activity demonstrates the different levels at which they felt capable of being autonomous from logging into and navigating the site in their free-time to 'reactively' engaging with the expert-led *RTR* forum, demonstrating their proactive capacity to take responsibility, make decisions and exercise control over their learning through independent thought, action and interaction in response to the structure of the VLE. Student accounts of the value of reading classmates' posts were corroborated by site records, providing insights into the value of implicit (reading) interaction and the notion of relatedness that gives shape to the internal-cognitive and the socially interactive VLE-mediated web of interaction, and an ecological view of learner autonomy.

We should however be careful and avoid the dangers of 'artificially strengthening the apparent causal link between the medium and its pedagogical affordances' (Lamy and Hampel, 2007c:84). In comparing student perceptions of the value of the VLE with the reality of their online activity, there might be an identifiable connection between autonomy and technology in a language-learning context but the nature of this relationship is less clear.

The nature of the relationship between technology and expressions of learner autonomy and L2 free expression

We need to look beyond our view of the union between technology as the cause and autonomy as the effect and expand our breadth of vision. It is helpful to begin by returning to the suggestion that in order for the learner to behave autonomously, he should be able and know how to take charge of his learning, and that there should be a structure within which he can exercise his ability to do so (Holec 1981:7). This view highlights the link between the centrality of the individual and context. It would, however, be a misconception to suggest that autonomy is about the individual and 'individualism' (Esch 2009:34) because this detracts from the significance of the structure and context within which learning takes place. Furthermore it overlooks the view held by Little (1990:7) that 'As social beings our independence is always balanced by dependence, our essential condition is one of interdependence.' Misapprehensions have emerged about what it means to be an autonomous learner, failing to observe the delicate interplay between the individual and context relative to autonomy.

It is short-sighted to suggest that these learners simply responded to the direction suggested by screen-mediated activities and that instances of autonomy were unrelated to the technology. This overlooks the implications of context in shaping students' personal response to experience. Equally, it is too restrictive to suggest that autonomy emerged as a response to the virtual dynamic of the VLE, altering the dimensions of learner behaviour thereby liberating the individual from the constraints of the classroom and extending learning and language opportunities into the students' free time.

I propose that the nature of the relationship between autonomy and technology is a combination of the learners' response to the design intentions of screen-mediated activities, as well as a response to the transformation brought to the learning environment by introducing the technology. This corresponds to the view held by Esch (1996:36) that 'Humans are not only able to adapt to different languages and different learning conditions but also to progress in their ability to learn, by conceptualizing their learning experience.' It seems that technology can be successfully exploited to encourage students to deploy cognitive and metacognitive learning strategies, helping them to conceptualize new ideas and information (Esch and Zähner 2000:9).

Theoretical and pedagogical insights

The theoretical debate has predominantly questioned causal links and whether technology leads to good learning, but Blake (2008:2) describes technology as 'methodologically neutral', and Ganem Gutierrez (2006:244) argues that 'one cannot attribute the success [...] of a task solely to the medium of implementation'. In this book, I have questioned our understanding of the suggestion that technology creates opportunities that 'encourage students to strive for autonomy in the target language' (Kessler 2009:79) and that 'educational technology demonstrates its effectiveness as a purveyor of learner autonomy' (Murray 1999:296).

Theoretical insights

In seeking fresh insights into the nature of the relationship between autonomy and technology, I propose that we expand upon Little's (1990:7) notion of interdependence and the reciprocity between internal cognition and social interaction (Little 2007:18) and argue for an ecological version of learner autonomy. The theoretical insights that relate to notions of autonomy in a VLE rest upon the co-dependence and co-existence of the three findings relative to these students' personal response to the introduction of a VLE to support foreign language learning, indicated in Box 9.1:

> ### Box 9.1 Summary of findings
>
> 1. Learners have the potential for autonomous behaviour in the context of a VLE.
> 2. In light of Holec's (1981) condition that there should be a structure within which the learner can express his capacity for autonomy:
>   - Learners are able to express their capacity for autonomous behaviour in the context of a VLE in response to the structure and design intentions of technologically mediated stimuli rather than as a response to the functionality of the technology.
>   - The VLE structure creates a space within which the individual can exercise control over his learning and use of the target language.
> 3. The VLE structure introduces a virtual component, transforming the ecology of the learning environment and the learners' personal response to the technology reveals instances of autonomous behaviour in terms of:
>   - Proactive autonomy where the student takes charge of his own learning and directs activity (Littlewood 1999:75–6).
>   - Reactive autonomy where the student responds to direction, marshalling resources, and working with others to complete the task (ibid.).
>   - Networks of relationships in blended lessons and online 'totality of relationships' (van Lier 2004:3).
>   - Implicit (reading and listening) and explicit interaction (writing and speaking) in which language is defined *by* the task but equally, the language used by those who respond to the task *define* the context in which the interaction takes place (ibid.).
>   - VLE-mediated affordances enhance learner choice, freedom to choose and responsibility.

These findings add a virtual dimension to Holec's (1981:7) view of autonomy and reinforce Little's (1990:7) notion of interdependence between the individual and the context within which he exists. But significantly they acknowledge the implications of the transformative qualities brought to the learning experience by the introduction of a VLE, and an ecological version of autonomy with technology. Ecological autonomy in the context of a VLE acknowledges the dynamic connectivity between elements that contribute to events as they unfold in the learning environment. The notion of VLE-mediated ecological learner autonomy is anchored by the structure of the affordance, whether in the blended lesson or a forum thread. Ecological autonomy is a dynamic state that has the potential to be transformed by the learners' personal and cognitive response to ideas and the unpredictable web of social interaction, as individuals reflect and construct a response to the voices of those around them.

If, as educators, we hope to exploit and maximize the potential of technology as a means by which we can encourage our learners to be autonomous, we should do so from a basis of improved understanding about the nature of the relationship between technology and autonomy, so what pedagogical insights can be drawn?

Pedagogical insights

I suggest four conditions necessary as a means of informing and guiding educators towards an improved understanding about the nature of the relationship between autonomy and technology. The first condition is (Box 9.2):

Box 9.2 First condition necessary for understanding the nature of the relationship between autonomy and technology

A more robust understanding of the conceptual complexities and nuances of what it means to be an autonomous learner and user of the target language so that educators can recognize, build upon, respond to, create and evaluate opportunities for autonomous learning using technology.

Considering the significance attributed by Holec (1981:7) to the need for structure within which the learner can express his capacity for autonomy, the second condition necessary for understanding the nature of the relationship between autonomy and technology (indicated in Box 9.3) is that it depends upon:

Box 9.3 Second condition necessary for understanding the nature of the relationship between autonomy and technology

The provision of a clearly defined virtual structure with a transparency of purpose, within which individuals can express their innate capacity for autonomy. A virtual structure can:

- Mediate activities to which learners can respond in class or online.
- Reconfigure classroom space within which learners can make choices, interact and engage in the target language.
- Provide a virtual space within which learners can engage and collaborate.
- Acknowledge the 'essential human need to interact with others' (Pemberton 1996:3).

In isolation, the provision of a resource-rich virtual structure will not necessarily trigger the 'desired' response, because learners respond to some affordances but overlook others. In working towards a more profound understanding of the nature of relationship between autonomy and technology, the third condition indicated in Box 9.4 incorporates the notion of interdependence and the interplay between the internal cognitive (i.e. the individual) and external social and physical (i.e. the structure) dimensions of autonomy.

Box 9.4 Third condition necessary for understanding the nature of the relationship between autonomy and technology

Learners perceive, value and act upon opportunities for learning and development embedded within the structure that they identify as corresponding to personal language and development needs, according to their 'understanding of what is valuable and worth doing' (Wall 2003:307/8), and overlook those opportunities they perceive to be less helpful.

Technological affordances may lie dormant, but this is not to say they have no potential value. Learners will turn to an affordance, if it corresponds to a personally identified development need.

These three conditions do not explicitly address the significance of the virtual dimensions brought to the learning environment by introducing the technology, and with this in mind I turn to the final condition indicated in Box 9.5. If we are to understand the nature of the relationship between autonomy and technology, it is necessary to acknowledge and respond to the idea that:

Box 9.5 Fourth condition necessary for understanding the nature of the relationship between autonomy and technology

The technology introduces a virtual component that ecologically has the potential to transform the dimensions of the learning environment, altering the internal-cognitive/social-interactive (Little 2007:18) dynamic of human interaction as students selectively engage with screen-mediated affordances and the virtual structure.

If we are to create the right conditions in a technological learning environment so that learners might be able to express their potential capacity for autonomous behaviour, there is a need to raise awareness that the introduction of a VLE has an ecologically transformative effect on the learning environment and learners' responses. In looking beyond matters of whether technology improves learning, the challenge for teachers, teacher educators, materials designers and software developers lies in recognizing, understanding and harnessing the pedagogical value that might be achieved from the transformative effects of the digitalized learning environment.

In light of this fourth condition, Table 9.1 suggests the ways in which using a VLE for blended learning and free-time access can be physically, communicatively and virtually transformative. Improved awareness of the transformative implications (column two) of introducing a VLE will serve to inform educators about the development of best practice, materials writing and design so that we might create the right conditions in a technological learning environment for the autonomous learner to thrive.

Thinking forwards: Future research

The project described in this book was small scale and highly qualitative, it did not seek to make generalizations about the wider population. It shows how a monolingual class of advanced learners, one teacher and one institution from one culture responded to the introduction of a VLE in the context of a language-learning programme. Nevertheless, it has revealed fresh insights into the nature of the relationship between autonomy and technology making recommendations about how it might be possible to create the conditions necessary for autonomy to flourish in a technologically mediated language learning environment.

Mindful of the scale of this project, I would therefore propose the following recommendations for further research in order to refine and validate insights identified in this project. Table 9.2 proposes suggested models of studies that might be designed to pursue similar objectives and to expand upon the findings from this project, using different permutations of case samples and national contexts.

Closing remarks

The premise of this book is grounded in the intuitive but ambiguous relationship between technology and autonomy in the context of foreign language learning. In our increasingly digitalized world, my purpose has been to provide insights

Table 9.1 Implications of the transformative qualities of a VLE on the learning experience

Modes of transformation	Transformative implications of blended VLE learning and free-time use of the VLE
Physically transformative (Proactive autonomy, Littlewood 1999:75–6)	**Individual terminals in computer room** 1. Increased learner responsibility in class. 2. Private space between students in class. **VLE 'Hotmail' access beyond the classroom** 1. Course management – provision of online resources. 2. Responsibility to take charge of free-time learning. 3. Increased choice in selecting and engaging with online affordance. 4. Exchanging of information between school and home.<ul><li>Access to homework.</li><li>Writing and submitting assignments.</li><li>Marking and returning assignments.</li></ul>
Communicatively transformative (Reactive autonomy, Littlewood 1999:75–6)	**Explicit interaction in blended classroom** *speaking* in response to: 1. VLE-mediated stimuli. 2. Classmates' response to VLE-mediated stimuli. **Explicit interaction online** *writing* in response to: 1. VLE-mediated content in blended lessons (assignments, classroom writing). 2. Parent threads in VLE forum. 3. Ideas expressed by others in reply to parent threads. 4. Course management. **Implicit interaction in blended classroom** *listening and reflection*: Classmates and teacher's response to VLE-mediated content. **Implicit interaction online** *reading* in response to: 1. VLE-mediated content in blended lessons. 2. VLE-mediated additional resources. 3. VLE-mediated forums. 4. The internet.
Virtually transformative (Proactive and reactive autonomy, ibid.)	**VLE blended classroom** 1. VLE hyperlinks: Alters the pace of lesson. Smooth transition to and between VLE-embedded resources. 2. Internet-mediated access to information beyond the 'course book'. **'Hotmail' free-time access** 1. Technologically mediated access to lessons, online affordances. 2. Multiple levels of social interaction:<ul><li>Between tutors and students.</li><li>Responding and contributing to an online community.</li><li>Leaving and tracing an indelible mark online.</li><li>Awareness of the responsibilities associated with the potential to influence other's thinking.</li></ul>

Table 9.2 Recommendations for further research

Study one (this project): Monolingual group One country	One class	One teacher	Language level Advanced	One institution
Study two: Monolingual group One country	Two classes	Two teachers	Language level Advanced	One institution
Study three: Multilingual group UK-based English as *lingua franca*	One class	One teacher	Language level Pre-intermediate Intermediate +	One institution
Study four: Multilingual groups UK-based English as *lingua franca*	Two classes	Two teachers	Language level Pre-intermediate Intermediate +	One institution
Study five: Multiple groups Multiple countries English as *lingua franca*	Two + classes	Two + teachers	Language level Shared level	Two + institutions

into the nature of this relationship. In a technologically mediated context, learners' potential for autonomy can emerge proactively enabling them to take charge and determine learning objectives or reactively as they respond to direction, organizing their resources to achieve pre-determined learning objectives. Introducing a virtual component to the learning environment creates opportunities to observe students' capacity to cognitively transform and exchange ideas, characterizing autonomy as an interdependent, dynamic web of human interaction as they respond to VLE-mediated affordances. An ecological view provides insights into language and learning 'among learners and between learners and the environment' (van Lier 2000:258) by connecting cognitive and social processes (ibid.). It is a view that enhances our understanding of the nature of the relationship between autonomy and technology, which has the potential to inform the development of VLE content and online teaching methodologies so that teachers and learners can exploit and harness technology, striving for learner autonomy mediated by a VLE.

Bibliography

Allford, D. and Pachler, N. (2007). Autonomous language learning: radicalism and gradualism. *Language, Autonomy and the New Learning Environments* (pp. 139–65). Oxford; New York: Peter Lang.

Allwright, D. (1988). Autonomy and individualisation in whole class instruction. In A. Brookes and P. Grundy (eds), *Individualisation and Autonomy in Language Learning ELT Documents 131* (pp. 35–44). London: Modern English Publications and the British Council.

Arnold, N. and Ducate, L. (2006). Future foreign language teachers' social and cognitive collaboration in online environment. *Language Learning and Technology*, 10(1), 42–66.

Bandura, A. (1986). *Social Foundations of Thought and Action: A Social Cognitive Theory.* Englewood Cliffs, NJ: Prentice Hall.

Bax, S. (2003). CALL – past, present and future. *System*, 31(1), 13–28.

Benson, P. (1996). Concepts of autonomy in language learning. In R. Pemberton, E. S. L. Li, W. W. F Or and H. D. Pierson (eds), *Taking Control, Autonomy in Language Learning* (pp. 27–34). Hong Kong: Hong Kong University Press.

— (1997). The philosophy and politics of learner autonomy. In P. Benson and P. Voller (eds), *Autonomy and Independence in Language Learning* (pp. 18–34). London: Longman.

— (2000). Autonomy as a learner's and teacher's right. In B. Sinclair, I. McGrath and T. Lamb (eds), *Learner Autonomy, Teacher Autonomy: Future Directions* (pp. 11–117). Harlow: Longman.

— (2001). The history of autonomy in language learning. In C. N. Candlin and D. R. Hall (eds), *Teaching and Researching Autonomy in Language Learning* (pp. 7–22). Harlow: Pearson Education.

— (2007). Autonomy in language teaching and learning. *Language Teaching*, 40(1), 21–40.

— (2008). Teachers' and learners perspectives on autonomy. In T. E. Lamb and H. Reinders (eds), *Learner and Teacher Autonomy: Concepts, Realities and Responses* (pp. 15–33). Amsterdam: John Benjamins.

— (2009). Making sense of autonomy in language learning. In R. Pemberton, S. Toogood and A. Barfield (eds), *Maintaining Control: Autonomy and Language Learning* (pp. 13–26). Hong Kong: Hong Kong University Press.

Benson, P. and Chik, A. (2010). New literacies and autonomy in foreign language learning. In M. J. Luzon, M. N. Ruiz-Madrid and M. L. Villanueva (eds), *Digital*

Genres, New Literacies and Autonomy in Language Learning (pp. 63–80). Newcastle: Cambridge Scholars.

Benson, P. and Voller, P. (1997). Introduction. In P. Benson and P. Voller (eds), *Autonomy and Independence in Language Learning* (pp. 1–13). London; New York: Longman.

Bensousan, M., Avinor, E., Ben-Israel, B. and Bogdanov, O. (2006). CMC among multilingual students of English for academic purposes: linguistic and sociolinguistic communicative factors in online response. In *language@internet*. Retrieved 1 June 2010 from: www.languageatinternet.de/articles/LangInternetSpecialVolume1/370/index_html.

Blake, R. (2005). Bimodal CMC: The Glue of Language Learning at a Distance. *CALICO Journal*, 22(3), 497–511.

— (2008). *Brave New Digital Classroom, Technology and Foreign Language Learning*. Washington DC: Georgetown University Press.

Blin, F. (2004). CALL and the development of learner autonomy: towards an activity theoretical perspective. *ReCALL*, 16(2), 377–95.

Blyth, C. (2009). From textbook to online materials: the changing ecology of foreign language publishing in the era of ICT. In M. J. Evans (ed.), *Foreign Language Learning with Digital Technology* (pp. 174–202). London; New York: Continuum.

Boud, D. (1988). Moving towards autonomy. In D. Boud (ed.), *Developing Student Autonomy in Learning* (2nd edn, pp. 17–39). London: Kogan Page.

Breen, M. P. and Mann, S. J. (1997). Shooting arrows at the sun: perspectives on a pedagogy for autonomy. In P. Benson and P. Voller (eds), *Autonomy and Independence in Language Learning* (pp. 1321–49). London; New York: Longman.

Bronfenbrenner, U. (1979). *The Ecology of Human Development*. Cambridge, MA: Harvard University Press.

— (1993). The ecology of cognitive development: research models and fugitive findings. In R. H. Wozniak and K. W. Fischer (eds), *Development in Context: Acting and Thinking in Specific Environments* (pp. 3–44). Hillsdale, NJ: Erlbaum.

Candy, P. C. (1989). Constructivism and the study of self-direction in adult learning. *Studies in the Education of Adults*, 21, 15–21.

Chapelle, C. (1997). CALL in the year 2000: still in search of research paradigms? *Language Learning and Technology*, 1(1), 19–43.

Ciekanski, M. (2007). Fostering learner autonomy: power and reciprocity in the relationship between language learner and language earning advisor. *Cambridge Journal of Education*, 37(1), 111–27.

Cohen, L., Manion, L. and Morrison, K. (2003). *Research Methods in Education* (5th edn). London: Routledge Falmer.

Cole, J. (2005). *Using Moodle: Teaching with the Popular Open Source Course Management System*. Sebastopol, CA: O'Reilly Community Press.

Coomey, M. and Stephenson, J. (2001). Online learning: it's all about dialogue, involvement, support and control – according to the research. In J. Stephenson (ed.),

Teaching and Learning Online, Pedagogies for New Technologies (pp. 38–51). London: Kogan Page.

Cotterall, S. (1995). Developing a course strategy for learner autonomy. *ELT Journal*, 49(3), 210–27.

— (2000). Promoting learner autonomy through the curriculum: principles for designing language courses. *ELT Journal*, 54(2), 109–17.

Crook, C. (1994). *Computers and the Collaborative Experience of Learning: A Psychological Perspective.* London: Routledge.

Dam, L. (1990). Learner autonomy in practice: an experiment in learning and teaching. In I. Gathercole (ed.), *Autonomy in Language Learning: Papers from a Conference Held in* Britain in *January 1990* (pp. 16–37). London: Centre for Information on Language Teaching and Research.

— (2009). The use of logbooks – a tool for developing learner autonomy. In R. Pemberton, S. Toogood and A. Barfield (eds), *Maintaining Control: Autonomy and Language Learning* (pp. 125–44). Hong Kong: Hong Kong University Press.

Deci, E. L. and Flaste, R. (1996). *Why We Do What We Do: Understanding Self-Motivation.* New York: Penguin Books.

Dede, C. (1995). The evolution of constructivist learning environments: immersion in distributed, virtual worlds. *Educational Technology*, 35(5), 46–52.

Denscombe, M. (2003). *The Good Research Guide for Small-Scale Social Research Projects.* Maidenhead: Open University Press.

Denzin, N. K. and Lincoln, Y. S. (2008). *Collecting and Interpreting Qualitative Materials.* London: Sage Publications.

Dickinson, L. (1987a). Why self instruction? *Self Instruction in Language Learning* (pp. 1–35). Cambridge: Cambridge University Press.

— (1987b). Supporting the learner in self-instruction. *Self Instruction in Language Learning* (pp. 88–105). Cambridge: Cambridge University Press.

— (1989). Learner training. In A. Brookes and P. Grundy (eds), *Individualisation and Autonomy in Language Learning, ELT Documents 131* (pp. 45–53). London: Modern English Publications and the British Council.

— (1994). Learner autonomy: what, why and how? In J. V. Leffa (ed.), *Autonomy in Language Learning*. Porto Alegre: UFRGS (pp. 2–12). Retrieved 9 April 2010 from: http://w3.ufsm.br/desireemroth/publi/autonomy.pdf#page=15.

— (1995). Autonomy and motivation a literature review. *System*, 23(2), 165–74.

Dillenbourg, P., Schneider, D. and Synteta, P. (2002). Virtual learning environments. In A. Dimitracopoulou (ed.), Proceedings of the 3rd Hellenic Conference 'Information & Communication Technologies in Education' (pp. 3–18). Greece: Kastiniotis Editions. Retrieved 11 April 2009 from: http://hal.archivesouvertes.fr/docs/00/19/07/01/PDF/Dillernbourg-Pierre-2002a.pdf.

Driscoll, M. (2002). *Blended Learning: Let's Get Beyond the Hype.* Retrieved 1 June 2010 from: www.-07.ibm.com/services/pdf/blended.

Ellis, G. and Sinclair, B. (1989). *Learning to Learn English Teacher's Book*. Cambridge: Cambridge University Press.

Esch, E. (2009). Crash or clash? Autonomy 10 years on. In R. Pemberton, S. Toogood and A. Barfield (eds), *Maintaining Control: Autonomy and Language Learning* (pp. 27–44). Hong Kong: Hong Kong University Press.

Esch, E. and Zähner, C. (2000). The contribution of Information and Communication Technology (ICT) to language learning environments, or the mystery of the secret agent. *ReCALL,* 12(1), 5–18.

Esch, E. M. (1996). Promoting learner autonomy. In R. Pemberton, E. S. L. Li, W. W. F. Or and H. D. Pierson (eds), *Taking Control: Autonomy in Language Learning* (pp. 35–48). Hong Kong: Hong Kong University Press.

— (1997). Learner training for autonomous language learning. In P. Benson and P. Voller (eds), *Autonomy and Independence in Language Learning* (pp. 164–77). London; New York: Longman.

Evans, M. (1993). Flexible learning and modern language teaching. *Language Learning Journal,* 8(1), 17–21.

Evans, M. J. (2009). Digital technology and language learning: a review of policy and research evidence. In M. J. Evans (ed.), *Foreign Language Learning with Digital Technology* (pp. 7–31). London; New York: Continuum.

Felix, U. (2005). E-learning pedagogy in the third millennium: the need for combining social and cognitive constructivist approaches. *ReCALL,* 17(1), 85–100.

Finley, S. (2008). Arts-based inquiry: performing revolutionary pedagogy. In N. K. Denzi and Y. S. Lincoln (eds), *Collecting and Interpreting Qualitative Materials* (pp. 95–113). London: Sage Publications.

Fisher, L., Evans, M. J. and Esch, E. (2004). Computer-mediated communication: promoting learner autonomy and intercultural understanding at secondary level. *Language Learning Journal,* 30(1), 50–8.

Flannery, J. L. (1994). Teacher as co-conspirator: knowledge and authority in collaborative learning. In K. Bosworth and S. J. Hamilton (eds), *Collaborative Learning: Underlying Processes and Effective Techniques* (pp. 15–23). San Francisco, CA: Jossey Bass.

Ganem Gutierrez, G. A. (2006). Sociocultural theory and its application to CALL: a study of the computer and its relevance as a mediational tool in the process of collaborative activity. *ReCALL,* 18(2), 230–51.

Garrison, R. (2000). Theoretical challenges for distance education in the 21st century: a shift from structural to transactional issues. *The International Review of Open and Distance Learning,* 1(1). Retrieved 16 December 2008 from: www.irrodl.org/index.php/irrodl/article/view/2/333.

Godwin-Jones, R. (2011). Emerging technologies: autonomous language learning. Learner autonomy and new learning environments. *Language Learning and Technology,* 15(3), 4–11.

Gonzalez-Lloret, M. (2003). Designing task-based CALL to promote interaction: en busca de Esmeraldas. *Language Learning and Technology,* 7(1), 86–104.

Goodfellow, R. and Hewling, A. (2005). Reconceptualising culture in literal learning environments: from an 'essentialist' to a 'negotiated' perspective. *E-Learning*, 2(4), 355–67.

Gregg, K. R. (1996). The logical and developmental problems of second language acquisition. In W. C. Ritchieand T. K. Bhatia (eds), *Handbook of Second Language Acquisition* (pp. 49–80). London: Academic Press.

Gremmo, M. J. and Riley, P. (1995). Autonomy, self-direction and self-access in language teaching and learning: the history of an idea. *System,* 23(2), 151–64.

Groult Bois, N. (no date). Formar asesores de centros de auto-acceso a distancia: una nueva modalidad para aprender y enseñar, n.p. Centro de Enseñanza de Lenguas Extranjeras, Universidad Nacional Autónoma de México. Retrieved as PDF on 8 June 2010 from: www.santiago.cu/hosting/linguistica/Descargar.php?archivo … groult.pdf.

Guba, E. G. (1990). *The Paradigm Dialog.* Newbury Park, CA: Sage Publications.

Hafner, C. A. and Miller, L. (2011). Fostering learner autonomy in English for Science: a collaborative digital video project in a technological learning environment. *Language Learning and Technology,* 15(3), 68–86.

Hamilton, M. L. J. (2009). Teacher and student perceptions of e-learning in EFL. In M. J. Evans (ed.), *Foreign Language Learning with Digital Technology* (pp. 149–73). London; New York: Continuum.

Hawisher, C. (2000). Accessing the virtual worlds of cyberspace. *The Journal of Electronic Publishing*, 6(1), n.p.

Hawisher, G. and Selfe, C. (1991). The rhetoric of technology and the electronic writing class. *College Composition and Communication*, 42(1), 55–65.

— (2000). Introduction: testing the claims. In G. Hawisher, C. Selfe (eds), *Global Literacies and the World-Wide Web* (pp. 1–4). London: Routledge.

Hernández Cuevas, L. A. (2004). Mediatecas de la UNAM. 12 años de autonomía en el aprendizaje de lenguas. In *Lenguas en Aprendizaje Autodirigido: Revista Electronica de la Mediateca del* CELE-UNAM. Retrieved 26 April 2010 from: http://cad.cele. unam.mx/leaa/cont/ano01/num00/0001ind.html.

Hitchcock, G. and Hughes, D. (1989). *Research and the Teacher.* London: Routledge.

Holec, H. (1981). *Autonomy and Foreign Language Learning* (Council of Europe Modern Languages Project). Oxford: Pergamon Press.

— (2000). The C.R.A.P.E.L. through the ages. In *Mélanges CRAPEL* n°25. Retrieved 26 April 2010 from: www.univ-nancy2.fr/CRAPEL/histoire.htm.

Holliday, A. (2003). Social autonomy: addressing the dangers of culturalism in TESOL. In A. Palfreyman and R. Smith (eds), *Learner Autonomy across Cultures* (pp. 110–26). Basingstoke: Palgrave Macmillan.

Horwitz, E. (1987). Surveying student beliefs about language learning. In A. Wenden and J. Rubin (eds), *Learner Strategies in Language Learning* (pp. 119–29). New York: Prentice-Hall.

Hutchby, I. (2001). The communicative affordances of technological artefacts. *Conversation and Technology from the Telephone to the Internet* (pp. 13–34). Malden, MA: Blackwell.

Illich, I. (1971). *Deschooling Society*. London: Calder and Boyars.
Jiménez Raya, M. and Perez Fernández, J. M. (2002). Learner autonomy and new technologies. *Education Media International*, 39(1), 61–8.
Jones, J. F. (1995). Self-access and culture: retreating from autonomy. *English Language Teaching Journal*, 49(3), 228–34.
Kern, R. (1995). Restructuring classroom interaction with networked computers: effects on quantity and characteristics of language production. *Modern Language Journal*, 79(4), 457–76.
— (2000). Notions of literacy. In *Literacy and Language Teaching* (pp. 13–39). Hong Kong: Oxford University Press.
— (2006). Perspectives on technology in learning and teaching languages. *TESOL Quarterly*, 40(1), 183–210.
Kern, R. and Warschauer, M. (2000). Theory and practice of network-based language teaching. In M. Warschauer and R. Kern (eds), *Network-Based Language Teaching: Concepts and Practice* (pp. 1–19). Cambridge: Cambridge University Press.
Kessler, G. (2009). Student-initiated attention to form in Wiki-based collaborative writing. *Language Learning and Technology*, 13(1), 79–95.
Kitade, K. (2008). The role of offline metalanguage talk in asynchronous computer-mediated communication. *Language Learning and Technology*, 12(1), 64–84.
Kohonen, V. (1992). Experiential language learning: second language learning as cooperative learner education. In D. Nunan (ed.), *Collaborative Language Learning and Teaching* (pp. 14–39). Cambridge: Cambridge University Press.
Kol, S. and Schcolnik, M. (2008). Asynchronous forums in EAP: assessment issues. *Language Learning and Technology*, 12(2), 49–70.
Kozulin, A. (2002). *Thought and Language/Lev Vygotsky Translation, Cambridge* (pp. 6–57). London: MIT Press.
Kramsch, C. (2002). Introduction 'How can we tell the dancer from the dance?' In C. Kramsch (ed.), *Language Acquisition and Language Socialisation: Ecological Perspectives* (pp. 1–30). Bath: Continuum.
Kreijns, K., Kirschner, P. A. and Jochems, W. (2002). The sociability of computer-supported collaborative learning environments. In *Educational Technology & Society*, 5(1), 1–19. Retrieved 5 May 2009 from: www.ifets.info/journals/5_1/kreijns.html.
Labour, M. (2001). Social constructivism and CALL: evaluating some interactive features of network-based authoring tools. *ReCALL*, 13(1), 32–46.
Lai, C. and Zhao, Y. (2006). Noticing and text-based chat. *Language Learning and Technology*, 10(3), 102–20.
Lam, W. S. E. (2004). Second language socialisation in a bilingual chat room: global and local considerations. *Language Learning and Technology*, 18(3), 44–65.
Lamb, T. E. (2006). Backward planning for lifelong language learning. In *Lenguas en Aprendizaje Autodirigido. Revista Electrónica de la Mediateca del CELE-UNAM*.

[en línea] México: UNAM, CELE, 1(2). [consulta: 1 junio 2007]. Retrieved 26 April 2010 from: http://cad.cele.unam.mx/leaa/0102a01-A.html, n.p.

— (2009). Controlling learning: learners' voices and relationships between motivation and learner autonomy. In R. Pemberton, S. Toogood and A. Barfield (eds), *Maintaining Control: Autonomy and Language Learning* (pp. 67–86). Hong Kong: Hong Kong University Press.

Lamy, M. N. and Hampel, R. (2007a). Learning theories. *Online Communication in Language Learning and Teaching* (pp. 19–30). Basingstoke: Palgrave Macmillan.

— (2007b). Teaching online. *Online Communication in Language Learning and Teaching* (pp. 61–75). Basingstoke: Palgrave Macmillan.

— (2007c). Learner experience, online communication. *Online Communication in Language Learning and Teaching* (pp. 76–87). Basingstoke: Palgrave Macmillan.

Lantolf, J. P. (2000). Introducing sociocultural theory. *Sociocultural Theory and Second Language Learning* (pp. 1–27). Oxford: Oxford University Press.

— (2002). Sociocultural theory and second language acquisition. In R. B. Kaplan (ed.), *The Oxford Handbook of Applied Linguistics* (pp. 104–14). Oxford: Oxford University Press.

— (2003). Intrapersonal communication and internalisation in the second language classroom. In A. Kozulin, B. Gindis, V. Ageyer and S. Miller (eds), *Vygotsky's Educational Theory in Cultural Context* (pp. 349–70). Cambridge: Cambridge University Press.

Lantolf, J. P. and Thorne, S. L. (2006a). Introduction. *Sociocultural Theory and the Genesis of Second Language Development* (pp. 1–23). Oxford: Oxford University Press.

— (2006b). Mediation: Theoretical framework. *Sociocultural Theory and the Genesis of Second Language Development* (pp. 59–81). Oxford: Oxford University Press.

— (2006c). The Zone of proximal development. *Sociocultural Theory and the Genesis of Second Language Development* (pp. 263–90). Oxford: Oxford University Press.

LeCompte, M. and Preissle, J. (1993). *Ethnography and Qualitative Design in Educational Research* (2nd edn). Orlando: London Academic Press Ltd.

Lee, L. (2011). Blogging: promoting learner autonomy and intercultural competence through study abroad. *Language* Learning and Technology, 15(3), 87–109.

Lincoln, Y. S. and Guba, E. G. (1985). *Naturalistic Inquiry*. Beverly Hills, CA: Sage Publications.

Little, D. (1990). Autonomy in language learning – some theoretical and practical considerations. In I. Gathercole (ed.), *Autonomy in Language Learning: Papers from a Conference Held in January 1990* (pp. 7–15). London: CiLT.

— (1991). *Learner Autonomy: Definitions, Issues and Problems*. Dublin: Authentik.

— (1995). Learning as dialogue: the dependence of learner autonomy on teacher autonomy. *System*, 23(2), 175–81.

— (1996). Freedom to learn and compulsion to interact: promoting learner autonomy through the use of information systems and information technologies. In R. Pemberton, E. S. L. Li, W. W. F. Or and H. D. Pierson (eds), *Taking Control,*

Autonomy in Language Learning (pp. 203-18). Hong Kong: Hong Kong University Press.
— (1999). Learner autonomy is more than a Western cultural construct. In S. Cotterall and D. Crabbe (eds), *Learner Autonomy in Language Learning: Defining the Field and Effecting Change* (pp. 11-18). Frankfurt: Peter Lang.
— (2000). Learner autonomy and human interdependence: some theoretical and practical consequences of a social-interactive view of cognition, language and learning. In B. Sinclair, I. McGrath and T. Lamb (eds), *Learner Autonomy, Teacher Autonomy: Future Directions* (pp. 15-24). Harlow: Longman.
— (2003). Learner autonomy and second/foreign language learning: guide to good practice. *Subject Centre for Languages, Linguistics and Area Studies*. Retrieved 15 September 2010 from: www.llas.ac.uk/resources/gpg/1409, n.p.
— (2007). Language learner autonomy: some fundamental considerations revisited. *Innovation in Language Learning and Teaching*, 1(1), 14-29.
— (2009). Learner autonomy, the European Language Portfolio and teacher development. In R. Pemberton, S. Toogood and A. Barfield (eds), *Maintaining Control: Autonomy and Language Learning* (pp. 147-73). Hong Kong: Hong Kong University Press.
Littlewood, W. (1996). 'Autonomy': an anatomy and a framework. *System*, 24(4), 427-35.
— (1999). Defining and developing autonomy in East Asian contexts. *Applied Linguistics*, 20(1), 71-94.
Lund, A. (2006). The multiple contexts of online language teaching. *Language Teaching Research*, 10(2), 181-203.
Macaro, E. (1997). *Target Language, Collaborative Learning and Autonomy* (pp. 167-89). Clevedon: Multilingual Matters.
— (2008). The shifting dimensions of language learner autonomy. In T. E. Lamb and H. Reinders (eds), *Learner and Teacher Autonomy, Concepts and Realities* (pp. 47-63). Amsterdam: John Benjamins.
Manteca Aguirre, E., Fischer, R., Vargas Rodríguez, S. and Pereyra, A. (2006). Lengua Extranjera, Inglés *Secretaría de Educación Pública* (pp. 3-31) México, D. F. Retrieved 28 April 2010 from: www.reformasecundaria.sep.gob.mx/doc/FUNDAMENTACIONES/INGLES.pdf.
Mason, R. (2001). Effective facilitation of online learning: the Open University experience. In J. Stephenson (ed.), *Teaching and Learning Online, Pedagogies for New Technologies* (pp. 67-75). London; New York: Routledge Falmer.
Mitchell, R. and Myles, F. (2004). Socio-cultural perspectives on second language learning. *Second Language Learning Theories* (pp. 193-222). London: Hodder Arnold.
Moustakas, C. (2001). Heuristic research: design and methodology. In K. L. Schneider, J. F. T. Bugental and J. Fraser Pierson (eds), *The Handbook of Humanistic Psychology – Leading Edges in Theory, Research and Practice* (pp. 263-75). Thousand Oaks, CA: Sage Publications.

Müge Satar, M. and Özdener, N. (2008). The effects of synchronous CMC on speaking proficiency and anxiety: text versus voice chat. *The Modern Language Journal*, 92(4), 595–613.

Murray, G. L. (1999). Autonomy and language learning in a simulated environment. *System*, 27(3), 295–308.

Neumeier, P. (2005). A closer look at blended learning – parameters for designing a blended learning environment for language learning and teaching. *ReCALL*, 17(2), 163–78.

O'Dowd, R. (2007). Evaluating the outcomes of online intercultural exchange. *English Language Teaching Journal*, 61(2), 144–52.

O'Rourke, B. and Schwienhorst, K. (2003). Talking text: reflections on reflection in computer-mediated communication. In D. Little, J. Ridley and E. Ushioda (eds), *Learner Autonomy in the Foreign Language Classroom: Learner, Teacher, Curriculum and Assessment* (pp. 47–60). Dublin: Authentik.

Ohta, A. S. (2000). Rethinking interaction in SLA: developmentally appropriate assistance in the zone of proximal development and the acquisition of L2 grammar. In J. P. Lantolf (ed.), *Sociocultural Theory and Second Language Learning* (pp. 51–77). Oxford: Oxford University Press.

Oshana, M. (2003). How much should we value autonomy? In E. P. Frankel, F. D. Miller and J. Paul (eds), *Autonomy* (pp. 99–127). Cambridge: Cambridge University Press.

Oxford, R. L. (2003). Towards a more systematic model of L2 learner autonomy. In D. Palfreyman and R. C. Smith (eds), *Learner Autonomy across Cultures: Language Education Perspectives* (pp. 75–91). Basingstoke: Palgrave Macmillan.

— (2008). Hero with a thousand faces: learner, learning strategies and learning tactics in independent language learning. In S. Hurd and T. Lewis (eds), *Language Learning Strategies in Independent Settings* (pp. 41–63). Clevedon: Multilingual Matters.

PACCIT (2005). Putting People @ the Centre of Communication and Information Technologies. In L. Lilley (ed.), *Social Sciences,* issue 59 (p. 3). Retrieved 26 May 2010 from: www.esrcsocietytoday.ac.uk/ESRCInfoCentre/about/CI/CP/Social_Sciences/issue59.

Pachler, N. (2007). Technological advances and educational changes. In D. Allford and N. Pachler (eds), *Language, Autonomy and The New Learning Environments* (p. 220). Germany: Peter Lang.

Palfreyman, D. (2003). Introduction: culture and learner autonomy. In D. Palfreyman and R. C. Smith (eds), *Learner Autonomy across Cultures: Language Education Perspectives* (pp. 1–19). Basingstoke: Palgrave Macmillan.

Pelletieri, J. (2000). Negotiation in cyberspace: the role of chatting in the development of grammatical competence. In M. Warschauer and R. G. Kern (eds), *Network-Based Language Teaching: Concepts and Practice* (pp. 59–87). Cambridge: Cambridge University Press.

Pemberton, R. (1996). Introduction. In R. Pemberton, E. S. L. Li, W. W. F. Or and H. D. Pierson (eds), *Taking Control: Autonomy in Language Learning* (pp.1–8). Hong Kong: Hong Kong University Press.

Pemberton, R., Toogood, S. and Barfield, A. (2009). Maintaining control: an introduction. In R. Pemberton, S. Toogood and A. Barfield (eds), *Maintaining Control: Autonomy and Language Learning* (pp. 3–10). Hong Kong: Hong Kong University Press.

Pennycook, A. (1997). Cultural alternatives and autonomy. In P. Benson and P. Voller (eds), *Autonomy and Independence in Language Learning* (pp. 35–54). London; New York: Longman.

Pica, T., Lincoln Porter, F., Paninos, D. and Linnell, J. (1996). Language learners' interaction: how does it address the input, output and feedback needs of L2 learners? *TESOL Quarterly*, 30(1), 59–84.

Piccoli, G., Ahmad, R. and Ives, B. (2001). Web-based virtual learning environments: a research framework and a preliminary assessment of effect. *MIS Quarterly*, 25(4), 401–26.

Reinders, H. and White, C. (2011). Commentary, learner autonomy and new learning environments. *Language Learning and Technology*, 15(3), 1–3.

Ribé, R. (2003). Tramas in the foreign language classroom: autopoietic networks for learner growth. In D. Little, J. Ridley and E. Ushioda (eds), *Learner Autonomy in the Foreign Language Classroom Curriculum and Assessment: Learner, Teacher* (pp. 47–60). Dublin: Authentik.

Riley, P. (1989). Learners' representations of language and language learning. *Melanges Pedagogiques* (pp. 65–72). Retrieved 2 June 2010 from: http://revues.univnancy2.fr/melangesCrapel/IMG/pdf/6riley-4.pdf.

— (2009). Discursive dissonance in approaches to autonomy. In R. Pemberton, S. Toogood and A. Barfield (eds), *Maintaining Control: Autonomy and Language Learning* (pp. 45–63). Hong Kong: Hong Kong University Press.

Robson, C. (2002). *Real World Research* (2nd edn). Oxford: Blackwell Publishing.

Rubin, H. J. and Rubin, I. S. (2005). *Qualitative Interviewing: The Art of Hearing Data*. London: Sage Publications.

Ryan, R. M. (1991). The nature of self in autonomy and relatedness. In J. Strauss and G. R. Goethals (eds), *The Self: Interdisciplinary Approaches* (pp. 208–38). New York: Springer.

Sarantakos, S. (2005). *Social Research* (3rd edn). Basingstoke: Palgrave Macmillan.

Scharle, Á. and Szabó, A. (2000). *Learner Autonomy: A Guide to Developing Learner Responsibility*. Cambridge: Cambridge University Press.

Schneider, K. L., Bugental, J. F. T. and Fraser Pierson, J. (2001). *The Handbook of Humanistic Psychology – Leading Edges in Theory, Research and Practice*. Thousand Oaks, CA: Sage Publications.

Schwienhorst, K. (2003). Neither here nor there? Learner autonomy and intercultural factors in CALL environments. In D. Palfreyman and R. C. Smith (eds), *Learner Autonomy across Cultures: Language Education Perspectives* (pp. 164–80). Basingstoke: Palgrave Macmillan.

— (2008). *Learner Autonomy and CALL Environments*. New York: Routledge.

Shachaf, P. and Hara, N. (2002). *Ecological Approach to Virtual Team Effectiveness.* Retrieved 4 May 2009 from: https://scholarworks.iu.edu/dspace/bitstream/handle/2022/1017/WP02-08B.html.

Sheerin, S. (1997). An exploration of the relationship between self-access and independent learning. In P. Benson and P. Voller (eds), *Autonomy and Independence in Language Learning.* London; New York: Longman.

Shekary, M. and Tahririan, M. H. (2006). Negotiation of meaning and noticing in text-based online chat. *The Modern Language Journal,* 90(4), 557-73.

Smith, B. (2003). Computer-mediated negotiated interaction: an expanded model. *The Modern Language Journal,* 87(1), 38-57.

Sotillo, S. M. (2002). Constructivist and collaborative learning in a wireless environment. *TESOL Journal,* 11(3), 16-20.

Stake, R. E. (1995). *The Art of Case Study Research.* Thousand Oaks, CA: Sage Publications.

Stephenson, J. (2001). Introduction. In J. Stephenson (ed.), *Teaching and Learning Online, New Pedagogies for New Technologies* (pp. ix-xi). London; New York: Routledge Falmer.

Stepp-Greany, J. (2002). Student perceptions on language learning in a technological environment: implications for the new millennium. *Language Learning and Technology,* 6(1), 165-80.

Stickler, U. and Hampel, R. (2007). 'What I think works well . . .': Learners' evaluation and actual usage of online tools (pp. 1-20). In *Paper from Conference ICL2007, September 26-28, 2007.* Villach: Austria.

Swain, M. (2000). The output hypothesis and beyond: mediating acquisition through collaborative dialogue. In J. P. Lantolf (ed.), *Sociocultural Theory and Second Language Learning* (pp. 97-114). Oxford: Oxford University Press.

Swain, M. and Deters, P. (2007). 'New' mainstream SLA theory: expanded and enriched. *The Modern Language Journal,* 91(5), 820-36.

Swain, M. and Lapkin, S. (1995). Problems in output and the cognitive processes they generate: a step towards second language learning. *Applied Linguistics,* 16(3), 371-91.

Sykes, J. M., Oskoz, A. and Thorne, S. L. (2008). Web 2.0 synthetic immersive environments, and mobile resources for language education. *CALICO Journal,* 25(3), 528-46.

Thorne, K. (2003). *Blended Learning: How to Integrate Online and Traditional Learning.* London; Sterling: Kogan Page.

Trebbi, T. (2008). Freedom – a prerequisite for learner autonomy. In T. E. Lamb and H. Reinders (eds), *Learner and Teacher Autonomy Concepts and Realities* (pp. 33-47). Amsterdam: John Benjamins.

van Lier, L. (1997). Approaches to observation in classroom research. *TESOL Quarterly,* 31(4), 783-86.

— (2000). From input to affordance: social interactive learning from an ecological perspective. In J. Lantolf (ed.), *Socio-Cultural Theory and Second Language Learning* (pp. 245-59). London: Oxford University Press.

— (2004). *The Ecology and Semiotics of Language Learning.* Norwell, MA: Kluwer Academic Publishers.
— (2007). Action-based teaching, autonomy and identity. *Innovation in Language Learning and Teaching*, 1(1), 46–65.
Villanueva Alfonso, M. L. (2009). ICT paradoxes from the point of view of autonomy training and plurilingualism, In *Mélanges CRAPEL* no. 28. Retrieved 2 June 2010 from: http://revues.univ-nancy2.fr/melangesCrapel/IMG/pdf/1_VILLANUEVA.pdf.
Villanueva, M. L., Ruiz-Madrid, M. N. and Luzon, M. L. (2010). Digital genres, new literacies and autonomy in language learning (pp. 81–99). Newcastle: Cambridge Scholars.
Vygotsky, L. (1978). *Mind in Society.* Cambridge, MA: Harvard University Press.
Wall, S. (2003). Freedom as a political ideal. In E. Frankel, F. D. Paul and J. Miller (eds), *Autonomy* (pp. 307–34). Cambridge: Cambridge University Press.
Warschauer, M. (1996a). Motivational aspects of using computers for writing and communication. In M. Warschauer (ed.), *Telecollaboration in Foreign Language Learning: Proceedings of the Hawai'i Symposium* (pp. 29–46). Hawai'i: Second Language Teaching and Curriculum Center. Retrieved 22 October 2006 from: www.lll.hawaii.edu/nflrc/NetWorks/NW1.
— (1996b). Comparing face-to-face and electronic discussion in the second language classroom, University of Hawaii at Maoa. *Calico Journal*, 13(2 and 3), 7–26.
— (1997). Computer-mediated collaborative learning: theory and practice. *The Modern Language Journal*, 81(4), 470–81.
— (1999). CALL vs. electronic literacy: reconceiving technology in the language classroom. On *CILT Research Forum – Information Technology*. Retrieved 11 April 2009 from: www.cilt.org.uk/research/papers/resfor2/warsum1.htm.
— (2002a). Networking into academic discourse. *Journal of English for Academic Purposes*, 1(1), 45–58.
— (2002b). A developmental perspective on technology in language education. *TESOL Quarterly*, 36(3), 453–75.
Warschauer, M. and Healey, D. (1998). Computers and language learning: an overview. In *Language Teaching*, 31(2), 57–71. Retrieved 7 March 2009 from: www.gse.uci.edu/person/markw/overview.html.
White, C. (2006). State of the article: distance learning of foreign languages. *Language Teaching*, 39(4), 247–64.
Whitworth, A. (2005). The politics of virtual learning environments: environmental change, conflict and e-learning. *British Journal of Educational Technology*, 46(4), 685–91.
Wiśniewska, D. (2009). *Introducing Autonomy in the Foreign Language Classroom: Qualitative Research on Teacher's Practice and Problems Encountered (Occasional Papers no. 69).* Dublin: Trinity College, Centre for Language and Communication Studies.
Yin, R. (2003). *Case Study Research – Design and Methods.* London: Sage Publications.

Index

Page numbers in **bold** denote boxes, figures or tables.

affordance(s) 76-7, 172, 200, 203-4, 205, 206, 209, 213, 216, 217, 218
  see also ecology
  mediated by the VLE (in class and free-time access),
    autonomous view, the 209-11
    eclectic view, the 215-16
    guided view, the 203-4
Allford, D. 21, 22, 26
Allwright, D. 27, 139, 156
Arnold, N. 76, 95, 130
autonomous individual 3
  Wall's interpretation of 3
autonomous language learning in Mexico 6
  the British Council approach 7
  British Council versus CRAPEL 8
  the CRAPEL approach 7-8
autonomous learner 72
autonomous learning behaviour 79-80
  case study, the 83-9
  conceptual framework for **79, 199**
    autonomous pedagogical approach **81**
    eclectic pedagogical approach **81**
    an ecological representation 198
    guided pedagogical approach **80**
    notions of autonomy within 200-1
autonomy 17-47
  as attitude 25
  as a communicator 41, 44
  conditions necessary for **4**
  framework in a VLE 44, **45**, 45-6
  frameworks for 38-43
    from Benson **39**
    from Littlewood **40**
    from Macaro **42**
  versus independence 1, 219
  Kohonen's description of 20
  as a pedagogical ideal 3
  philosophical dimensions of 19-20
  and technology 1-3, **2**, **10**, 224-5
    and language learning 3-5
    pedagogical insights 227-9
    theoretical insights 225-7
  theoretical definition in a VLE 37-8
  versions of 23-37 *see also* cultural autonomy political autonomy psychological autonomy technical autonomy
  and virtual language learning 216-18

Bandura, A. 68, 183, 198
Bax, S. 90
Benson, P. 7, 10, 12, 18, 19, 20, 21, 22, 23, 24, 26, 28, 34, 35, 38, 40, 41, 44, 51, 55, 76, 111, 115, 117, 130, 131, 135, 139, 141, 142, 158, 175, 176, 192, 196, 200, 205
Bensousan, M. 76
Bijiker, W. 175
Blake, R. 20, 54, 59, 60, 64, 65, 68, 93, 212, 225
blended learning,
  interpretations of **90**
Blin, F. 57, 69
Blyth, C. 64, 75, **80**, 187
Boud, D. 18, 38
Breen, M. P. 29, 34, 41
Bronfenbrenner, U. 66, 138, 143, 148, 153, 157

CALL (computer-assisted language learning) 11 *see also* CMC; CMCL; EI; VLE
Candy, P. C. 34, 57
Centro de Enseñanza de Lenguas Extranjeras (CELE) 7
Chapelle, C. 53, 56, 58, 95
Chik, A. 51, 192

Ciekanski, M. 2, 18, 19, 37, 151
Cohen, L. 26
computer-mediated communication learning (CMCL) 58
computer-mediated communication (CMC) 51
connectedness 30
constructivism 21, 22
Coomey, M. 61, 76
Cotterall, S. 27, 36
Council of Europe's Modern Language Project, the 24
Crook, C. 21, 53, 54, 56, 57, **80**, 91, 123, 149, 174, 199
cultural autonomy 35–7 *see also* autonomy, versions of

Dam, L. 25
Deci, E. L. 1, 30, 219
Denscombe, M. 82
Deters, P. 30, 68
Dickinson, L. 12, 13, 24, 25, 26, 27, 36, 114, 122
Dillenbourg, P. 13, 49, 76, 79, 123, 130, 135, 138, 141, 155, 172, 174, 183
discovery learning 21 *see also* positivism
Driscoll, M. 90
Ducate, L. 76, 93, 130

ecology *see also* affordance(s)
    as a theoretical approach 75–6
    totality of relationships, the 77–8
Ellis, G. 18, 27
Engestrom, Y. 51
English,
    in EI lessons 139–42
    as the lingua franca of the internet 2, 51
English as a foreign language (EFL) 51
English for Academic Purposes (EAP) 65
English International (EI) 14, 89–109
    see also virtual learning environment (VLE)
    approaches to CALL 91–7
        EI lesson, to an **97**
    blended learning 90
    blended lessons **92**, **95**, **96**, 101–9
    EI lessons, reasons for using English in 139–42

    free-time access to 91
        EI VLE free-time access overview 97–8
    learning tools and modes of delivery **89**
    Your space' forums 98, **99**, 99–100
Esch, E. 4, 5, 12, 22, 26, 28, 29, 30, 35, 43, 53, 113, 117, 151, 154, 156, 158, 175, 185, 196, 212, 217, 220, 224, 225
ESRC (Economic and Social Research Council) 3
Evans, M. 56, 57, 59, 60, 63, 91, 96, 97, 207

Felix, U. 50, 56, 63, 68
Fisher, L. 23, 50, 54, 62, 67, 205
Flannery, J. L. 31
Flaste, R. 1, 30, 219

Ganem Gutierrez, G. A. 5, 9, 54, 55, 96, 151, 193, 195, 197, 199, 225
Garrison, R. 54, 56
globalized online spaces 192
Godwin-Jones, R. 61
Gonzalez Lloret, M. 54, 59, 76
Goodfellow, R. 68
Groult Bois, N. 7
Gruba, P. 59, 96
guided learning 21

Hafner, C. A. 55
Hamilton, M. L. J. 56
Hampel, R. 3, 52, 53, 55, 57, 58, 65, 96, 224
Hara, N. 13, 206
Hawisher, G. 3, 44, 52, 53, 57, 64, 66, 67, 112, 179, 181, 212, 216, 220
Healey, D. 54, 55, 57, 58, 61, 62, 63, 67, 95, 96, 97, 121, 122
Hernández Cuevas, L. A. 7
Hewling, A. 68
Holec, H. 4, 12, 17, 18, 21, 22, 23, 26, 61, 62, 67, 70, 116, 125, 126, 135, 174, 176, 181, 192, 196, 198, 217, 220, 224, **226**, 227
Holliday, A. 23
Hutchby, I. 5, 13, 54, 66, 175, 190, 203

information computer technology (ICT) 51
interdependence 201, 216, 218, 225, 226, 228 *see also* Little

Jimenez Raya, M. 53, 56
Jones, J. F. 56

Kern, R. 5, 11, 18, 41, 43, 44, 49, 50, 53, 54, 55, 56, 57, 59, 60, 64, 66, 76, 121, 129, 153, 214, 217
Kessler, G. 1, 2, 12, 50, 61, 65, 66, 76, 96, 117, 192, 225
Kitade, K. 64, 65, 66, 96, 117, 207, 211
Kohonen, V. 20
Kol, S. 65, 66, 67, 96, 142, 209, 212
Kramsch, C. 64, 207
Kreijns, K. 52

L2 free expression,
   patterns of use of target language 135–9
Lai, C. 59, 96
Lamb, T. E. 35
Lamy, M. N. 3, 52, 53, 58, 96, 224
language learning *see also* technology, learner confidence in
   potential capacity for autonomy in 125–31
     with technology 129–31
   student perceptions of 111–19
     classroom interaction and the target language 114–15
     conflicting perceptions 117–19
     EFL learning environment 111–12
     learning environment **128**
     patterns of interaction in the target language 115–17
     pedagogical culture 112–13
language mediated by the VLE (in class and free-time access)
   autonomous view, the 211–13
   eclectic view, the 216
   guided view, the 204–6
Lantolf, J. P. 12, 30, 37, 50, 67, 69, 115, 141, 149, 153, 172, 175, 216, 223
Law, 175
Leander, K. 51
learner autonomy,
   Dickinson's definition of 26
   Holec's definition of 17, 46
   Little's definition of 28
   within EI VLE blended lessons 149–62
     blended classroom autonomy in EI **150**

     classroom freedom 155–6
     computer room freedom 152–4
     interactivity beyond the VLE to the internet 161–2
     interactivity within the VLE 159–61
     site activity (EI access) 157–9
learners' assignments 142, 143, **144**, 144–7
   recurring themes 143–7
     texting and context 145, **146**
     texting and saving time **147**
     texting as a fashion 145, **146**, 147
   as a reflection of engagement in class 148–9
Lee, L. 50, 51, 185
Little, D. 4, 12, 20, 21, 22, 28, 29, 30, 31, 34, 36, 37, 39, 43, 44, 46, 77, 78, **81**, 114, 116, 126, 135, 138, 140, 147, 156, 176, 185, 194, 201, 206, 213, 217, 218, 221, 224, 225, **228**
   see also interdependence
Littlewood, W. 18, 31, 32, 33, 36, 38, 40, 41, 43, 44, 46, 80, 133, 148, 172, 181, 200, 203, 204, 205, 209, 210, 212, 214, 215, 217, 221, 222, 223, **226**, **230**
Lund, A. 51

Macaro, E. 22, 38, 41, 42, 43, 44, **81**, 90, 133, 140, 213
Mann, S. J. 29, 34, 41
Manteca Aguirre, E. 6
Mason, R. 5, 13, 67, 69, 181, 220
mediated mind, the 63, 67
   see also Vygotsky
Miller, L. 55
Mitchell, R. 172
Moodle 89
Müge Satar, M. 76, 96
Murray, G. L. 1, 2, 22, 23, 50, 69, 156, 197, 202, 214, 225
Myles, F. 172

network-based language learning (NBLL) 49, 64
Neumeier, P. 63, 90

Ohta, A. S. 64
online spaces 51 *see also* globalized online spaces

O'Rourke, B. 23
Oskoz, A. 51
Oxford, R. L. 34, 36, 39, 46
Özdener, N. 76, 96

PACCIT (People at the centre of Communication and Information Technologies) 3, 5, 9, 11
Pachler, N. 21, 22, 26, 52
Packer, M. J. 153
Palfreyman, D. 36
Pelletieri, J. 58, 59, 60, 66, 96
Pemberton, R. 3, 4, 20, 34, 223, 227
Pennycook, A. 18, 19, 20, 33, 35, 39, 213
Perez Fernández, J. M. 53, 56
personal response 17
Pica, T. 41, 65, 182
Piccoli, G. 64, 77, 138
political autonomy 34–5
   see also autonomy, versions of
positivism 21
proactive autonomy 31, **32**, 32–3, 172, 209, 212, 217
   in the context of a VLE **33**
psychological autonomy 28–33
   see also autonomy, versions of
   difficulties associated with **31**
   individual personal autonomy 29
   in a VLE **31**

reactive autonomy 31, **32**, 32–3, **80**, 172, 181, 203, 209, 212, 217, 223
   in the context of a VLE **33**
relatedness 31
   and ecology 31
Ribé, R. 23
Riley, P. 22, 127
Ryan, R. M. 31, 40

Scharle, Á. 28
Schcolnik, M. 65, 66, 67, 96, 142, 209, 212
Schwartz, B. 135
Schwienhorst, K. 23, 53, 208
second language acquisition (SLA),
   virtual promise of technology in, the 50–2
   virtual reality of technology in, the 52–5
Selfe, 3, 44, 52, 53, 64, 66, 67, 112, 179, 181, 212, 216, 220
self-instruction 25

Shachaf, P. 13, 206
Sheerin, S. 27
Shekary, M. 96
Sinclair, B. 18, 27
Smith, B. 52, 59, 60, 96
Sotillo, S. M. 64, 186, 202
Stephenson, J. 53, 57, 61, 65, 76
Stickler, U. 55, 57, 65
supportive dialogue 172
Swain, M. 30, 59, 68, 130
Sykes, J. M. 51, 193, 216
Szabó, A. 28

Tahririan, M. H. 96
technical autonomy 23–8
   see also autonomy, versions of
   learner training and 26–8
technology, digital 49–70 *see also* language learning
   CALL 55–68
      Communicative CALL 58–62
      Integrative CALL 62, **63**, 63–8
      Structural CALL 55–7
   learner confidence in 119–24
   online language practice exercises 121–4
   virtual promise in SLA, the 50–2
   virtual reality in SLA, the 52–5
Thorne, K. 30, 51, 90, 115, 153
totality of relationships (mediated by the VLE in class and free-time access)
   autonomous view, the 206–9
   eclectic view, the 214–15
   guided view, the 202–3
Trebbi, T. 19, 37, 148, 176

Universidad Nacional Autónoma de México (UNAM) 7

van Lier, L. 5, 9, 11, 12, 31, 33, 37, 38, 61, 64, 66, 69, 75, 76, 77, 78, 79, 80, 117, 138, 139, 140, 143, 147, 148, 156, 159, 182, 185, 190, 192, 198, 199, 200, 201, 202, 203, 204, 206, 208, 210, 212, 213, 214, 215, 216, 218, 222, 223, **226**, 231
Villanueva, M. L. 25, 50, 51, 192, 194
virtual learning environment (VLE) 35
   see also English International (EI)
   characteristics of **49**

students' response to 221–4
   transformative qualities, implications
      of **230**
VLE autonomy framework **72–3**
   blended learning framework with EI **135**
   free-time framework 172, **173**
      discussion forums 174–5, 176, **177**
      forum writing 185
      implicit interaction within 182–5
      RTR posts 178–82
      similarities between posts 186–90
      student perceptions of the value
         of 193–6
Voller, P. 7, 12, 18, 19, 24, 111, 139, 158, 175, 176, 196
Vygotsky, L. 30, 64 *see also* mediated mind; ZPD

Wall, S. 13, 19, 51, 138, 151, 155, 175, 195, 219, 228
Warschauer, M. 5, 51, 52, 53, 54, 55, 56, 57, 58, 59, 60, 61, 62, 63, 64, 67, 75, 76, 90, 91, 95, 96, 97, 121, 122, 129, 181, 214, 217, 223
Weaver, S. 26
Web 2.0 13, 219 *see also* VLE
White, C. 50, 135
Wiśniewska, D. 20, 23, 26, 29, 34

Yin, R. 82

Zähner, C. 26, 35, 113, 154, 185, 212, 225
Zhao, Y. 59, 96
Zone of Proximal Development (ZPD) 64
   see also Vygotsky